Y0-BZL-026

The Guide to
EVERYTHING
JEWISH IN
NEW YORK

The Guide to EVERYTHING JEWISH IN NEW YORK

Nancy Davis
Joy Levitt

Adama Books

Acknowledgments

Help and encouragement for this book took many forms, from saying "you're crazy to take this on but go ahead" to spending hours on the telephone sharing information with us about Jewish resources—or even taking us on tours of particular neighborhoods. We wish we could thank everyone who gave us tips on new kosher restaurants or encouraged us during the research and writing of this book; the following people deserve special thanks: Misha Avramoff, Doug Balin, Helen Barer, Moshe Birnbaum, Esther Cohen, Susan Cohen, Rachel Falkove Diana Galer, Sandy Kadet, Susan Katz, Stephie Kirschner, Yaakov Kornreich, Deborah Levitt, Diane Levitt, Shirley Levitt, Claire Marcus, Egon Mayer, Irene Schiffman, Bliss Siman, Chuck Simon, Roger Streit, Betsy Platkin Teutsch, and David Teutsch.

No part of this publication may be reproduced, stored in a retrieval system, or transmitted in any form or by any means, electronic, mechanical, photocopying, recording or otherwise (brief quotations used in magazines or newspaper reviews excepted), without the prior permission of the publisher.

Copyright © 1986 Nancy Davis and Joy Levitt
All rights reserved

Library of Congress Cataloging-in-Publications Data

Levitt, Joy.
  The guide to everything Jewish in New York.

  1. Jews—new York (N.Y.)—Directories. 2. Jews—New York (N.Y.)—Societies, etc.—Directories. 3. New York (N.Y.)—Directories.
I. Davis, Nancy, 1947- . II. Title.
F128.9J5L48 1986   974.7'1004924'0025 86-10927 ISBN 0-915361-47-7

Printed in Israel
Design by Irwin Rosenhouse

Adama Books, 306 West 38 Street, New York, N.Y. 10018

To Ed and Lee, both real New York Jews
even though they were born in Philadelphia.

CONTENTS

HOW TO USE THIS BOOK

This guide is a selective and comprehensive look at New York's Jewish resources. All facts in this book have been researched carefully. Information was checked and re-checked and—when we had conflicting information—checked again. Nevertheless, New York is a city where many things happen in a flash; shops and businesses open and close quickly, and even major organizations go through changes or move offices. Hours change too, and this is particularly true in the Jewish community where hours are often dictated more by the rising and setting of the sun than by the hands of the clock. It is always a good idea to call and verify.

In most of the book we have put our listings in alphabetical order; however, in certain sections we have listed the most significant or larger organizations first because they serve as umbrellas for many activities. Unless otherwise indicated, all telephone numbers are for area code 212. Where a telephone number does not appear, the organization or synagogue either has no telephone or has an unlisted number.

As much as we like all of New York, we have restricted the scope of this book to Manhattan in order to maintain a manageable size. Just look at the number of Jewish organizations in Manhattan alone and you'll know why.

This guide to Jewish New York was researched and written independently; no agencies or organizations funded any of the research or made decisions about what should be included in the book. Restaurants were visited anonymously; no shops, organizations, or individuals paid for listings or were promised space in our book for any reason.

We welcome comments, suggestions and reactions for updated editions. Write to us c/o
ADAMA BOOKS
306 West 38th Street
New York, New York 10018

Introduction

Harry Golden wrote, "If you wanted to find the American Jewish community in 1900, a New York cop would tell you to get off at the Houston Street stop on the Third Avenue El. . . . The streets would be jammed with Jews. There would be as many coffee shops as there were pushcarts and inside there would be old men sipping tea and debating Talmudic law or socialism."

After nearly 100 years, finding New York's Jewish community is not as simple as a trip downtown. There are still about 35,000 Jews living on the Lower East Side and it is undoubtedly the place to find a *tallit* for a Bar or Bat Mitzvah, but there are far more Jews, affiliated and unaffiliated, living all over Manhattan, from Soho to the Upper East Side to Washington Heights.

These days, we identify ourselves in many different ways. Some of us observe only by putting *mezuzot* on our doors, and some of us observe by not riding on Shabbat. We worship in different ways too, in small and informal *havurot* or fellowships, in traditional and modern Orthodox synagogues, in large Reform and Conservative congregations, even at lunchtime *minyanim* in the offices of midtown corporations. Even the most assimilated yuppie still craves a knish, and New York is where you will find the most authentic knishes outside Bialystok. We eat blintzes in dairy restaurants on Essex Street, kosher pizza in the diamond district, nouvelle kosher cuisine on the Upper West Side, and hot pastrami at the Stage Delicatessen.

We study Talmud and Yiddish, and Israeli folk dancing, and contemporary Jewish literature, and kosher Chinese cooking. We go to groups to help us find a Jewish husband or wife and groups to find help dealing with problems of raising children in an intermarried family. We attend High Holiday services for singles and luncheon clubs for seniors. The miracle of it is that no matter how we see ourselves as Jews, we have an opportunity in New York to find a place for ourselves.

Chapter 1
CHILDREN

Jewish tradition describes a scene when the Israelites were about to receive the Torah (which everyone else had apparently rejected). Before God would hand over the precious words, however, the Israelites were asked for guarantors. Their ancestors, their sages, their prophets were all suggested, to no avail. Only when the children were offered did God give the people of Israel the Torah. Children are indeed our most precious resource, and in this chapter we describe programs to help nurture and educate, care for and enjoy them.

PREGNANCY AND GENETIC COUNSELING

Jewish tradition places a high value on the propagation of the Jewish people, specifically achieved through procreation. So it is a time of great happiness and rejoicing within both families and the community when a woman becomes pregnant. But it is also a time of some concern, particularly for a number of Jewish couples who may be carriers of genetic diseases that appear mostly among Jews of Eastern European backgrounds. Tay-Sachs is perhaps the most widely known of this group of genetic disorders that include such diseases as Gaucher and Niemann-Pick. Tay-Sachs is a fatal disease causing the progressive destruction of the central nervous system. Deterioration continues relentlessly; death between the ages of three and five is inevitable. There is no prevention and no cure. Testing for Tay-Sachs, however, has been available for some time now, and a simple blood test can tell whether you or your partner is a carrier. Since Tay-Sachs is transmitted through recessive genes, both partners need to carry the gene for there to be a possibility of a Tay-Sachs child. Obviously, it is best to have such a test before you conceive, but the blood test is also possible once you are pregnant, and should it be determined that both you and your spouse are carriers, amniocentesis testing will tell whether the baby has Tay-Sachs disease.

Several Manhattan-area hospitals offer genetic screening and testing, both for Tay-Sachs and some of the less common genetic diseases. Appointments are needed at each of these hospitals, but they are easy to get. If you are already pregnant, be sure to communicate that when you make your appointment. Most of these programs encourage both partners to come in.

Beth Israel Medical Center
  10 Nathan Perlman Place 10003   420-2000
Columbia Presbyterian Medical Center
  Babies Hospital South, Room 202
  3959 Broadway 10032   305-6731
Mount Sinai Hospital
  Fifth Avenue and 100th Street 10029   650-6500
New York University Medical Center
  550 First Avenue 10016   340-7300

In addition to these hospital testing centers, there are occasional testing or information programs in Jewish community centers and synagogues throughout the metropolitan area. The National Tay-Sachs and Allied Diseases Association helps groups in Manhattan and nationwide to offer low-cost testing for Tay-Sachs and other genetic disorders. To find out where and when such testing programs are scheduled near you, or to arrange for such a testing program at your synagogue or organization, call the Association (1-516-569-4300). For information about Jewish genetic disorders for which there is no prenatal screening, but for which support systems do exist within the community, see Chapter 11.

Losing a baby before it is born can be a devastating experience for a woman, her husband, and her family. To help women cope with the array of emotions at this difficult time, a new program has been developed in the Jewish community.

Pregnancy Loss Peer-Counseling Group
Jewish Women's Resource Center
National Council of Jewish Women,
New York Section
9 East 69th Street 10021   535-5900

> Calling itself a support group, not a therapy group, the Pregnancy Loss Peer-Counseling Group offers a place where women who have experienced pregnancy loss can help each other through this difficult time. There is also a telephone counseling service for people who need more immediate personal attention.

ADOPTION

Resources in the Jewish community for couples seeking to adopt healthy infants are not unlike those in the general community—scarce indeed. Effective sex education and birth control, as well as legalized abortion, have drastically reduced the number of babies (Jewish and non-Jewish) available for adoption. If you're interested in adopting a child through an agency under Jewish auspices, there are still some options, but you should be aware that it won't necessarily be a baby whose birth parents are Jewish.

Louise Wise Services
12 East 94th Street 10028   876-3050

> This well-known agency, formally called the Jewish Unmarried Mothers Association, was founded in 1916 to help Jewish couples adopt babies. It still tries to do that, now not only for Jewish couples but for any appropriate couple (the agency, like other UJA–Federation constituents serves the total New York population, not just Jews); there is a long waiting list for healthy infants. They also place toddlers and adolescents, of all races. Hardest to place are infants and older children with physical or mental handicaps, although the agency offers a full range of follow-up services and resources to help parents. In addition to its adoption services, Louise Wise maintains an East Side townhouse for mothers and their babies, providing day care for mothers who work or go to school. There is also a residence for pregnant, unmarried girls, where prenatal care is provided, as well as educational programs. Louise Wise offers temporary and long-term foster care for children whose family problems make removal from the home necessary. For

more information about Louise Wise and what it does, see section on Children in Need.

Jewish Child Care Association
345 Madison Avenue 10017   490-9160, ext. 210
This UJA–Federation-supported agency maintains several residential facilities for emotionally disturbed children and has an Adoption Services Unit for appropriate children in their programs. The department actively recruits homes for children and provides follow-up support services for the child and the adoptive parents. The agency also maintains NAP, the Networking Adoption Program, which helps couples sort through the various options available to them.

BIRTH

COVENANTAL CEREMONIES FOR BABIES

It's a boy! How wonderful, how exciting! But wait. There's a bris to plan, a *mohel* to call, people to invite, food to prepare, a name to choose, and suddenly delivering the baby seems easy compared to what's ahead. Take a deep, cleansing breath and relax. Here are some resources for you.

FINDING A *MOHEL*

The person who circumcises your infant may be a doctor in the hospital or a *mohel,* a religious practitioner trained by physicians and other *mohelim.* Unless the child is ill, ritual circumcision must be done by a *mohel* on the eighth day, although exceptions may be made in communities where there is no *mohel* handy. In that case, a Jewish doctor who is familiar with the ritual side of the procedures is often called. Manhattan has no shortage of *mohelim.* Many have been trained in a program that used to be operated at Mount Sinai Hospital. To get the name of a trained *mohel,* ask your obstetrician or pediatrician. The hospital where you give birth will also have certified *mohelim* on their staff, or keep a list of *mohelim* who are authorized to perform circumcisions at that hospital. You may also call one of the following organizations, which provide referrals.

Brith Milah Board of New York
10 East 73rd Street 10021   879-8415
This agency is run by the New York Board of Rabbis. It

certifies and supervises *mohelim*. It publishes a pamphlet for parents as well. They've certified an estimated 35 *mohelim* in Manhattan and 200 throughout the country.

Reform Brit Milah Board
Hebrew Union College-Jewish Institute of Religion
1 West 4th Street 10013   674-5300

This new program was started to meet an increasing need among liberal Jews to have ritual circumcision ceremonies that more closely match the rest of their religious lives. The *mohelim* trained by this program are not necessarily Orthodox. All are Jewish physicians (both men and women) who maintain an affiliation with a hospital and active membership in a Reform congregation. They adhere to Reform practices regarding the definition of Jewish identity, which holds that the child of a Jewish parent (mother or father) is a Jew. Since Orthodox interpretation determines Jewish identity through the mother and not the father, in cases where the father is Jewish and the mother is not, traditional *mohelim* treat the bris as part of a conversion process. These new Reform *mohelim* handle such ceremonies as a regular bris for a Jewish child.

NAMING CEREMONIES FOR GIRLS

It's a girl! How wonderful, how exciting! But wait. How do you enter this baby daughter into the convenant of the Jewish people? How do you give her a Hebrew name? Traditionally, a baby girl is named by her father in the synagogue on the first Sabbath following the birth. Usually the mother and baby are still at the hospital, or resting at home, and in any event would not be called to the Torah for an *aliya*. If you want a more egalitarian ceremony, for both mother and daughter, you have a few choices. Most Conservative synagogues in Manhattan, and all Reform and Reconstructionist synagogues, invite both men and women to the Torah for an *aliya*, and welcome couples with their newborn at services either on Friday night or Saturday morning. Some have elaborate naming ceremonies that enable the entire family to participate—parents, grandparents, and siblings. If you'd like a synagogue naming ceremony and you are affiliated with a synagogue, discuss your interest with your rabbi, preferably before giving birth, if you want to participate in the planning. You can also arrange a naming ceremony in your home, either with the help of a rabbi or by yourselves. To help you plan a naming ceremony for your baby daughter, call The Jewish Women's Resource Center of the National Council of Jewish Women, New York Section, 9 East 69th Street, 10021 (535-5900).

THE PARTY

If your mother lives in Florida and you can't stand your mother-in-law's cooking, you'll need to think about food for after the ceremony. Assuming that neither of you is going to have much time or energy for this, you might want to call one of the places listed below. For more information about them, as well as caterers and take-out places, many of whom will handle smaller parties, see our chapter "Where We Eat." Remember that not all "Jewish-style" delis or caterers are rabbinically certified as kosher; if they have supervision, we've listed that. Others may claim to be kosher, or have kosher products, but have no rabbinic supervision; still others simply specialize in Jewish-style food. Most of these places deliver, but if you're interested in having help serving and cleaning up, be sure to ask if they provide such a service.

Barney Greengrass
541 Amsterdam Avenue 10024   724-4707

Bernstein-on-Essex
Supervision: Harav Jacov Yitzchok Spiegel
135 Essex Street 10002   473-3900

Broadway Kosher Deli
321 Broadway 10013   964-2116

Broadway's Jerusalem II
Supervision: Va'ad Harabonim of Flatbush
1375 Broadway 10018   398-1475

Carnegie Deli
854 Seventh Avenue   757-2245

Cornucopia Kosher Deli and Appetizers
1651 Second Avenue 10021   879-0733

Deli King
1162 First Avenue   355-5577

Famous Dairy
Supervision: K'hal Adath Jeshurun of Washington Heights
222 West 72nd Street 10023   595-8487

Fine & Shapiro
138 West 72nd Street 10023   877-2874

Henry's Delicatessen and Restaurant
 Supervision: Rabbi G. Taylor
 195 Houston Street 10002   260-0491

Just-A-Bite
 Supervision: Va'ad Harabonim of Bensonhurst
 106 Greenwich Street 10013   425-5470

Kaplan's Deli
 71 West 47th Street 10036   391-2333

Katz's
 205 East Houston Street 10002   254-2246

Kirschenbaum's Deli Restaurant
 18 East 33rd Street 10016   683-0748

Kosher Delight
 Supervision: Rabbinical Board of Flatbush
 1365 Broadway 10036   563-3366

Levana
 Supervision: OK Labs
 141 West 69th Street 10023   877-8457

Macabeem Restaurant
 Supervision: Orthodox Union
 147 West 47th Street 10036   575-0226

Mama Leah's Restaurant & Blintzeria
 1400 First Avenue 10021   570-2010

Moshe Peking
 Supervision: Orthodox Union
 40 West 37th Street 10018   594-6500

New Gross Restaurant
 Supervision: Orthodox Union
 1372 Broadway 10018   921-1969

The New York Delicatessen
 104 West 57th Street   541-8320

Pastrami Factory
 7 West 47th Street 10036   819-0202
 333 East 23rd Street 10010   689-8090

Ratner's
 138 Delancey Street 10002   677-5588

Sabra
 Supervision: Rabbi Avraham Fishelis
 505 Grand Street   260-6330

Second Avenue Deli
 156 Second Avenue 10003   677-0606

Lou G. Siegel
 209 West 38th Street 10018   921-4433

Someplace Special
  Supervision: Orthodox Union
  401 Grand Street 10002   674-0980
Stage Delicatessen
  834 Seventh Avenue 10019   245-7850
Wolf's Sixth Avenue Deli
  101 West 57th Street   765-1016
Yonah Schimmel
  137 East Houston Street 10002   477-2858
Zooky's
  180 Third Avenue 10003   982-4690

ANNOUNCEMENTS

Some people say it's a good thing that we send out birth announcements because otherwise we might never agree on a name for our child! If you're planning to send out birth announcements and would like the Hebrew name and birth date of your child printed or done in calligraphy, ask the store where you're ordering if they carry work by Art Scroll. This company prints many birth announcements and wedding invitations and does a lot of work with Hebrew. Although they don't deal directly with the public, you can call them (924-2413) and find out where their brokers are so you can see what they have to offer. Another good resource for Hebrew typefaces is Crown Thermography (691-3066). If you would like someone to do this for you, Iris Levitsky (628-2380) handles Hebrew engraving and invitations.

Many if not most of the calligraphers whom we have described in our section on Artists in Chapter 7 will also do birth announcements.

CONVERSION OF INFANTS

Before the growth of denominational movements in Jewish life, conversion was somewhat simpler. You found a rabbi who arranged the conversion for you. Though it's still more or less that way, now you need to decide whether you would like a Reform, Reconstructionist, Conservative or Orthodox conversion. This is all quite complicated, and is best discussed with your rabbi, if you have one. With the movements warring with one another as they are at the time of this writing, Jewish identity has become a sensitive question. We've heard stories about rabbis not accepting one another's conversions, while the poor parents and baby are caught in the middle, unaware of the political infighting that's going on. This worldwide problem also affects Manhattan residents. Each of the four movements has a Manhattan office, and if you would like help in arranging for the conversion of your baby, you can call them. (The philosophies of the various movements are described in Chapter 13, under Religious Organizations.)

Federation of Reconstructionist Congregations and Havurot *Reconstructionist*
270 West 89th Street 10025 496-2960
Central Conference of American Rabbis *Reform*
21 East 40th Street 10016 684-4990
Rabbinical Assembly *Conservative*
3080 Broadway 10027 678-8060
Rabbinical Council of America *Orthodox*
275 Seventh Avenue 10001 807-7888

DAY CARE PROGRAMS

In 1982, Sharon Strassfeld (coeditor of *The Jewish Catalogs*) called for the Jewish community to pay some attention to the needs of working parents by creating more Jewish day care programs. Day care programs were springing up all over town, everywhere except within the the Jewish community, which seemed still to believe that every Jewish mother was at home fingerpainting with her children. The issue was not only that of the changing role of Jewish women, either. Fundamental questions were raised about how Jewish women ought to be spending their time, and what was best for the Jewish child. The American Jewish Committee, the National Council of Jewish Women and the Union of American Hebrew Congregations, all undertook studies to ascertain the needs of the community. And slowly, very slowly, the programs began. Because these programs are constantly changing, be sure to call for updated information. Some organizations, including the Educational Alliance, run day care programs that have no Jewish content, and aren't really aimed at the Jewish community. We have listed only those programs that claim to be "Jewish" day care programs, with some Jewish programming, though not necessarily servicing only Jewish children. Please note that these centers are early childhood programs, with age-appropriate nursery schools within them.

You might also want to try a workshop at the 92nd Street Y, entitled "Child Care Options," which is run out of their Parenting Center and helps parents find appropriate child care. Call the Y (427-6000) for more information.

National Council of Jewish Women, New York Section
69th Street and Madison Avenue 10021   535-5900, ext. 33

The Council operates a day care center in cooperation with the Federation of Jewish Agencies, designed specifically for the children of employees of Jewish communal agencies. Housed in the garden room of NCJW headquarters, the center has fifteen children who are two-and-a-half through four years old. They meet Monday–Friday, 8:00 A.M.–6:00 P.M. Jewish holidays are celebrated, and each Friday afternoon there is an *Oneg Shabbat,* a special Sabbath ritual, before the kids go home for the weekend. Children may bring their own food.

92nd Street YM–YWHA
1395 Lexington Avenue 10128   427-6000, ext. 206

The Y runs what's called the Jewish Family Child Care Network, which trains people who are interested in setting up family day care programs in their homes, and refers parents to certified day care providers in their neighborhoods. In addition, there are periodic training workshops. Family day care through this program is offered to working and nonworking parents in the neighborhood in which they live, and generally takes place between 8:30 A.M. and 6:00 P.M. Rates are reasonable.

Stephen Wise Free Synagogue
30 West 68th Street 10023   877-4050

This special synagogue, with its emphasis on community outreach, has the only synagogue day care program in Manhattan. They take kids as early as eighteen months, and will look after children up to four years old. The program runs from 8:00 A.M. to 6:00 P.M., but there are part-time options available. There is a good amount of Jewish content in the program, Shabbat and holidays are celebrated, and only dairy is served.

Washington Heights YM–YWHA
54 Nagle Avenue 10040   569-6200

The Y in Washington Heights operates a Jewish day care

program for children between the ages of two and five-and-a-half years old. It operates ten months a year, *kashrut* is observed, and Jewish holidays are celebrated. There are some scholarships available for this program. There are lots of schedule options, with the half-day choice of morning or afternoon, a full day from 9:00 A.M. to 3:45 P.M., and an extended day which begins at eight in the morning and finishes for the day at six in the evening.

Yaldenu 251 West 100th Street 10025 866-4993, ext. 162

Yaldenu, like Congregation Ansche Chesed where it rents space, is one of the sparkling new institutions conceived by members of the *havurah* movement. Yaldenu takes children, from eighteen months to three years, and has both full-day (8:30 A.M.–6:00 P.M.) and half-day options. Children are asked to bring dairy only into the school. There is substantial Jewish content in this program (although not all the kids happen to be Jewish), including a Jewish musical specialist a few times a week. The number of Israeli kids here makes for a kind of bilingual program, with lots of Hebrew being both spoken and informally taught.

PRESCHOOL PROGRAMS AND PLAYGROUPS

If you're looking for activities for your preschooler, from infancy through the age of two or two-and-a-half, be sure to call the YM–YWHA's throughout Manhattan. They each have Parenting Centers, offering classes for parents as well as recreational and cultural programs for both parents and children, some of which are popular enough to have waiting lists. Some synagogues also have programs for infants. One is Central Synagogue, 123 East 55th Street, which has a Parenting Center for children ages twelve to twenty-seven months and their parents. Once a week the program includes a one-and-a-half hour session, with the children singing and playing in one room with a teacher, while the parents meet across the hall in a Parents' Group.

Pripetchik, a new and unique Yiddish playgroup, sponsored by Yugntruf Youth for Yiddish, is for children between the ages of three and seven. It meets on Sunday morning at the Yorkville Synagogue, 352 East 78th Street, and has grown by leaps and bounds in the course of a few years. To enroll your child, you or your spouse must speak Yiddish. Call 654-8540 for more information.

NURSERY PROGRAMS

Watching the smiling, eager faces of children in good Jewish nursery school programs leads one to wish such delight could be bottled and preserved for their whole education. For at few points in the life of an average Jew is learning so marvellous as at the nursery level.

Jewish nursery schools in Manhattan fall roughly into four categories. Those that are part of day care centers have been listed above. Others are part of day schools that also have elementary and sometimes secondary programs as well. Still others are affiliated with synagogues, and a few are independent both of synagogues and day schools. Again, we are listing only those programs that have Jewish content; occasionally you'll find a nursery school housed in a synagogue but devoid of Jewish programming.

Abraham Joshua Heschel School
270 West 89th Street 10024   595-7087

The Heschel School, Manhattan's newest Jewish school, has just begun a three-year-old's program, which is a five day a week full-day nursery program. The Heschel school is not affiliated with any movement, and children from all backgrounds attend its programs. For a more comprehensive description of the philosophy of this school, look under Day Schools in this chapter.

Central Synagogue   123 East 55th Street 10022   838-5122

This large Reform synagogue has a nursery school with Jewish content, mostly concerned with holidays, for children ages two-and-a-half to five. The littlest kids go two or three mornings a week, while the three year olds go five mornings a week and the older kids go from 9:00 A.M. to 2:00 P.M., except on Fridays, when they have a shorter day.

Educational Alliance
197 East Broadway 10002   475-6200

In addition to its Head Start program, the Educational Alliance runs a co-op nursery school and kindergarten for kids between the ages of twenty-one months and five-and-a-half years. The program is five days a week (younger children, between ages one and two-and-a-half, can go two or three days instead), with either half or full days. For those interested in a traditional

Hebrew-English program, the Alliance offers *Beit Ha Yeled*. Kosher food is provided. There is an extended-day option available.

Emanu-El Midtown YM–YWHA

344 East 14th Street 10003   674-7200

One of the oldest nursery schools in New York, founded in 1905, this school is for children between the ages of two and six. The youngest kids come two days a week, while older kids can choose a three or five day program, either half or full days. Conversational Hebrew is part of the program for four and five year olds, and Jewish holidays are celebrated at every level.

Gani Nursery School and Early Childhood Center

P.S. 3, Hudson and Grove Streets 10014   420-1150

This new program, sponsored by the Educational Alliance West, takes children beginning at age two-and-a-half. It offers a fully-equipped nursery, housed in a public school, and provides children an introduction to Jewish holidays and customs. In addition to the program for the kids, workshops on child development are held in the evening to accommodate working parents. You can select either the half-day or full-day options, either on a three or five day a week schedule.

Lincoln Square Synagogue Nursery School

200 Amsterdam Avenue 10023   874-6100

Here's yet another program offered by this dynamic Upper West Side Orthodox synagogue. Small classes and parental involvement are characteristic of the Lincoln Square program, which offers both half and full-day options for children ages three to six.

Manhattan Day School

310 West 75th Street 10023   595-6800

This traditional day school has a preschool program for three and four year olds; the younger children come a half day, either morning or afternoon, while the older kids come a full day. This is a Yeshiva, though the school welcomes children from diverse backgrounds. There is a great deal of Jewish content to this program, as would be expected from a traditional Jewish school.

92nd Street YM–YWHA

1395 Lexington Avenue 10128   427-6000

People have been known to move to the Carnegie Hill neighborhood just to improve their chances of enrolling their children in this highly popular nursery program (preference is given to neighborhood residents). Its small size and high quality make this one of the Y's more sought-after programs. It begins with a toddler program for two year olds two or three days a week, while the three year olds go from 9:00 A.M. to 12:00 noon, with an afternoon option, and the older fours and fives come a full day. Nursery school kids are taken by their teachers after school to other popular Y programs such as the Red, Yellow, Blue and Glue art program. Shabbat is observed every Friday, and holidays are celebrated as well.

Park Avenue Synagogue
50 East 87th Street 10028 831-8686

This popular nursery school has programs for children ages two to four, with the youngest kids coming two mornings a week and the oldest coming mornings and afternoons every day. There is a fair amount of Jewish content. The program is open to nonmembers of the synagogue; if you're interested in registering your child, call a year in advance—that's how long the waiting list is.

Park East ESHI Day School
164 East 68th Street 10021 737-6900

This Upper East Side nursery school is part of the day school affiliated with the Park East Synagogue. The school is Orthodox, and begins at age two-and-one-half, with both half-day and full-day programs, and runs through kindergarten. There are about one hundred children in the nursery division, and much attention is paid to Jewish holidays, celebrations, music and values.

Ramaz 125 East 85th Street 10028 427-1000

Called the "pride and joy of Ramaz," the primary school at this prestigious traditional Upper East Side day school holds classes for three and four year olds in a half-day setting, though the four year olds come for a slightly longer time. It is part of the Ramaz Lower School, and incorporates both Judaic and general studies. The preschool has its own, separate outdoor play terrace, with a custom-designed play sculpture.

Rodeph Sholom Nursery Division
7 West 83rd Street 10024 362-8800

The nursery school of Rodeph Sholom is affiliated with both the synagogue and its day school. Registration in the program also includes membership in the synagogue itself. Programs for two, three, and four year olds are held at the Temple House, a block away from the synagogue and elementary division. Toddlers come for two or three days a week, while three year olds take in a half day, five days a week. The four year olds have a full day–full week program. The nursery division has its own gym facilities, library, and of course a distinct curriculum, which has some Jewish content. Shabbat is celebrated each week, as are other Jewish holidays as they occur. (See also under Day Schools; for a general description of the synagogue itself, see Chapter 8.)

Temple Emanu-El 1 East 65th Street 10021 744-1400

The largest synagogue in the world, this Reform synagogue offers a nursery program with only limited Jewish content. There is a long waiting list for programs for children ages two to five. One unusual feature here is that older four and five year olds go for a full day, from 9:00 A.M. to 4:00 P.M.

Westside Jewish Center Nursery

131 West 86th Street 10024 873-6464

This school was once affiliated with the Society for the Advancement of Judaism, but is now independent, though it rents space from the Jewish Center. The program, for two–four year olds, meets five days a week, half days for younger kids and a full day for the four year olds. On Fridays, parents come in with challah and grape juice to begin the celebration of Shabbat, and there is a model seder for parents and grandparents.

Yeshiva Chofetz Chaim

346 West 89th Street 10024 362-1436

Yeshiva Chofetz Chaim, housed in a landmark building on Riverside Drive, has a nursery program for boys and girls (after kindergarten, there are only boys at the school), ages three to five. Children come five days a week, from 9:00 A.M. to 1:30 P.M. Classes are small, and great emphasis is given to communicating the Jewish values propounded by the Chofetz Chaim rebbe whose name the school bears, values such as lovingkindness, respect for others and good citizenship.

Yeshiva Tifereth Jerusalem

141–7 East Broadway 10002 964-2830

This very Orthodox Yeshiva has grandparents studying along with grandchildren, because it begins with a nursery program for three and four year olds, and continues through graduate school. The little children attend school from 9:00 A.M. to 4:00 P.M. at this Yeshiva that has been open for eighty years.

Yeshiva Rabbi Samson Raphael Hirsch

85–93 Bennett Avenue 10033 586-6200

This Orthodox Yeshiva of the Washington Heights Breuer community begins at nursery school, with a full-day, five day a week program.

DAY SCHOOLS

Within the traditional Jewish community, Jewish parochial schools (day schools) have always been the educational program of choice. A comprehensive Jewish education, including fluency in Hebrew, familiarity with Jewish texts, literature and history, is simply not achievable in two to six hours a week, no matter how successful the afternoon program is. For Orthodox Jewish parents, day school is usually the only avenue that will give their child the intensity of educational and social experience they desire. But in recent years, interest in day schools has extended beyond the Orthodox community. Clearly some interest is related to the decline of the New York City public schools. Some parents, not necessarily Orthodox or even very Jewishly oriented, figured that if they had to send their kids to private school anyway, they might as well find a Jewish school that would also take care of the child's Jewish education. The rise of interest in, attendance at and number of day schools serving the non-Orthodox community is also a reflection of a greater interest in things Jewish across the spectrum. Parents who regretted not getting a "solid" Jewish education in their own youth sometimes elect to send their kids to Jewish day schools, even if their own life style may be out of sync with some of the customs of the school.

Only a few of the day schools in Manhattan have high school divisions at the present time. Others are only high schools, while some operate through only the second or third grade. The overwhelming majority of the day schools is Orthodox, either by affiliation or style, and the degree of openness to non-Orthodox children varies widely.

Abraham Joshua Heschel School
270 West 89th Street 10024   595-7087

The newest day school in Manhattan, the Heschel School is also the only nondenominational Jewish day school in Manhattan. Furthermore, it is one of the few day schools that bills itself as innovative, and that it is. "Innovative" is not to be confused with flaky: this is a serious school, run by dedicated and experienced Jewish educators who are committed to offering quality Jewish and secular education in an open and supportive environment. At the time of this writing, the Heschel School goes through the eighth grade, though there may eventually be a high school as well, given the general enthusiasm of parents, teachers and administrators, to say nothing of financial supporters. When one parent was asked whether she had any complaints about the Heschel School, she quickly responded, "Only one—that I can't go too!"

Beth Jacob School   142 Broome Street 10002   473-4500

The Beth Jacob School, located on the Lower East Side, is a strictly Orthodox school for girls from religious families. It draws children from both Brooklyn and Manhattan, and runs from kindergarten through the eighth grade.

Park East ESHI Day School
164 East 68th Street 10021   737-6900

Originally a day school serving the Lower East Side Jewish community, ESHI moved uptown and merged with the Orthodox Park East Synagogue, on the Upper East Side. The school has approximately 200 students, equally divided between the Lower school (kindergarten through the sixth grade) and the Upper school (grades seven and eight). Secular studies are taught for half the day, and Jewish studies comprise the other half. Four days a week there is an after-school enrichment program, held from 3:30–4:30 P.M., which offers classes in chess, drama, computers and science, among other subjects.

Ramaz   125 East 85th Street (Lower school)
60 East 78th Street (Upper school)   427-1000

One of the oldest (founded in 1937) and largest (over 800 students) Jewish day schools in Manhattan, Ramaz was originally established by Rabbi Joseph Lookstein of Congregation Kehilath Jeshurun, an Upper East Side Conservative synagogue. His son Haskel is now the principal of this prestigious and highly competitive school. The Lower and Upper schools are seven blocks apart, the latter housed in a new facility that has gained wide attention for its architectural and educational qualities. In addition to a serious and wide-ranging academic program in both Jewish and secular subjects, there are special programs for students with minor learning disabilities.

The Upper school instituted a new curriculum in 1983, individualizing programs and maintaining its honors program in Talmud. After-school activities are extensive, including courses in karate, typing and driver's education, as well as student-run clubs.

Rodeph Sholom Day School
10 West 84th Street 10024   362-8769

In recent years, the Reform movement has made tentative moves toward a more positive view of Jewish day schools, even while maintaining its commitment to the public school system.

Meanwhile, the Rodeph Sholom School has been going about its business as the first Jewish day school founded by a Reform synagogue. Almost thirty years later, this Upper West Side elementary school is an integral part of the synagogue (you must be a member of the synagogue to attend the school). There are special school-congregational events coordinated throughout the year as well. The Jewish studies program, covering major areas such as literature, history, values, holidays and Hebrew language, is taught within the framework of Reform Jewish practice. In this liberal Jewish school, subjects like Torah and Bible, as well as later Jewish writings, history and practice are dealt with very differently than at a place like Ramaz, for example. Although children are exposed to traditional Judaism in a variety of ways, the goal of Rodeph Sholom is to acquaint students with the diversity of Jewish life, and with the changes that have taken place in it over the centuries of Jewish history. Jewish Studies are handled both as a separate curricular program, with separate faculty and classes, and as a thread woven into the secular program. There is an after-school program, from 3:30–5:00 P.M. (4:30 on Fridays), which offers classes in cooking, art, photography, gymnastics, story telling and computer literacy, among other subjects. Students can even go to Rodeph Sholom when it's closed! There's now a vacation program that runs during winter and spring recesses, with many of the same classes that are offered after school during the year. Both the afterschool and vacation programs are open to children in the community who are not students at the school.

Yeshiva Chofetz Chaim
346 West 89th Street 10024   362-1436

The Chofetz Chaim rebbe, whose name was given to this school by its founder, the rebbe's son-in-law, considered kindness toward others, appropriate behavior and *menchlichkeit* to be of supreme importance. So this Orthodox Yeshiva places great emphasis on these teachings. It has a coed nursery and kindergarten, but from fifth grade through the eighth grade it takes only boys. The school is small, approximately fifty students.

Yeshiva Ohr Torah–Manhattan Day School
308 West 75th Street 10023   595-6800

The Manhattan Day School was founded as the Jewish Community School in 1943, and moved to its current West Side site in 1972. Its four floors include classrooms, a science laboratory, cafeteria, art room, gymnasium and library, in addition to offices. This is a traditional school, with a traditional approach. Although no affiliation is required of parents, there is an emphasis on the Orthodox tradition, and children are encouraged to put into practice what they have learned. The school offers a *mechina* (preparatory) program for students who come in at the third grade or higher from secular schools; these children take secular classes with their peers and *mechina* courses for Hebrew studies with other students of similar backgrounds. It also offers a special education program for children with learning disabilities, maintaining three separate classes with a student-teacher ratio of three to one.

Yeshiva Rabbi Samson Raphael Hirsch
85–91 Bennett Avenue 10033   568-6200

This is the Yeshiva of the Breuer community, extremely Orthodox German Jews who have settled in Washington Heights. The program begins with a nursery school and continues through high school. It's a large school, with about seven hundred students, with after-school programs, and a branch of PTACH, the program for children with learning disabilities.

Yeshiva Tifereth Jerusalem
141–7 East Broadway 10002   964-2830

The late, renowned Rabbi Moshe Feinstein was the dean at this Orthodox school, which begins at nursery level and runs straight through until graduate school. There are several hundred students here, who study at the elementary and high school levels from 9:00 A.M. to 6:00 P.M. It is a school for very religious children.

Yeshiva University High School for Boys–The Marsha Stern Talmudical Academy
2540 Amsterdam Avenue 10033   960-5337

Founded in 1916, this high school of Yeshiva University was the first Jewish-sponsored high school in the United States. Committed to the concept of *Torah U'Mada* (Torah learning and general academic study), which is the motto of the University itself, TMSTA concentrates on an intensive course of Jewish as well as secular studies. Rooted in traditional Judaism, it draws most of its student body from the Orthodox community, though there is a *mechina* (preparatory) program for students who have not received an intensive Jewish elementary education. PTACH (Parents for Torah for All Children) runs a program at the school for students with learning disabilities. Although most students at TMSTA commute (there are special buses servicing Long Island, Brooklyn, Manhattan, the Bronx and Westchester), there is housing available at the Joseph and Dora Strenger Residence Hall, a high school dormitory. TMSTA accepts only students who have attended elementary day schools or some equivalency program, who are observant Jews with strong academic backgrounds and a high motivation for learning.

Yeshiva University High School for Girls—Tonya Soloveitchik High School

Olga Gruss Lewin Educational Center
425 Fifth Avenue 10016 340-7800

The girls' division of the Yeshiva University High School system, originally part of Girls High School in Brooklyn, was founded in 1959 as its Manhattan branch. Now a part of Yeshiva, TSHSG, like its male equivalent, offers an intensive Jewish and secular education on the high school level for Orthodox women who have been educated at elementary day schools and are interested in a serious and competitive program. There are differences between the boys' and girls' division, to be sure; young women at TSHSG do not study Talmud. However, they do study Bible, Jewish history, Hebrew language, Jewish philosophy and practice, in addition to their secular studies. All students commute to the midtown campus. Like the boys' division, TSHSG has PTACH classes for learning-disabled students.

AFTER-SCHOOL RELIGIOUS EDUCATION

Living as we do in two civilizations, American and Jewish, presents special problems for the education of our children, problems hardly imagined by our parents and grandparents who attended only Jewish schools (the *heder*). For those parents who choose public or nonsectarian private schools for their children, finding a good way to give them a Jewish education can be quite a challenge. No afternoon Hebrew school can do what a day school does; that isn't its purpose. These schools teach a degree of skill in Hebrew reading and conversation, along with a general curriculum of history, ethics, holidays, prayer and Bible study. What they try to do, and the good ones do it quite well, is provide children with a strong Jewish identity, which may or may not be something the kids get at home, a fact recognized by these schools. Many try to involve the whole family when possible, realizing that often the parents are not much more learned than their children. The principals in these afternoon schools know that for many of their students, Judaism is seen as an option, and it must be made attractive to be chosen.

Most Conservative, Reconstructionist and Reform congregations maintain afternoon religious schools, usually for their members only. A few Orthodox synagogues do also, apparently because not every child whose parents belong to an Orthodox synagogue goes to a religious day school. Most of these synagogues have a three, four, or five year residency requirement at the school in order to become a Bar or Bat Mitzvah, although some make exceptions in certain cases. Many of these schools have primary programs that meet on Sundays or one another day of the week. Religious school generally begins in the third grade and continues through the seventh grade, at which time a child usually becomes a Bar or Bat Mitzvah.

Hebrew high school can run from eighth to twelfth grade, depending on the program. Afternoon Hebrew schools vary from one to four days a week.

Central Synagogue Reform
123 East 55th Street 10022 838-5122

Civic Center Synagogue Orthodox
49 White Street 10013 966-7141

Congregation B'nai Jeshurun Conservative
257 West 88th Street 10024 787-7600

Congregation Emunath Israel Orthodox
236 West 23rd Street 10011 675-2819

Congregation Habonim Reform
44 West 66th Street 10023 787-5347

Congregation Kehilath Jeshurun Orthodox
125 East 85th Street 10028 427-1000

Congregation Nodah Bi Yehudah Orthodox
392 Ft. Washington Avenue 10033 795-1552

Congregation Ohab Zedek Orthodox
118 West 95th Street 10025 749-5150

Congregation Rodeph Sholom Reform
7 West 83rd Street 10024 362-8800

Congregation Shearith Israel Orthodox
8 West 70th Street 10023 873-0300

Conservative Synagogue of Fifth Avenue
11 East 11th Street 10003 929-6954

East End Temple Reform
398 Second Avenue 10010 254-8518

Fifth Avenue Synagogue Orthodox
5 East 62nd Street 10021 838-2122

First Roumanian American Congregation Orthodox
89-95 Rivington Street 10002 673-2835

Hebrew Tabernacle Congregation Unaffiliated
551 Ft. Washington Avenue 10033 586-8304

Lincoln Square Synagogue Orthodox
   200 Amsterdam Avenue 10023   874-6105

Metropolitan Synagogue of New York Reform
   10 Park Avenue 10016   679-8580

Park Avenue Synagogue Conservative
   50 East 87th Street 10028   369-2600

Park East Synagogue Orthodox
   163 East 67th Street 10021   737-6900

Society for the Advancement of Judaism Reconstructionist
   15 West 86th Street 10024   724-7000

Stephen Wise Free Synagogue Reform
   30 West 68th Street 10023   877-4050

Sutton Place Synagogue Conservative
   225 East 51st Street 10022   593-3300

Temple Emanu-El Reform
   1 East 65th Street 10021   744-1400

Temple Israel of the City of New York Reform
   112 East 75th Street 10021   249-5000

Temple Shaaray Tefila Reform
   250 East 79th Street 10021   575-8008

Tifereth Israel–Town and Village Conservative Synagogue
   334 East 14th Street 10003   677-8090

Village Temple Reform
   33 East 12th Street 10003   674-2340

West End Synagogue Reconstructionist
   270 West 89th Street 10024   595-7929

There are a few afternoon Hebrew schools that are not affiliated with synagogues. The Havurah School is housed at Ansche Chesed, 251 West 100th Street (662-3436), but not affiliated with it. Children between five and thirteen meet once a week and participate in an open-classroom educational program. Another program, limited to high school students, is Prozdor, affiliated with the Jewish Theological Seminary, 3080 Broadway (678-8824). Students study at the Seminary on Sundays and at local centers during the week. The 92nd Street Y also offers CONNECT After-School Program, 1395 Lexington Avenue (427-6000, ext. 245), which provides children between the ages of four and twelve a chance to study Hebrew, Bible and Jewish subjects. The Jewish Family School of the Educational Alliance, 197 East Broadway (475-6200), has after-school religious instruction, actually the only one of its kind now on the Lower East Side. The school educates children between the ages of three and thirteen, with some classes attended by parents as well.

AFTER-SCHOOL CULTURAL PROGRAMS

After-school and weekend cultural Jewish programs give children an opportunity to experience things Jewish in a less structured way than is typical in day schools and Hebrew schools. Several programs have lots of Jewish content, from ethnic cooking classes to Israeli folk dancing. Others have a less Jewish focus, but are operated under Jewish auspices and tend to have a great many Jewish children participating in them. All of these programs seek to strengthen Jewish identity through informal and enjoyable social activities.

Educational Alliance
197 East Broadway 10002 475-6200

After-school programs here include crafts, sewing, dancing, woodwork, and gym for the younger kids, while teenagers have a lounge, a teen council, athletic activities and Friday Night programs. The *Kol Tov* and *B'nos Agudath* programs on weekends are designed for Orthodox youth.

Educational Alliance West
51 East 10th Street 10003 420-1150

The Children's Network is this Y's commitment to providing well-supervised after-school care for elementary school children in the Village, Soho, and Lower West Side areas. Programs are held Monday–Friday and children may attend as many days as they like. There is some transportation from area public schools. Activities include sports, crafts and creative dance, as well as drama and puppetry.

Emanu-El Midtown YM–YWHA
344 East 14th Street 10003 674-7200

The Midtown Y has a "Playland" for kids from nursery school age through the fifth grade (and other programs for older kids), which runs five days a week after school, with bus pick-up at local schools available on request. Athletic activities, arts and crafts, dramatics, as well as a full range of individual and group musical intruction are offered. This Y also has a Hebrew School, held in cooperation with the Town and Village Synagogue down the street, which is designed for children with no previous Jewish background. Affiliation at the synagogue or the Y is not required.

Hebrew Arts School
129 West 67th Street 10023 362-8060

This major center for music education, located on the Upper West Side, offers individual and group musical instruction after school. There are also Israeli dance programs and special classes in Jewish music. Sunday programming includes choirs for children and teenagers, which concentrate on Hebrew and Jewish music.

92nd Street YM–YWHA (After-school on the West Side)
427-6000, ext. 179

The Upper East Side Y has begun a westside program in an attempt to fill in a gap in cultural programming for the Upper West Side Jewish community. At P.S. 75, on 96th Street and West End Avenue, students participate in recreational, arts and crafts, and science classes after school. On Friday afternoons and Sundays, Young Israel of the West Side houses a program for children of Orthodox families.

92nd Street YM–YWHA
1395 Lexington Avenue 10128 427-6000

The NOAR after-school program at the Y offers classes in art, dance, swimming, gymnastics, fencing and the like. A full range of music, art and physical education classes is available. There is also a Sunday program called V.Y.P. (Very Young People), offering entertainment for children ages three to six and their families. There are "tween and teen" programs after school as well.

Rodeph Sholom Day School
19 West 84th Street 10024 362-8800

This Reform day school has an extensive after-school program that is open to children between the ages of four and twelve, whether or not they attend the day school itself. The programming is fairly secular, and includes arts and crafts activities, sports and audiovisual classes.

YM–YWHA of Washington Heights and Inwood
54 Nagle Avenue 10040 569-6200

Activities here for kids ages five to fourteen include bowling, carpentry, cooking, science, puppet making and swimming. Transportation is available. There is also a Yeshiva program on Sundays, designed specifically for Orthodox youngsters.

The Jewish Museum 1109 Fifth Avenue 10128 860-1888
The Jewish Museum sponsors some creative programming for elementary school children, usually on Sundays and often

related to an upcoming holiday. These programs, billed as Family Programs, make use of the museum's extensive facilities in an age-appropriate manner.

BAR AND BAT MITZVAH

It used to be, when a boy turned thirteen, you took him to *shul*, he was called to the Torah, and you provided the *shnaps* for the *Kiddush*. Such was the Bar Mitzvah of our grandfathers in Poland. So, things have changed a bit! Now it's not only for boys, but more and more often for girls too, and they are usually required to do part of a Friday night or Saturday morning service as well. As for the *shnaps,* there's plenty of that, and it's still the parents' responsibility to provide it, but it's often accompanied with enough food to have fed all the Jews in our grandfathers' shtetlach for a year.

Although Jewish tradition recognizes this time in a family's life as one of great rejoicing, most parents (and their thirteen year olds) experience some anxiety as well. As the child struggles with a cracking voice and a few out of control hormones, parents are trading off worries about their child's progress (what will Uncle Abe say if he can't read Hebrew?), with concerns about the band (will it be too loud?), and the chopped liver (will there be enough?) and the seating arrangements at the party (are Jack and June still married?). Here is some help with the details.

PREPARATIONS

Most kids in Manhattan prepare for their Bar or Bat Mitzvah ceremony by going to either a day school or afternoon Hebrew school and studying with a tutor. Because this ceremony is so linked to entrance into the Jewish community, it's rare to find a synagogue that will allow a nonmember to hold a Bar or Bat Mitzvah service in its chapel or sanctuary. However, most synagogues offer alternative times when a Bar or Bat Mitzvah may be held for a child who has not attended the requisite amount of school. For a list of synagogues, community centers, and other places that offer Jewish education for children, see the section on After-School Religious Education in this chapter. There are some *shuls* without schools; other unusual situations might also require a special tutor. You can try calling the Jewish Theological Seminary (678-8000) or Hebrew Union College (674-5300), both of which have rabbinical and cantorial schools and often have students willing to do private tutoring.

For children who are developmentally or learning disabled, special Bar or Bat Mitzvah tutoring is available. See Chapter 11, or call Rabbi Martin Schloss, Director of Special Education at The Board of Jewish Education (245-8200).

INVITATIONS

Many of the calligraphers described under Artists will design a Bar or Bat Mitzvah invitation, and usually arrange for its printing as well. Art Scroll printing company specializes in Hebrew invitations; if you can't find any where you usually order invitations, have the store call them (929-2413). Another good source for Hebrew invitations is Crown Thermography (691-3066).

YARMULKES AND *TALLITOT*

Although most synagogues that require yarmulkes (skull caps) have sufficient numbers of them for your guests, many people prefer to order their own, choosing a special color and having the name of the Bar or Bat Mitzvah child and the date imprinted on the inside. A few stores on the Lower East Side manufacture yarmulkes and will accept orders from individuals. Many Judaica stores can also provide you with quantities of yarmulkes; when ordering, be sure to allow enough time for special colors and imprints.

H & M Skullcap Manufacturing Co.
  46 Hester Street 10002   475-1977
Israel Gifts
  575 Seventh Avenue 10018   391-4928
Israel Wholesale Import Corp.
  21 Essex Street 10002   228-1661
J. Levine
  58 Eldridge Street 10002   966-4460
  5 West 30th Street 10001 695-6888
Kipah Or
  49 Essex Street 10002   260-3252
Shaller's Bookstore
  2555 Amsterdam Avenue 10033   928-2140

Louis Stavsky Bookstore
  147 Essex Street 10002   674-1289
Weinfeld Skullcap Manufacturing Co.
  19 Essex Street 10002   254-9260
West Side Judaica
  2404 Broadway 10024   362-7846
Zion Talis Mfg. Co., Inc.
  48 Eldridge Street 10002   925-8558

Taking your son or daughter to buy a *tallit* (prayer shawl) or *tefillin* (phylachteries) can be one of the most special family occasions in preparation for the big day. These religious items aren't what they used to be, especially the *tallit*, which is now available in every color of the rainbow, and in many styles. One father we know took his daughter to a store on the Lower East Side, warning her to pretend that the *tallit* they were about to purchase for her Bat Mitzvah was really being bought for her brother. The father feared that the merchants might be traditionally opposed to selling a *tallit* to a young woman. At the store, the father asked if his daughter could try a few on, since she and her brother were about the same size. The merchant obliged, and when she tried on a purple-striped one she had eyed when they first entered the store, the merchant smiled and said to the young girl, "Take the purple. It looks good on you!" How the world has changed!

Most of the bookstores we listed above for yarmulkes also carry a wide assortment of *tallitot* and *tefillin*. One of the biggest selections is at Zion Talis, which claims to be the largest manufacturer of *tallitot* in the world. J. Levine is another good place to check; they have handwoven *tallitot* by the well-known Israeli weaver, Malka Gabreili.

Should you be interested in a handwoven *tallit,* you can also speak to the people at In the Spirit (861-5222). This gallery of Judaica, described more fully in Chapter 7, is in touch with artists around the world and can have a handwoven *tallit* made for you. You can also call Rona Rones (607 West End Avenue, 10024, 873-5276), a weaver who specializes in Judaica.

ENTERTAINMENT

There probably isn't a band in Manhattan that can't play a hora or sing a few Israeli songs, so if that's what you're looking for in terms of entertainment at a Bar or Bat Mitvah reception, rest assured that here everyone's a Jewish entertainer, no matter what the name of the band leader happens to be. Klezmer music, the music of Eastern European Jews, has been experiencing a renascence of late, thanks to Giora Feidman and others who have been performing in this lively style. Although the overwhelming number of Jewish bands and klezmer musicians seem to be located in the outer boroughs and elsewhere, you can get their names from the classified ads in most of the major Jewish weeklies. There is one unusual klezmer band in Manhattan: *Klezmeyd-lekh*, an all-women's quartet, is probably the only one of its kind, and plays authentic klezmer music. You can reach them at 222-5507. Another source for out-of-town musicians and entertainers who work with Jewish themes is *In the Jewish Tradition: A Directory of Performing Artists,* published in 1985 by the Federation of Jewish Philanthropies of New York (980-1000). You should also ask your caterer for recommendations. Also see our section on Entertainers in Chapter 7, especially if you're looking for something a little different.

CATERERS

Most of the synagogues in New York that have reception rooms for Bar and Bat Mitzvah parties also have either a house caterer or an approved list from which you can choose. A few will let you bring in your own caterer, though there may be restrictions related to *kashrut*. If your party is elsewhere, or at home, see Chapter 10, where we list all Manhattan caterers. Many good caterers located outside Manhattan will service synagogues and other facilities in the city.

SPECIAL OPPORTUNITIES

Twinning. In recent years, some children and their parents have sought different ways to make the Bar or Bat Mitzvah experience more meaningful. One opportunity has been provided by the Coalition to Free Soviet Jewry, 8 West 40th Street, Suite 602, 10018 (354-1316). Formerly called the New York Conference on Soviet Jewry, this organization helps students find Soviet Jewish kids who are also thirteen, but who cannot become a Bar or Bat Mitzvah because of conditions in the Soviet Union. The program is called Twinning, because the American child actually becomes a Bar or Bat Mitzvah both for him or herself and, in absentia, for the Russian teenager. The Coalition has a package of materials they will be happy to send you, which includes the name of a Russian teen, and suggestions for things you and your family can do before, during and after the service.

The Israel Option. One woman we know, after looking at the caterer's estimate, and contemplating decisions about invitations, bands, clothing and the like, threw up her hands and said, "There's got to be another way." She found one. The whole family got on a plane and went to Israel, where her son became a Bar Mitzvah on Masada. This can be a wonderful experience for the whole family, and resources exist to help you put it all together. Several options are available. You can hold a service on Masada, which may be arranged through the Israel Government Tourist Office (560-0650). They bring the rabbi and Torah, you bring the people. Both Bar and Bat Mitzvah services are held on Masada, and men and women may sit together. They will also arrange a Bar or Bat Mitzvah at the Western Wall in Jerusalem. Here there is a *mechitza* (separation of men and women). You can also contact Hebrew Union College (674-5300) if you're interested in a Bar or Bat Mitzvah service at the synagogue of their Jerusalem campus, or United Synagogue (533-7800) for availability of such a service at the Conservative synagogue in Jersusalem. Many travel agencies arrange tours for families or groups that include Bar and Bat Mitzvah ceremonies. You can also check the World Zionist Organization, Department of Education and Culture (752-0600). Finally, a few organizations sponsor summer programs for teenagers that include becoming a Bar or Bat Mitzvah.

Betar   9 East 38th Street   10016   696-0080
> This Zionist Youth organization sponsors a six-week trip to Israel for Bar and Bat Mitzvah-age kids. The trip includes touring as well as a day-long ceremony at the Western Wall accompanied by parties, singing and dinner.

Zionist Organization of America
4 East 34th Street   10016   481-1500
> Z.O.A. has a teenage camp in Israel for thirteen and fourteen year olds, which includes a regular camp program, touring the country and the option of a Bar or Bat Mitzvah ceremony at the Western Wall.

Hadassah 50 West 58th Street 10019 355-7900

This Zionist women's organization has a travel department that aids people in planning individualized trips to Israel that include Bar or Bar Mitzvah celebrations. They'll help you arrange a ceremony practically anywhere (Hadassah Hospital is one location) in Israel.

YOUTH GROUPS

Jewish youth groups provide teenagers with a link to the Jewish community, a social network with other Jewish kids and a sense of Jewish identity. Some of these groups belong to religious or communal organizations, while others have Zionist affiliations. Some of them, especially those connected with denominational organizations, may require synagogue or organizational membership to join, so be sure to ask.

Agudath Israel 5 Beekman Place 10038 964-1620

This Orthodox group has several youth programs. B'nos Agudath Israel is the girls' division, while boys join Pirchei Agudath Israel.

B'nai Brith Youth Organization
823 United Nations Plaza 10017 490-2792

BBYO has chapters throughout the city, and over 25,000 members nationwide. There are recreational, cultural and social programs for children ages thirteen and older.

B'nei Akiva of North America New York Region
25 West 26th Street 10010 889-5992

This is one of the largest religious Zionist youth organizations in North America (affiliated with Hapoel Hamizrachi) and has *snifim* or local branches in most major cities. Boys and girls ages nine to seventeen belong to these groups, which are involved in religious, social and educational activities. There are also regional groups that bring together high school kids from a larger geographical area. For information about where local groups meet, call the number listed above.

Educational Alliance 197 East Broadway 10002 475-6200

In partnership with the United Jewish Council, the Educational Alliance employs a Youth Programmer, who works with Jewish kids from all backgrounds. There is a lounge program, athletic events, social programs and other activities.

Federation of Reconstructionist Congregations and Havurot   270 West 89th Street   10024   496-2960

The Reconstructionist movement is developing a nationwide youth program, and has sponsored *kallot* (weekend get-togethers) throughout the United States and Canada.

Habonim Dror   27 West 20th Street   10011   255-1796

Habonim Dror is the worldwide Labor Zionist Youth Movement, affiliated with the United Kibbutz Movement in Israel, the Labor Zionist Alliance, and Na'amat USA. Among its many activities, Habonim Dror sponsors local youth groups for children ages nine to sixteen. These groups meet on weekends for social and educational activities, largely related to Zionism and Israeli life.

Jewish Public School Youth
197 East Broadway   10002   475-6200

JPSY goes to seventeen public high schools throughout the five boroughs, in order to strengthen Jewish identification. Weekly activities include informal Jewish education and socialization, long weekend seminars, film programs and weekend trips.

National Conference of Synagogue Youth
45 West 36th Street   10018   563-4000

This is an Orthodox youth program, typically run out of Orthodox synagogues, but open to nonaffiliated teens as well. The group sponsors twenty-five weekend conventions in different places, with the kids staying in people's homes. NCSY also has special programs for deaf Jewish youth.

National Young Judaea   New York City Regional Division
141 West 28th Street   10001   736-8330

Young Judaea, one of the oldest Jewish youth agencies in the country, is sponsored by Hadassah, the Zionist women's organization. It is part of Hashachar, the umbrella youth and young adult organization under Hadassah's auspices, and involves students from age nine through their last year in high school. Clubs are divided by grade levels: *ofarim*, grades four through six; *tsafim*, grades seven and eight; and *bogrim*, grades nine through twelve. For information about Hashachar's college and young adult programs, see Summer and All-Year Programs in Israel in this chapter. The clubs try to combine an appreciation for things Jewish and things Israeli. For information about a group in your neighborhood, call the regional office, whose number is listed above.

National Federation of Temple Youth CRaFTY Region
838 Fifth Avenue 10021 249-1011

> This is the Reform movement's youth arm, with chapters
> throughout the United States and Canada. The CRaFTY
> region (City Region at Federation of Temple Youth) services
> the city, with individual chapter meetings and programs, as
> well as regional and national events. You usually need to be a
> member of a Reform synagogue to enter the youth group,
> although each synagogue may decide for itself how to handle
> that issue, and sometimes unaffiliated kids are permitted to
> join.

United Synagogue Of America
Department of Youth Activities, METNY Region
155 Fifth Avenue 10011 533-7800

> The synagogue arm of the Conservative movement runs
> programs nationally for over 30,000 young people, ages ten to
> eighteen, through its Kadima and USY (United Synagogue
> Youth) divisions. These programs are operated through
> synagogues, and normally you need to be a member of the
> synagogue to join. Many Manhattan Conservative synagogues
> have active chapters of both Kadima and USY, and United
> Synagogue will be happy to tell you where they are. In
> addition to local chapter meetings and programs, there are
> regional weekend events and summer programs, both in the
> United States and Israel.

SUMMER PROGRAMS

Once upon a time it looked like the Jewish community folded up
for the summer. Then we learned that it hadn't closed, it had
just moved to the Catskills. Today, the Jewish community runs
summer programs for kids ages six to eighteen all over. In
Manhattan, there are organizations, synagogues and day schools
running day camps, sleepaway camps, teen trips and programs
in Israel. Some of these programs vary from year to year; be
sure to call your local synagogue or community center for new
programs that may have developed since we went to press.

DAY CAMPS

The Federation of Jewish Philanthropies of New York operates,
through its Ys and community centers, day camps for children
ages three to seventeen. Programs are held at local facilities, as
well as at other area locations. The Federation also maintains

campgrounds on Long Island, Staten Island and at Pearl River, N.Y., all within easy reach of the community centers sponsoring the camp. For more information concerning the specific programs, call your local community center.

Educational Alliance   197 East Broadway   475-6200

Emanu-El Midtown YM–YWHA   344 East 14th Street   674-7200

92nd Street YM–YWHA   1395 Lexington Avenue   427-6000

YM–YWHA of Washington Heights and Inwood 54 Nagle Avenue   569-6200

SLEEPAWAY CAMPS

Jewish sleepaway camps have proved to be valuable tools in developing Jewish identity, as well as offering a wonderful opportunity for city kids to get out into the fresh air. We found camps sponsored by a variety of organizations, each seeking to combine an intense Jewish experience with the flavor of its particular philosophy, along with a healthy, enjoyable time. Please remember that we have listed only those programs whose base is in Manhattan; many sleepaway camps have their main offices in Brooklyn, or other parts of the country. A good resource for information concerning UJA–Federation-sponsored camps, as well as many independent camps throughout the country, is the Association of Jewish Sponsored Camps, which has a pamphlet of member camps, describing facilities, programs and the like. You can write or call this group, 130 East 59th Street, 10022 (751-0477).

There are also many private sleepaway camps that, while having no organizational affiliation, are mainly comprised of Jewish kids, and have some Jewish arts and crafts. Although we have not listed these, you can call the American Camping Association (986-8877), if you're interested in such a program.

Camp Agudah–Camp B'nos   Ferndale, N.Y.   Agudath Israel 5 Beekman Street 10038   791-1800

> These two camps, Agudah for boys and B'nos for girls, have Orthodox programs run by Agudath Israel. Religious activities, athletics and cultural programs are structured for children and teenagers. Of course, dietary laws are observed.

American Jewish Society for Service
15 East 26th Street 10010   732-7400

> This independent national social service organization runs three or four summer work camps for high school kids. It seeks to put the Jewish value of righteousness into practice by enabling young people to work in deprived communities. The work is usually physical, building schools and repairing bridges. Camp sessions last seven weeks, with sixteen to eighteen teenagers at each location.

B'nai B'rith Perlman   Starlight, Pa.
B'nai B'rith Youth Organization
823 United Nations Plaza 10017   490-3327

> This camp has a Jewish cultural bent, with emphasis on outdoor activities. Both boys and girls ages eight to sixteen attend the camp for three, four, or seven weeks. Kids come from all over the country to this Pennsylvania site. Dietary laws are observed.

Cejwin   Port Jervis, N.Y.
15 East 26th Street 10010   696-1024

> This is a nondenominational private camp with a creative Jewish program. Kids ages six to sixteen come for one or two months for a full camp program, as well as some unusual activities such as photography and electronics. Dietary laws are observed.

Chavatzeleth   Woodbourn, N.Y.
142 Broome Street 10002   473-4500

> This is a strictly Orthodox camp, run through the Beth Jacob School. Girls ages six to fifteen come for eight weeks, for a full summer-camp program. The camp is glatt kosher.

Eisner Camp Institute   Great Barrington, Mass.
Union of American Hebrew Congregations
838 Fifth Avenue 10021   249-0100, ext. 496

> This Reform movement camp serving the Greater New York area (as well as Northeast Canada and New England) has a strong liberal Jewish program. Both boys and girls, ages eight to seventeen, participate in either four- or eight-week programs. Dietary laws are not observed.

Galil   Oatsville, Pa   Habonim Camping Association
27 West 20th Street 10011   255-1796

> This Zionist camp tries to approximate a kibbutz-like atmosphere, while running a full camp program for children ages eight to sixteen. Hebrew is taught and informal discussions are held concerning Jewish topics such as social justice, Israel and Jewish history. Dietary laws are observed.

Kinderland   Tolland, Mass.   Friends of Camp
Kinderland   1 Union Square West   10003   255-6283

This is another Yiddish camp that has a Jewish secular program
and also teaches the Yiddish language. Children ages seven to
sixteen-and-a-half come for three-, four- or seven-week
programs. Dietary laws are not observed.

Kinder Ring   Hopewell Junction, N.Y.
Workman's Circle
45 East 33nd Street   10016   889-6800

This is a Yiddish cultural camp that also happens to have a nine-
hole golf course and a ham radio club. Kids ages seven through
fifteen come for one or two months. Dietary laws are not
observed.

Camp Kutz   Warwick, N.Y.
838 Fifth Avenue   10021   249-0100

This is the national teen camp of the Reform movement, taking
kids recommended by Reform congregations, who are fourteen
and over. The camp offers a college campus–style atmosphere,
with programming in Jewish studies, Hebrew, the arts and other
camping activities. Kids come for three or seven weeks.

Leah   Bear Mountain, N.Y.   Educational Alliance
197 East Broadway   10002   475-6061

This camp has a Jewish cultural program. It serves the greater
New York region, taking children ages seven-and-a-half to
sixteen. There is a three-, six- or nine-week option. Dietary laws
are observed.

Mogen Avraham—Chaim Heller   Swan Lake, N.Y.
114 Fifth Avenue   10011   691-5548

This camp is oriented specifically towards Orthodox Yeshiva
students. It serves only boys, ages seven to sixteen. There is a
full camp program along with daily study. It is glatt kosher.

Moshava   Indian Orchard, Pa.
B'nei Akiva of North America
25 West 26th Street   10010   683-4484

B'nei Akiva is one of the largest religious Zionist youth groups
in North America, and operates a summer camp for boys and
girls ages nine to fifteen. There is a full camp program, along
with Hebrew speaking and instruction. Children go for either
four or eight weeks, and there is an emphasis on outdoor
activities.

Poyntelle–Ray Hill and Lewis Village Teen Camp
Poyntelle, Pa.   253 West 72nd Street 10023   787-7974

These two camps serve kids ages seven to thirteen at one facility
and ages fourteen to seventeen at the other. They are full camp
programs offering both four- or eight-week options. Dietary
laws are observed.

Camp Ramah in the Berkshires   Wingdale, N.Y.
Jewish Theological Seminary of America
3080 Broadway 10027   749-0754

The Conservative movement sponsors sleepaway camps
throughout the United States and Canada; the facility in the
Berkshires serves the greater metropolitan area. Children ages
nine to fifteen participate in daily services and classes in Hebrew
and Jewish civilization and texts. Recreational activities are all
run in Hebrew, as are other programs throughout the camp.
What you don't know at the beginning of July, you're bound to
pick up by the end of August. Only children recommended by
Conservative synagogues or day schools attend Camp Ramah,
which observes the dietary laws.

Shomria   Liberty, N.Y.   Hashomer Hatzair
150 Fifth Avenue, Suite 709 10011   929-4955

This Zionist camp, affiliated with Hashomer Hatzair, has a
Jewish secular program oriented towards kibbutz values.
Hebrew is taught to the children, ages nine to sixteen, who come
for six weeks. Dietary laws are not observed.

Sternberg—Anna Heller   Narrowsburg, N.Y.
114 Fifth Avenue 10011   691-5548

Sternberg serves Orthodox girls, ages eight through fourteen.
There is daily study, as well as a full camp program, which girls
attend for three or six weeks. It is glatt kosher. Heller, also
Federation-sponsored and serving Orthodox girls, is for
teenagers from fourteen to sixteen, and runs for four weeks.

Surprise Lake Camp   Cold Spring, N.Y.
Surprise Lake Camp   80 Fifth Avenue 10011

Surprise Lake Camp has a Jewish and Israeli cultural program,
along with a full camping program. Children ages seven
through fifteen-and-a-half come for either one or two months.
Dietary laws are observed.

Sussex   Sussex, N.J.
Camp Sussex, Inc.   1140 Broadway 10001   683-8528

This private camp serves the Greater New York area and takes
children ages seven to twelve for a three-week session, and
thirteen to fifteen year olds for a two-week program. What
makes Camp Sussex unique on the camping scene is that it is
free. The camp is large, with about 800 children, and provides a

full range of programs, including Sabbath services. Dietary laws are observed.

Tel Yehuda/Camp Young Judaea–Sprout Lake
Barryville, N.Y. and Verbank, N.Y.
Hadassah Zionist Youth Commission
50 West 58th Street 10019 255-7900

Tel Yehuda and Sprout Lake, both part of the Hashachar Zionist Youth Program of Hadassah, have strong Jewish and Israeli cultural programs. In fact, Israeli children live with the American campers. Tel Yehuda is for teenagers between the ages of fourteen and eighteen, while Sprout Lake is for younger children, ages nine to thirteen.

SUMMER TRIPS IN AMERICA

92nd Street YM–YWHA
1395 Lexington Avenue 427-6000

For years, the 92nd Street Y has been running bicycle tours, in different parts of the country, for teenagers. There isn't much Jewish content to these programs, although most of the participants are Jewish.

USY on Wheels 155 Fifth Avenue 10010 533-7800, ext. 2314

This program, now over twenty-five years old, takes several groups of forty-five teenagers, between the ages of fourteen-and-a-half and eighteen, on a bus trip throughout the United States. Sponsored by the youth arm of the Conservative movement, the program provides experiences in intensive Jewish living while on the road, observing *kashrut* and Shabbat, and linking up with Conservative congregations at various times.

PROGRAMS IN ISRAEL

American Zionist Youth Foundation
515 Park Avenue 10022 751-6070

Affiliated with the American Zionist Federation, an umbrella group of Zionist organizations in the United States, AZYF sponsors several trips to Israel for American high school students. Six-week trips include programs of touring, kibbutz work, study, sports and arts, with lots of combinations. There are also special trips for religious youth.

Betar Summer Programs
9 East 38th Street 10016 696-0080

In addition to the Bar or Bat Mitzvah program, Betar

sponsors several different trips to Israel for teenagers, with programs of touring, photography, learning and sports. Trips to Europe are often included at the end of the Israel trips.

B'nei Akiva of North America
25 West 26th Street 10010 889-5992

B'nei Akiva runs two Israel programs for religious teenagers who have completed the tenth grade. One is essentially a tour program, while the other focuses on a work-study program on a kibbutz, with a two-week touring program.

Hashachar of Hadassah
141 West 28th Street 10001 736-8330

Hashachar, the organization for youth activities of Hadassah, runs two Israel programs for high school students. The Hashachar Israel experience, open to all interested teenagers between the ages of fifteen and eighteen, is a six-week touring and study program. The Hadracha Seminar, also six weeks long, is designed for specially selected Young Judaeans (the youth group of Hadassah) who have demonstrated leadership ability and commitment to the movement.

Hashomer Hatzair 150 Fifth Avenue 10011 929-4955
This Zionist youth movement, with over ninety kibbutzim in Israel and a wide array of youth activities and summer programs here in the United States, has a leadership program in Israel for sixteen-year-olds.

Kibbutz Aliya Desk
575 Avenue of the Americas 10011 255-1338

This central office, representing the kibbutzim in Israel, has various programs for teens who are interested in spending some time on a kibbutz.

Masada of the Zionist Organization of America
4 East 34th Street 10016 481-1500

In addition to the teenage camp for thirteen and fourteen-year-olds, Masada has several trips, including programs of touring, leadership development, kibbutz work, hiking and camping, arts and sports.

National Conference of Synagogue Youth
45 West 36th Street 10018 563-4000

Under the auspices of the Orthodox Union, NCSY sponsors several Israel programs for high school students, including one that takes kids to a religious army base.

Nativ—USY Year Program in Israel
155 Fifth Avenue 10010 533-7800

Under the auspices of the United Synagogue, an arm of the

Conservative movement, Nativ is linked academically with Hebrew University in Jerusalem, and offers special Hebrew language and culture classes in addition to a full semester of work, which may be accepted by American universities. Social, cultural and religious programming is included. The program is geared for students in their last year of high school.

NFTY-High School Programs in Israel
838 Fifth Avenue 10021 249-0100

The Reform movement's commitment to the state of Israel is reflected in its several summer programs there for high school kids. Most are six weeks long (there's also an eight-week ulpan program for students who are serious about learning Hebrew), and feature a variety of special programs. The NFTY Israel Academy is a combination tour and volunteer work program, while the Israel Safari stresses travel with a special emphasis on nature. There is a program for students who are especially interested in participating in archaeological digs, and, finally, a Mitzvah Corps program where students work together with Israeli youth in a youth village.

USY Pilgrimage   155 Fifth Avenue 10010   533-7800

This program, run by the Conservative movement's youth division, is designed for high school students between the ages of fifteen and eighteen-and-a-half who are members of Conservative synagogues. It is six weeks in length, and combines travel through Israel with study. In 1986, there was also an added week in Poland, with special emphasis on the Holocaust and the history of Polish Jewry.

World Zionist Organization, American Section, Inc.
515 Park Avenue 10022   752-0600

WZO runs two programs for high school students who are interested in studying in Israel for a year. Tenth graders enroll in the America-Israel Secondary School program at Kibbutz Kfar Blum, where they attend the Huleh Valley Regional High School. Eleventh graders join the Beit Hashita program, attending the Kibbutz Beit Hashita High School. American curricula are offered, taught in English, with Hebrew language and literature offered as well. Both programs are integrated into kibbutz life: students work on the kibbutz and participate in social and cultural events. In most cases, credit received through these programs is transferable to American secondary schools.

Chapter 2
PROGRAMS FOR COLLEGE STUDENTS

Years ago, Jewish parents sent their sons and daughters off
to college with a dictionary and the address of the local
Hillel House, "so you'll have a place to eat on Shabbes."
Although there's still a good deal of eating going on in the
Jewish campus groups throughout the city, there are also
politics, dancing and singing, worship, socializing, study
and social service work taking place, largely under the
auspices of B'nai B'rith Hillel–Jewish Association for College Youth, 95 Madison Avenue, Suite 401–402, 10016
(696-1590). JACY, as the agency is known, is actually a
coordinated effort between B'nai B'rith Hillel, whose base
is in Washington and whose involvement in campus work
has been diminishing in the last several years, and the
Federation of Jewish Philanthropies, which prior to this
joint venture had a smaller Jewish group that was present
on some of the campuses in the city. In 1981, the two
groups joined forces and today have Jewish groups on five
Manhattan campuses.

CAMPUS PROGRAMS

City College of the City University of New York
475 West 140th Street 10031 234-7317

JACY estimates that about five percent of the 18,000 students at City College are Jewish. A wide range of religious, cultural, educational and social programs take place here, including a weekly Friday evening Shabbat program. Hebrew and Yiddish are usually taught, and there's Israeli dancing.

Columbia University 105 Earl Hall 10027 280-5111

Columbia has a Jewish chaplain as well as a staff person from JACY, who also happens to be the associate Jewish chaplain. Together and separately these two rabbis work with fifteen student groups at Columbia and Barnard. Activities include outreach to the campus through cultural and social events, religious programming for undergraduates and graduate students, a theatre group, a Homelessness project, a Jewish women's group and interfaith activities.

Hunter College 47 East 65th Street 10021 734-2600

Located at Roosevelt House, the interfaith student activities center of Hunter, the B'nai B'rith Hillel–Jewish Association for College Youth program here is attuned to the needs of a commuter population. Events are scheduled during the "Dean's Hour," when there are no classes, and include lectures, films, discussion groups and holiday celebrations. There is a library of Judaica, a kosher kitchen, and a lounge at Roosevelt House, which provide an opportunity for social interaction among Jewish students at Hunter.

New York University Jewish Culture Foundation
Loeb Student Center, Room 715
566 LaGuardia Place 10012 982-0428

There are actually two groups at NYU, the primary one being the Jewish Culture Foundation, which is related not to JACY, but to the Hebrew Culture Department of the University itself. JCF publishes a newspaper, with a circulation of 19,000, for Jewish students and faculty. There are social action committees, Israeli dancing once a week and daily religious services. A kosher meal plan and individual kosher meals are offered through the Kosher Kitchen. JACY is also at NYU, with a dormitory outreach program to provide programming, a student group interested in Israeli politics and a Campus UJA Campaign.

Pace University Downtown 41 Park Row 10038 488-1590

This largely non-Jewish commuter campus has a Jewish

Student Association that focuses on providing community through Shabbat dinners, holiday programs and outreach programs.

Although B'nai B'rith Hillel–JACY serves all Jewish students, there are other groups on campuses in Manhattan specifically directed to students with particular denominational concerns.

National Council of Young Israel Campus Outreach Program (Orthodox)
3 West 16th Street 10011 929-1525

NCSY Alumni Services (Orthodox)
45 West 36th Street 10018 563-4000

OMETZ (Conservative)
Jewish Theological Seminary 3080 Broadway 10027 678-8000

UAHC College Education Department (Reform)
838 Fifth Avenue 10021 249-0100

CITY-WIDE PROGRAMS

American Zionist Youth Foundation, University Service Department 515 Park Avenue 10022 751-6070

The central address for assistance to campus groups and those interested in Zionist activities, USD has representatives on campuses throughout Manhattan who promote study in Israel for college and graduate students, especially at the five Israeli universities who have overseas programs for English-speaking students.

B'nai B'rith–JACY 95 Madison Avenue 10016 696-1590

JACY also has several city-wide programs for Jewish students, including a Department of Graduate Programs, primarily at the Business and Law Schools of NYU, which holds lectures, cultural events, parties and holiday celebrations. The Special Projects Departmment has been involved in sending city students to Israel, organizing voter registration within the Jewish campus population and city-wide fund raising. JACY sponsors a Summer Internship Program, where students work in Jewish organizations to gain first-hand experience. The Jewish Communal Services Fellowship at JACY provides professional training experience for potential Jewish communal leaders. Students interested in volunteering their time to a Jewish organization can do so through the Community Service Volunteer Internship at JACY. Since college students in Manhattan are often in the city during the summers, JACY sponsors Summer in the City, with social, educational and cultural events in town and around the area.

Dorot   251 West 100th Street 10025   864-7410

This is a UJA–Federation-supported group that helps Upper West Side Jews in need, largely through the help of volunteers, many of whom are college and graduate students in Manhattan.

Israel Student Organization
515 Park Avenue 10022   688-6796

The Israel Student Organization is a resource in the United States for Israeli students studying here. It holds social, cultural and educational events on a periodic basis.

Jewish Student Press Service
15 East 26th Street 10010   679-1411

JSPS puts out a monthly packet of articles on Jewish life, serving both as an information resource for Jews on campuses throughout the country and as a vehicle for student journalists.

Kiruv Program   Yeshiva University
500 West 185th Street 10033   960-5262

This is an outreach program to unaffiliated or isolated Jewish students in American colleges and universities throughout the Northeast. It is a student-operated program with forty or fifty volunteers (mostly from Yeshiva) who give their time to present Jewish identity programs at college campuses with few or no Jewish resources. Often their focus is on schools with fairly high intellectual standards and a sort of "hidden Jewish population." They travel to twenty-five or thirty campuses a year, including several in the metropolitan area, presenting programs on topics like "Jewish Conceptions of Sexuality" or celebrating Jewish holidays away from home. The program is jointly sponsored by Yeshiva University and the Rabbinical Council of America.

North American Jewish Students Appeal
15 East 26th Street 10010   679-2293

This student fund-raising group devotes itself to helping support its constituent groups, which include Student Struggle for Soviet Jewry, Yugntruf–Youth for Yiddish, *Response* magazine and the Jewish Student Press Service. The group also raises money for local and regional Jewish student programs throughout the country.

North American Jewish Students' Network
1 Park Avenue   Suite 418 10016   689-0790

The umbrella group for all Jewish student groups through North America, NAJSN sponsors seminars and conferences and maintains a resource center and speakers bureau.

Progressive Zionist Caucus
27 West 20th Street 10011   675-1168

> Habonim Dror, the Labor Zionist Youth Group, has a college division, and offers a political, left-wing perspective on Israeli activities. There are active groups at NYU and Columbia.

Project Ezra   197 East Broadway 10022   982-4124

> This independent agency that services the Lower East Side Jewish community does so with the help and support of its volunteers, many of whom are college and graduate students in Manhattan.

Student Struggle For Soviet Jewry
210 West 91st Street 10024   799-8900

> This national group is committed to educating the world to the plight of Jews in the Soviet Union. Through study groups, publications, cultural programming and political action, SSSJ works toward freedom for the oppressed Jews in Russia.

Task Force on Missionaries and Cults
Jewish Community Relations Council
111 West 40th Street 10018 221-1535

> Established to educate and sensitize the Jewish community to the dangers of cults and missionary activity, this JCRC group has an outreach worker, who, in conjunction with B'nai B'rith Hillel–JACY, organizes programs to alert college students to these dangers. Workshops have been held at NYU, Stern and Yeshiva University in Manhattan.

ISRAEL TRAVEL, STUDY AND WORK PROGRAMS

There are several programs designed specifically for college and graduate students who want to spend time in Israel, whether to work, study, travel or engage in other creative activities.

American Zionist Youth Foundation
515 Park Avenue 10022   750-7773

> AZYF, an independent branch of the Zionist movement, runs many student groups to Israel, and their college-age programs include straight tours and many combinations of sightseeing and working on a kibbutz for various lengths of time. There is also an archaeology program at Hebrew University, a workshop at the Jerusalem Film Center and an intensive study program at the Pardes Institute of Jewish Studies. Through *Sherut La'Am*, graduate students (and others who have

graduated college) spend six months or a year in Israel, working in their chosen fields (medicine, law, the sciences, education, etc.), or exploring a new one.

Betar   9 East 38th Street 10016   696-0080

Betar is a Zionist group affiliated with Israel's Herut party. It sponsors a variety of Israel trips for several age groups and runs two special college programs. One combines travel through Israel with a personalized program that might include working on a *moshav*, volunteering on an army base, study or being on one's own. The other is a six-week program for "activists" that combines volunteering on special projects for the state of Israel, and three weeks of studying about Israel politics and visiting Betar's new settlements, located beyond the Green Line.

Kibbutz Aliya Desk   27 West 20th Street 10011 255-1338

This umbrella group that coordinates programs for those interested in making *aliya* runs several programs in Israel for college students, including a six-month kibbutz study program (accredited by many universities), shorter summer kibbutz ulpan, kibbutz work programs, Israeli university programs and combination work-study kibbutz programs.

NCSY Israel Programs
45 West 36th Street 10018   563-4000

The youth movement of the Union of Orthodox Jewish Congregations sponsors a Yeshiva trip to Israel for college students who want to combine travel and study.

NFTY College Programs in Israel
838 Fifth Avenue 10021   249-0100

The Reform movement runs both summer and year-long programs in Israel. College credit for work in Israel may be obtained through study at Hebrew Union College in Jerusalem. There are college-kibbutz combinations, with travel dimensions as well.

Zionist Organization of America
4 East 34th Street 10016   481-1500

The Masada program of ZOA runs a college-student tour throughout Israel, as well as a seminar program for those students who wish to combine a full touring itinerary with study and field work and an opportunity to get to know the people as well as the land.

Chapter 3
SINGLES

Back in the fifties and sixties, senior girls who returned to school after winter vacation without a rock on the appropriate finger were to be pitied. Those who didn't marry as soon as they finished school, found jobs or did volunteer work while waiting for Mr. Right. The late sixties turned the world upside down, and in the seventies and eighties women have been more interested in moving rapidly up the corporate ladder than down the aisle to stand under the *chuppah*. Career opportunities and a climbing divorce rate may have made marriage less central, but still, the Big Apple can be a lonely place for singles. Anyone who reads the personals in the back of *New York* magazine or *The Village Voice* can see that.

The 1984 American Jewish Yearbook lists more than 54,000 young Jewish singles and more than 33,000 mature Jewish singles in Manhattan, and the Jewish community is attempting to respond strongly to their needs. Since Judaism has always viewed marriage as the preferred state, Jewish matchmaking and dating services (both professional and amateur) have long existed, but now synagogues, which used to be thought of only as family places, are making serious attempts to reach the singles community. Singles are welcomed as members, and many synagogues have special singles clubs, social events, discussion groups and even *minyanim*. "Take a course, maybe you'll meet someone nice," our mothers always said. Actually it's not a bad way to meet people, and you may enjoy doing this at one of the Ys or organizations we've listed in our chapters on learning or culture. In any case, there's a lot going on for Jewish singles these days, and if you've had enough of singles bars we hope you'll try some of our listings.

If you've just arrived in New York and are having difficulty finding an apartment, you should know that the 92nd Street Y has a residence for young men and women between the ages of eighteen and twenty-six right in its building on Lexington Avenue. There are simply-furnished single and double rooms, shared baths and kitchens (as well as a separate central kosher kitchen) and weekly cleaning and linen service. There is a lounge, twenty-four hour security, and of course there are all those Y services, including classes, performing arts, music school and library. This is not a transient hotel, and the minimum residence requirement is three months, with a maximum of three years. Applicants must complete forms that include references and be accepted by an admissions committee. Most of the 350 young people who use the residence are students attending metropolitan area schools, but it would be a good place for someone just starting a job in New York to get a feel for the city and live in a comfortable atmosphere with lots of Jewish activity, all in one of the best neighborhoods in Manhattan. Another residence, this one on the Upper West Side, is popular among young Orthodox men and women. The Esplanade, 305 West End Avenue (874-5000), rents rooms by the day.

SYNAGOGUE SINGLES GROUPS

If you've ever been to Friday evening services at Lincoln Square or Sutton Place synagogues, you'll know where some Jewish yuppies park their briefcases when the sun goes down. Programs can vary drastically from synagogue to synagogue, and some are geared to specialized groups, such as the divorced or widowed, so you should call your neighborhood synagogue for information. We are listing here those synagogues that have made a commitment to singles by providing substantial programs. By the way, if you already belong to a synagogue and are interested in starting a singles group, the Task Force on Jewish Singles of the Commission on Synagogue Relations of UJA–Federation has published a booklet called "Reaching Out," which includes tips on planning, programming, developing a mailing list and attracting leaders.

The Brotherhood Synagogue *Conservative*
28 Gramercy Park South 10003 674-5740

The singles group here, which meets as often as twice a week, is open to anyone and particularly focuses on people in their forties, fifties, and sixties. There is a mixture of social events, including lectures, discussions and communal meals. Discussions seem to zero in on topics relevant for the group, which might include talking about new relationships in mid-life. There are many events on Sundays. A small contribution is asked for each individual event.

Central Synagogue *Reform*
652 Lexington Avenue 10022 939-5122

Makor, Central Synagogue's group for twenty-five to forty year olds, is open to singles and couples, but most of those who attend programs are singles, and there are usually fifty to eighty people. They meet one Friday evening a month for a service, guest speaker and *Oneg Shabbat.*

Congregation Kehilath Jeshurun *Orthodox*
125 East 85th Street 10028 427-1000

Kehilath Jeshurun holds Shabbat dinners for singles a few times a year, and they have other get-togethers with pizza and socializing. They usually have about 100 people attending. You don't need to be a member of the synagogue and you can call to get on their mailing list.

Congregation Rodeph Sholom *Reform*
7 West 83rd Street 10024 362-8800

Rodeph Sholom's young adults group is open to singles and marrieds from twenty-five to forty-six years old, and meets every six weeks for a program that might include dinner and a speaker or a film and dessert. The programs are open to nonmembers, and there is a fee for each event, which draws between forty and eighty people.

Lincoln Square Synagogue *Orthodox*
200 Amsterdam Avenue 10023 874-6105

Although there is no regularly scheduled program, the singles events at Lincoln Square, which are geared to those in their midtwenties to early forties, often draw as many as 300 people. Events are open to nonmembers, and they have a mailing list of about 2000 singles. They suggest mailing in a request with your name and address to get on the list and receive information about singles events.

Maimonides Temple *Unaffiliated*
P.O. Box 20374 10017 722-6984

This new synagogue is *devoted to singles;* it began in the fall of 1985 with a blurb in *New York* magazine promising that singles who felt unwelcome at more traditional family-oriented synagogues would find a haven here. Since that time, the rabbi says that there have been several hundred at each of the monthly Friday night services. With that success behind it, the synagogue has continued its commitment to fulfill not just the spiritual needs of singles but also their cultural and social interests, "to create a real sense of community for singles." It tries to fill these combined needs in its programming, and has been holding monthly Friday night Sabbath dinners before services. Dinners are kosher style and there is singing and plenty of socializing, followed by an *Oneg Shabbat* (coffee and dessert) and then services. Since there are no membership dues for Maimonides Temple, there is a contribution for these monthly services, and you can attend the dinner and services, or just the services and *Oneg*. Included with the reservation form for the dinner is a questionnaire that includes room for personal data about yourself, as well as a chance to indicate what services you would like to see the Maimonides Temple provide. Services have been held at the United Engineering Center at 345 East 47th Street.

Mt. Sinai Jewish Center *Orthodox*
135 Bennett Avenue 10033 928-9870

This progressive Orthodox congregation in Washington Heights draws many students from Yeshiva University and has become something of a center for young singles in this neighborhood.

Park Avenue Synagogue *Conservative*
50 East 87th Street 10028 368-2600

The Club 87, for twenty-one to thirty-one year olds has a monthly coffee house, and a committee also plans other events. There is a small charge to be included in their mailing list of about 100 people. The synagogue also has a club for thirty-one to fifty year olds (mostly divorced) that holds a service and *Oneg Shabbat* once a month.

Park East Synagogue *Orthodox*
163 East 67th Street 10021 737-6900

Park East Young Professionals Group is open to all Jewish
singles who wish to attend. The group sees itself as both an
educational and social forum and has monthly meetings with
speakers. Since this Upper East Side congregation has some of
New York City's movers and shakers as members (Seagrams,
Rothschilds and Ralph Lauren included) the monthly
programs of the group usually have prominent speakers.

Sutton Place Synagogue *Conservative*
225 East 51st Street 10022 593-3300

Sutton Place Synagogue has one of the strongest commitments
to singles in the city, and we know people who have joined
just because of that. Its Singles Havurah (Fellowship) has
strong programming throughout the year, including High
Holy Day singles services, an all-singles Passover seder,
monthly *Shabbaton* and many events incorporating worship,
study and socializing. There are brunches, parties, dances,
trips and guest speakers for discussion groups. Some social
events are for specific age groups. In addition, Sutton Place's
adult education catalogue includes several courses listed under
a "single and social" category, including "Picking a Partner"
and "How to Prepare a Simple Party (On Your Own)"; other
courses in their Center for Personal Enrichment would be of
interest to singles. Members of the synagogue are
automatically members of the Singles Havurah and can
participate in all events. Singles Havurah Affiliates who choose
not to join the synagogue as full members pay a separate
membership fee that entitles them to participate only in
Havurah events and the synagogue's adult education
programs.

Temple Emanu-El *Reform*
1 East 65th Street 10021 744-1400

The Emanu-El League, for singles between twenty-one and
forty, is an active social group with regular functions that are
usually attended by 50 or 100 people. Nonmembers may
attend an event or two, but then you must join the synagogue
to be part of the singles group. There is also a Temple Society
for singles between the ages of fifty and eighty that has its
own events.

SINGLES PROGRAMS AT Ys
AND OTHER ORGANIZATIONS

B'nai Zion Singles   136 East 39th Street 10012   725-1211

This fraternal organization, with chapters throughout the metropolitan area, sponsors singles dances at its different chapters. The dances are geared mainly to those between twenty-five and forty-nine, but because this organization performs varied functions (from fund raising to providing insurance plans for its members) and spans denominational and other differences, each chapter may have a different character, with predominantly Orthodox or liberal members as well as varied age groups. Since the separate chapters in the boroughs all hold social events, you might want to try different chapters until you find one that suits you. Call B'nai Zion for information about membership.

Educational Alliance West
51 East 10th Street 10003   420-1150

This Village Y is the center for Compatimates, Federation's new singles introduction and dating service, described in more detail under dating services. "Sunday Night Live," a series of lectures and discussions on topics ranging from politics to art, as well as subjects like stress and women's equality, is aimed at singles. There is a fee per evening (which covers the expense of the speaker as well as the wine and cheese served) and since space is somewhat limited at this Y, they recommend advance registration.

Emanu-El Midtown YM–YWHA
344 East 14th Street   674-7200

The Emanu-El Y sponsors the East Side Singles group for singles in their forties and fifties. They meet at the Town and Village Conservative Synagogue and the monthly programming includes parties, lecture-discussions and workshops led by psychologists or other experts in topics like Recognizing a Good Relationship. Group Yafa, designed for singles under forty, meets once a month for volley ball and swimming, entertainment, dancing and other social programs.

Mizrachi Young Leadership Council
25 West 26th Street 10010   684-6091

This social and educational coed Orthodox singles group caters to young professionals from twenty-two to thirty-five years old. They meet in different people's homes and often have outstanding personalities as speakers, including diplomats and well-known government people (they once had the Counsel

General of Israel and on another occasion the Jewish advisor to President Reagan). They have also begun to publish a serious journal. This is a serious, high-level organization, but it definitely is a social one too.

National Council of Young Israel

3 West 16th Street 10011   929-1525, ext. 19

Young Israel, a branch of the Orthodox movement, runs a Collegiate and Young Adult Group that provides social, educational and recreational activities for modern Orthodox young people, mostly between eighteen and twenty-seven. They sponsor ski trips, concerts and *Shabbaton* in other cities. There is great diversity in the events as well as the membership which numbers about 1000 (forty percent collegiate, sixty percent professional). They also sponsor some Israel-oriented programs. There is an annual membership fee.

92nd Street YM–YWHA

1395 Lexington Avenue 10128   427-6000

As part of its Group Service Department, the Y runs several different programs for singles. Social groups are for singles between the ages of twenty-one and sixty, and people within the same age range meet on Sunday afternoons with a Y coordinator who plans different activities, including parties, trips, picnics, concerts and lectures. In addition, there are discussion groups cosponsored by the Jewish Board of Family and Children's Services that cover topics pertinent to singles, such as the advantages of being single, difficulties in forming new relationships, ending relationships, and friendship. These groups, led by instructors, are divided by age category. Classes for singles run in three to six-week cycles and most cover cultural topics such as Early Film Classics, or appreciation of classical music for the concert goer, although we also saw listed a series of classes in social dance, finishing up with a trip to Roseland. "Sunday Evenings at the Y" are lectures by well-known guests, on topics as varied as Middle East politics and Sexuality in the 80s, presumably including discussion and also some socializing. In addition to all these classes, the Y runs a Singles Coffeehouse Series for singles under forty that meets at the Spanish Portuguese Synagogue on the Upper West Side, where a social hour and refreshments follow a presentation by a guest speaker.

Union of Orthodox Jewish Congregations of America

45 West 36th Street 10018   563-4000

The New York region's singles programs feature after-work buffet-lectures by prominent area rabbis and special weekends with religious, educational and social programs.

INDEPENDENT SINGLES GROUPS

Everything For Singles, Inc.
381 Park Avenue South   Suite 1112 10016   213-5515

This large company has several subdivisions that plan events for Jewish singles of various ages. Le Juda (213-3945) is their main organization for singles from twenty-two to thirty-nine. They began about ten years ago by sponsoring dances in synagogues, and now they run parties in New York at large clubs like Area and Tavern on the Green. They average one or two parties a week on Saturday or Sunday and charge per event. Their mailing list has over 2000 people and between 400 and 1000 usually show up for each event. You can call for information and get on their mailing list by attending one of the events. Weekend Rendezvous (213-3366) sponsors weekend trips to major hotels in the Catskills and the Poconos, often on a holiday weekend. They bring their own staff or organize activities like pool parties, aerobics and disco dancing, and the weekends usually draw more than 500 people. Kosher food is always available. Sports Mates (213-3368) is a new venture, offering volleyball games once a week at a gym on the East Side and other sports activities for singles. A new program called Rendezvous Packages, vacations for singles, is just beginning. The company maintains a 24-hour party hotline for information about upcoming events in all programs (213-3944).

Jewish Singles of Greater New York
530 Grand Street 10002   Call Charlie, 228-0128

The age range here is from graduate school to forty-five, and activities include weekends, parties and trips. They often meet in synagogues, and all food served is kosher. You can write or call to get on the mailing list.

West Side Jewish Singles   Call Beth, 222-2997

Most of the activities of this group for twenty-four to thirty-nine year old single Jews are geared to the outdoors, so there are trips, hikes and picnics planned for the warm weather. There are far fewer activities during the winter months, but they do sometimes have get-togethers or dances, and occasionally they meet at Congregation Ohab Zedek on West 93rd Street. There is a range of denominations represented, but all food is kosher. You can call Beth to get on the mailing list for future events.

DATING SERVICES

Compatimates Educational Alliance West
51 East 10th Street 10003 982-8196

> This UJA–Federation-sponsored dating service began two years ago in a Greenwich Village loft and has now moved into an office at the Village Y. After filling out a confidential application and paying a small registration fee, prospective members are given a "private, relaxed interview" by social work professionals to find out what they are looking for and how those needs could best be met. At the time of the interview a larger one-year membership fee is due; you will then receive a list of people, and others will be given your phone number. In addition there are small gatherings and special events (attendance optional) for which there is a small admission charge. Age eligibility goes up to sixty, and the clientele is divided into two age groups. There is also a separate service for Orthodox Jews with its own Orthodox social worker, since the service seeks to fulfill the needs of this growing group of singles. The emphasis at Compatimates is on shared interests and aspirations as well as Jewishness and on members who have an interest in "serious meaningful relationships"—with any luck, permanent.

Jewish Singles Date Phone
381 Park Avenue South Suite 1112 10016 213-3414

> This is part of the Le Juda–Everything for Singles company, and claims to be the original and most successful service of its kind in the country. Singles call the number above weekdays between 10:00 A.M. and 5:00 P.M. to register and make a tape-recorded message describing themselves. For a fee, your tape runs twenty-four hours a day for one week, with a file number to write to, and anyone who seems interested will write to you and the service will forward the letter. The company says that the average tape message gets twenty to twenty-five letters. To hear someone who might interest you, women should call 213-3505 for the bachelor line, and men should call 213-3506 for the bachelorette line.

One to One 15 West 44th Street 10036 921-8011

> Although this is not an exclusively Jewish agency, some of their advertising is directed to Jewish singles and they will honor requests for Jewish matches. The personal interview includes among other things your date, time and place of birth; they also find out what you are looking for in a date and you get a chance to see photos. For a fee you will receive the names of people to meet. This usually averages out to approximately six calls. The service includes Manhattan, all boroughs, and suburbs.

MATCHMAKING SERVICES

Field's Exclusive Service, Inc.

41 East 42nd Street, Room 1600 10017 391-2233

Russian-born Rabbi Joe Field (whose motto was "I can arrange") had such a knack for matchmaking that friends asked him to find husbands and wives for their children. He would invite couples for Friday night dinner; if they liked each other they would eventually sign a courting contract and, if the marriage took, Rabbi Field received a percentage of the dowry. The business has stayed in the family since the agency was founded in 1920, and Dan Field himself met his wife twenty-seven years ago when her parents placed her name on file with the agency. Today it is still often parents who come in to try to find matches for their children (who are then introduced as "friends of the family"). Field claims, however, that among his clients are single professionals who are tired of singles bars and short-term live-in relationships. This is not a dating club, but serious business. "We do not play games. Our clients want to get married. And we help them find a path to the altar." This is definitely not computer-style dating, for the first thing Dan Field says when you call is, "Come in, let's talk." Clients are screened very carefully and you can call for a free interview to discuss your needs. The fees charged depend on the amount of work, and he must love the labor because Field's is open seven days a week from 10:00 A.M. to 5:30 P.M.

Marriage Commission

Orthodox Union 45 West 36th Street 10018 563-4000

This dating program is for "seriously marriage-minded Orthodox individuals." There is extensive interviewing, a personal videotape session, and the service promises to be extremely private and confidential. Appointments can be made through Orthodox rabbis or by calling the commission directly.

The Perfect Match

301 East 49th Street, Suite 5C 10017 751-5430

A recent program from Le Juda—Everything for Singles, this is billed as an "old fashioned matchmaking service." After filling out a confidential application form with personal references and photo (no applications accepted without), you receive a telephone interview. For a three month membership fee you are guaranteed three matches (name and phone number given to both parties), although since their goal is "the best possible match . . . the perfect match!" you will receive only one name at a time. The pool of Jewish singles between twenty-two and fifty numbers about 750, and matches are based on common interests and hobbies, personal traits and religious beliefs.

Chapter 4
MARRIAGE

Many couples discover that deciding to marry is only the first decision of hundreds to come, all over planning the wedding! Even the smallest, most private ceremony requires some advance planning. You'll need to think about who will perform the ceremony (in New York, that means either a member of the clergy or the court), where it will be held, who will be present, and what kind of ceremony you want. If you're planning a reception, you'll need to think about caterers and bands also. Here are some resources to help you get through some of these decisions, so you can enjoy this special time in your lives.

FINDING A RABBI OR CANTOR

If you belong to a synagogue, it is customary to invite your rabbi to officiate at the ceremony. Sometimes, a cantor is asked, either to officiate or coofficiate. Often, both the bride's rabbi and the groom's rabbi share the honor. If you don't belong to a synagogue, or for some reason would like to explore other options, there are a few ways you can go about it. Word of mouth is usually a good method, provided your interests and those of your friends are similar. You can also visit several synagogues on a Friday night or Saturday morning and learn more about a particular rabbi or cantor and his or her style. Then you can call during the week and set up an appointment. At some of the larger synagogues, you can even ask the Executive Director for permission to attend a wedding in the near future, to see what kind of ceremony that particular rabbi or cantor performs.

You can also call one of the four offices of the denominational movements in search of a rabbi or cantor. Orthodox clergy naturally only officiate in traditional ceremonies, often with separate seating for guests. Conservative clergy generally follow the basic traditional format, but will often add explanations about what is going on. Reconstructionist and Reform clergy tend to involve couples in the creation of their ceremonies, though often retaining much of the traditional ceremony as well.

Central Conference of American Rabbis Reform
21 East 40th Street 10016 684-4990

Federation of Reconstructionist Congregations and Havurot
Reconstructionist
270 West 89th Street 10025 496-2960

Rabbinical Council of America Orthodox
275 Seventh Avenue 10001 807-7888

Rabbinical Assembly Conservative
3080 Broadway 10027 678-8060

American Conference of Cantors Reform
838 Fifth Avenue 10021 737-5020

Cantor's Assembly Conservative
150 Fifth Avenue 691-8020

Jewish Ministers Cantors Association of America Orthodox
3 West 16th Street 675-6601

FINDING A SYNAGOGUE

If you're a member of a synagogue and have asked your rabbi to officiate, check to find out about using your synagogue. Usually there's only a nominal rental fee for members. If you're not a member of a synagogue, or don't want to have your wedding in your synagogue, there are many Manhattan synagogues that will rent their sanctuaries or smaller chapels to nonmembers. Sometimes, a synagogue will allow you to bring in your own rabbi (provided your rabbi has contacted the rabbi of the synagogue you are using). At other times, however, the synagogue will require you to have the rabbi of the synagogue at least coofficiate with your rabbi. Be sure to ask what the policy is before you book the synagogue. The following Manhattan synagogues open their sanctuaries to nonmembers.

The Brotherhood Synagogue
28 Gramercy Park 10010   674-5750

This landmark building right on Gramercy Park has a Sephardic-style sanctuary, with the reader's desk in the center of the room. Weddings are held there as well, with guests encircling the wedding party. The sanctuary can accommodate about 500, and there is ample banquet space as well.

Central Synagogue   123 East 55th Street 10022 838-5122

One of the largest Reform synagogues in Manhattan, Central has a very formal sanctuary that can seat 1400 people. It's beautifully maintained and done in browns and Wedgwood blues, with wooden pews and a long central aisle. A smaller chapel is also available, which can accommodate 500 people, and the banquet hall seats 300.

Civic Center Synagogue   49 White Street 10013 966-7141

This Orthodox Wall Street synagogue, designed as a kind of sculptural abstraction by William N. Breger Associates, has a very modern sanctuary that seats close to 300 people and a banquet room that can handle 360.

Community Synagogue Center
325 East 6th Street 10003   473-3665

This is another Orthodox synagogue, originally built as a church in a kind of Romanesque style. The sanctuary can hold 600 people. It also has a very small chapel for 25 people, and a banquet facility that can handle 200.

Congregation Ansche Chesed
251 West 100th Street 10025   865-0600

This popular Upper West Side synagogue has no rabbi, but does rent its various sanctuary and ballroom spaces to nonmembers. The whole building is currently undergoing renovation, some of which is already complete. The sanctuary seats 1500, the more intimate chapel seats about 100, and the ballroom can handle 180 people.

Congregation Beth Simchat Torah
325 Bethune Street 10014   929-9498

The only Gay and Lesbian synagogue in Manhattan, this West Village *shul* has a sanctuary that can seat 1000, and a room for a reception that holds about 550 people. The decor throughout isn't fancy, but comfortable.

Congregation Emunath Israel
236 West 23rd Street 10011 675-2819

Emunath Israel is an old Orthodox synagogue that has a sanctuary that seats 700. There are stained-glass windows and marble walls, wooden pews, and an old feeling. The chapel accommodates about fifty people, and a banquet facility holds 300.

Congregation K'Hal Adath Jeshurun
85 Bennett Avenue 10033 923-3582

The home for the Breuer Orthodox community of Washington Heights, this synagogue has a large, almost stark sanctuary that seats 1000 people and a banquet hall that can accommodate 300.

Congregation Kehilath Jeshurun
125 East 85th Street 10028 427-1000

The sanctuary at this Upper East Side Orthodox synagogue has a kind of brown marble feeling. The *bimah*, where the rabbi stands, is in the center of the sanctuary in Sephardic styles, so there is no center aisle. There are stained-glass windows throughout, and an upstairs balcony for women.

Congregation Orach Chaim
1459 Lexington Avenue 10028 722-6566

This traditional Orthodox synagogue has a sanctuary that seats 500, with stained-glass windows, wooden pews with wine-colored cushions, a reader's desk in the center of the room, and a women's gallery upstairs. There is also a small chapel that can hold thirty people, and banquet facilities for about 150.

Congregation Rodeph Sholom
7 West 83rd Street 10024 362-8800

A Reform synagogue in the grand style, the sanctuary at this Upper West Side synagogue has an old traditional feeling, with lots of wood. It can seat more than 1300 people, and the banquet room is one of the largest in Manhattan, accommodating 600.

Congregation Shaare Hatikvah Ahavath Torah v'Tikvoh
Chadoshoh   711 West 179th Street 10033   927-2720

An Orthodox Washington Heights *shul*, the sanctuary here can accommodate 800 people, the banquet hall 200.

Congregation Shaare Zedek
212 West 93rd Street 10025 874-7005

This traditional Conservative Upper West Side synagogue has a pretty, light-colored wood-paneled sanctuary that seats 1000 in neat wooden pews. There is a small room for receptions that can accommodate 130 people.

Congregation Shearith Israel
8 West 70th Street 10023   873-0300

The oldest congregation in the United States, this prominent Sephardic synagogue is designed like the Spanish and Portuguese Synagogue in Amsterdam, with the *bimah* in the center of the room (though weddings are normally held in front of the ark) and pews around it, with a women's balcony above. The sanctuary seats 700. If you're interested in a smaller room, the chapel accommodates about 80 people and is a duplicate of the original chapel of this congregation, with colonial fixtures. The reception room can hold 150 people.

Congregation Ohav Sholaum
4624 Broadway 10040   567-0900

This Orthodux *shul* in Washington Heights has a sanctuary that seats 1000, and banquet facilities for 250.

Congregation Talmud Torah Adereth El
135 East 29th Street 10010   685-0241

This midtown Orthodox synagogue has a sanctuary that seats 300—with stained-glass windows depicting Jewish symbols and wooden pews with cushions—and a tiny chapel that can hold 30 people. There is banquet space for 200.

Conservative Synagogue of Fifth Avenue
11 East 11th Street 10003   929-6954

As its name says, this is a Conservative synagogue in the Village, housed in a small townhouse with a garden in the front. Its modest facilities include an eighty-five seat sanctuary and similar space for parties.

Fort Tryon Jewish Center
524 Ft. Washington Avenue 10033   795-1391

A Conservative synagogue in Washington Heights, Fort Tryon has a nice and comfortable sanctuary seating 425 people, with party facilities for 250.

Hebrew Tabernacle Congregation
551 Ft. Washington Avenue 10033   568-8304

Another synagogue in Washington Heights, Hebrew Tabernacle is an unaffiliated liberal congregation with a large and impressive sanctuary, designed in art deco style with a beautiful dome, that accommodates 850 people. A smaller chapel seats 250, and the banquet facilities can handle 250 people.

The Jewish Center   131 West 86th Street 10024   724-2700

A mainstay of the Upper West Side Orthodox community, the Jewish Center has a sanctuary on the second floor with a marble altar flanked by beautiful stained-glass windows. It seats 750 people, and there is also a tiny chapel for 40 people. Banquet facilities can accommodate a party of 200.

Lincoln Square Synagogue
200 Amsterdam Avenue 10023   874-6105

This beautiful modern Orthodox sanctuary, with its curved room and unusual *mechitza* (separation between men and women is accomplished by placing one section at one end of the circle and the other at the other end, slightly elevated), can seat 420 people. It has an "open *chuppah*" for those who wish to be married under the sky. A smaller chapel is also available, seating 100. Banquet facilities, newly redecorated, can accommodate 400.

Mt. Sinai Jewish Center
135 Bennett Avenue 10040   928-9870

This modern building has been redecorated recently, and is quite spacious. The sanctuary, which has a seating capacity of approximately 400, has a high ceiling and stained-glass windows depicting various Jewish symbols. There is a center section for men, with women's sections flanking both sides. There are banquet facilities for up to 250.

Park Avenue Synagogue
50 East 87th Street 10028   369-2600

Park Avenue Synagogue is a prominent Conservative synagogue on the Upper East Side with an impressive sanctuary, decorated in Moroccan style, with beautiful mosaics. The sanctuary can accommodate 1100 people in pews covered with red-velvet cushions; stained-glass windows cover the walls, with names of congregational benefactors etched in. The smaller chapel seats 125, and banquet facilities, recently renovated, can handle 300.

Park East Synagogue   163 East 67th Street 10021 737-6900

This landmark building has a beautiful sanctuary, designed in the Moorish style, with stained-glass windows and ornate decoration throughout. The balcony seating for women is supported by floor-to-ceiling columns with rounded arches. The seating capacity here is 1000, with a small chapel for 75 people. A room for receptions can accommodate 250 people.

Society for the Advancement of Judaism
15 West 86th Street 10024   724-7000

The SAJ, the first Reconstructionist Synagogue in the world, has a simple and tasteful sanctuary that can accommodate 500 people (there's also a balcony here, for latecomers and people who prefer to sit there, not specifically for women!). The reception room can handle 180 people.

Stephen Wise Free Synagogue
30 West 68th Street 10023   877-4050

The sanctuary here, which seats 1100, was designed by the Jewish artist A. Raymond Katz, who incorporated in the building many symbols of holidays during the Jewish year. Around the ark are representations of Jewish ethics. A small chapel, which seats 90, is used for weddings and other smaller events. Banquet facilities accommodate 200 to 300 people.

Sutton Place Synagogue
225 East 51st Street 10022   593-3300

The beautiful and modern sanctuary at this Conservative synagogue has stained-glass windows and lots of light. The seating capacity is 700, with banquet facilities for 200.

Temple Israel of the City of New York
112 East 75th Street   249-5000

With one of the most dramatic arks in the city (designed by Efrem Weitzman), this Reform synagogue's sanctuary is in the round and very modern. Stained-glass panels adorn the walls of the room, which can seat 1200 people. A smaller chapel holds about 100 people, and banquet facilities can accommodate 375.

Tifereth Israel–Town and Village Conservative
Synagogue   334 East 14th Street 10003   677-8090

The charming sanctuary at this Conservative synagogue on Fourteenth Street can accommodate 600 people, but still retains a warm feeling, with soft colors, a rosewood ark framed in gold, plenty of light, and stained-glass windows depicting the Twelve Tribes. A chapel holds 75, and there is room for a party of 200.

West End Synagogue
270 West 89th Street 10024   769-3100

Walk into the sanctuary of this brand-new Reconstructionist synagogue on the Upper West Side, with its wood-paneled walls, beamed ceiling, carved pews and rich furnishings, and you will think you have just entered a medieval European castle. The room seats about 200 people, and since the synagogue is housed at the Lindenbaum Center, there are other rooms available for receptions. For more information, call 595-7929.

PREPARING FOR THE CEREMONY

RITUALS

One of the components for most Jewish weddings is the signing of a *ketuba,* or marriage contract. Dating back to the middle ages, the traditional text contains promises (mostly financial!) made by bride and groom and witnessed by two Jews. The *ketuba* developed into a rather important Jewish art form, samples of which can be seen at the Jewish Museum. The text has also evolved over the years, so that now, in addition to the traditional text, there are Conservative and Reform texts, as well as several other liberal versions. Some people even write their own *ketubot,* seeing it as an important part of their prewedding preparation. Whatever you decide, be sure to discuss it with your rabbi. Some will insist on a particular form. *Ketubot* in their simplest form are available at most Jewish bookstores. Several of those stores also carry elaborate (and more costly) versions, many of which are one-of-a-kind, or limited edition silk screens. These are usually sent back to the artist' after they are purchased, so that pertinent information (names, place of the wedding) can be calligraphed by the artist. Finally, there are now several artists working in Manhattan who do one-of-a-kind commissioned *ketubot*. These are real works of art, suitable for framing, and are designed in consultation with the bride and groom. Most of these artists will work with any text you like, and many have sample texts at the studios that you can see. Below is a list of calligraphers we've found. For more information on them, see our lists of artists in Chapter 7.

Shoshana Averbach, 663-6886
Lee Bearson, 874-3531
Fran Farber, 431-8018
Sharon Frankel, 923-6736
Jay Greenspan, 496-5399
Claire Mendelson, 928-2732
Betsy Teutsch, 866-5448

Among the accoutrements that you may need for the ceremony are yarmulkes. For a complete list of places to order them in bulk, with your names imprinted inside if you wish, look in the section on Bar and Bat Mitzvah. A beautiful custom in Judaism is for the bride to present the groom with a *tallit*, a prayer shawl, at the time of the marriage. You can buy one where you purchase yarmulkes, or have one made by one of the weavers in our list of artists. *Benchers*, which contain the special prayers said after a wedding feast, can be obtained through your caterer, or at any of the bookstores listed in Chapter 7.

It is traditional for a woman to visit the *mikvah*, or ritual bath, right before her wedding. This ritual cleansing is done by all Orthodox women. Many others do it as well, for a kind of spiritual purification. There are three *mikvaot* in Manhattan; call them for an appointment as well as information about preparation.

Jewish Women's Club
234 West 78th Street 10024 799-1520

Mikvah of the East Side
313 East Broadway 10002 475-8514

Mikvah of Washington Heights
536 East 187th Street 10033 923-9548

THE PARTY

If you're being married in a synagogue, be sure to check with them about caterers; many have either a house caterer or an approved list from which you can choose. For a list of caterers in Manhattan, see Chapter 10. Remember that there are many good kosher caterers located in other parts of the city; check the ads in the Jewish weeklies for those.

Although most bands in New York know how to play a hora, there are also groups that specialize in Jewish music, and most of them are located in boroughs outside Manhattan. Check with your caterer, or in the back of Jewish weeklies for more information on them. For a list of Manhattan entertainers who specialize in Jewish themes, see our listings in Chapter 7. One unusual Manhattan Jewish band is the all-women *Klez-meyd-lekh* (222-5507).

For invitations, you can check with calligraphers listed in this section, or under Artists in Chapter 7. Also refer to our section on Bar Mitzvah preparations in Chapter 1. You can also call Iris Levitsky (628-2380), who will arrange it all for you.

IF YOU'RE INTERMARRYING

The high rate of mixed marriages in the United States has presented a great challenge both to couples and to the organized Jewish community. Programs for mixed-married couples are turning up all over town (see later in this section), and many rabbis are willing, even eager, to speak with couples who are intermarrying, although most will not officiate at such ceremonies. It is safe to say that no Orthodox or card-carrying Conservative rabbi will perform a mixed marriage ceremony. While Reconstructionist rabbis are permitted to follow their conscience on the matter, and many will work with couples who are being married in civil ceremonies, most do not officiate at mixed ceremonies. Reform rabbis fall into a similar category of freedom of choice, and most of the rabbis who officiate at mixed marriages are in fact Reform rabbis. Because the official policy of the Reform movement is not to encourage or endorse such unions, however, they are reluctant to recommend rabbis who will perform these ceremonies. A resource if you're looking for a rabbi willing to officiate at a mixed marriage is the Rabbinic Center for Research and Counseling. Although not located in Manhattan (it's at 128 East Dudley Avenue, Westfield, New Jersey, 201-233-0419), the Center keeps updated lists of rabbis in Manhattan and throughout the country who perform mixed marriages.

Programs for the Intermarried. Many non-Orthodox synagogues now sponsor groups, classes or programs for mixed-married couples (some are even starting groups for parents of mixed-married couples). Call your neighborhood synagogue to see if one exists there. Other programs around town include one at CONNECT, at the 92nd Street YM–YWHA, 1395 Lexington Avenue (427-6000). Through this Jewish outreach program at the Y, a workshop for interfaith couples is run by Rachel and Paul Cowan, who have been in the forefront of such programs. Many of the introduction to Judaism classes listed under Conversion in our chapter on "How We Learn" are designed for interfaith couples where the non-Jewish spouse isn't interested in converting, but wants to learn more about Judaism.

Chapter 5
SENIORS

America's population is growing older every year, as life expectancy increases and the birth rate decreases. It is no different for the Jewish population, and although Manhattan has the most "upscale" population and far fewer over-sixty-five year old Jews than Brooklyn, the Bronx or Queens (the Bronx rates highest with thirty-one percent of its Jewish population over sixty-five) the 1981 UJA–Federation population study of New York showed 46,300 Jews over the age of sixty-five living in Manhattan, or seventeen percent of the borough's Jewish population. (It lists another 30,600 or eleven percent in the fifty-five to sixty-four year old age group.) Many of these seniors live alone and survive on limited incomes. The Jewish community has many outreach programs to its senior population, and in our section on Services for the Elderly in Need you will see many programs for the poor, hungry, lonely, ill and homebound elderly, as well as information on hospitals and nursing homes. For the many seniors who don't need physical help but do need social and cultural activities geared to them (which often means daytime rather than evening events, since many are afraid to go out after dark), as well as peer support, we are listing the many programs offered in Manhattan. Since many classes serve as much of a social as an educational function, rather than dividing this section by need, we have listed activities by location or organization. Most Jewish centers and organizations have reduced rates for seniors, so be sure to ask.

PROGRAMS AT SYNAGOGUES

Central Synagogue   123 East 55th Street 10022 838-5122
The seniors program here meets every Tuesday. There are card games, dancing, trips and craft activities. Nonmembers are invited and they usually have quite a crowd.

Congregation Habonim
44 West 66th Street 10023   787-5347
The seniors here bring their lunches to the synagogue at noon on Thursdays, where they see movies, hear concerts or lectures. The synagogue provides the coffee and cake. Nonmembers are welcome.

Congregation Rodeph Sholom
7 West 83rd Street 10024   362-8800
Seniors meet once a month and for a modest fee have lunch, see a movie or hear a singer. Nonmembers are welcome.

Lincoln Square Synagogue
200 Amsterdam Avenue 10023   874-6105
The seniors group here usually meets on Mondays between 12:30 and 2:30 P.M., makes craft items for poor children and socializes.

Park Avenue Synagogue
50 East 87th Street 10028   369-2600
There is a group restricted to retirees only that meets once a week on Tuesdays.

Stephen Wise Free Synagogue
30 West 68th Street 10023   877-4050
The Golden Age Club meets every Wednesday from 10:00 A.M. to 3:00 P.M. and has classes in painting, singing and dancing, as well as discussion groups. There is an annual membership, or you can pay a minimal fee per session. Nonmembers are welcome.

Temple Emanu-El   1 East 65th Street 10021   744-1400
The seniors program meets here every Monday between October and May from 10:30 A.M. to 3:30 P.M. Activities include art, crafts, exercise and discussions of current events and recent books. The day usually ends with some kind of

entertainment. Members bring bag lunches and the synagogue supplies coffee and cake. There is a small annual fee for the program and nonsynagogue members are welcome.

Temple Shaaray Tefila
250 East 79th Street 10021   535-8008

On Mondays, beginning at 10:00 A.M. seniors have guest lectures, slide shows, aerobics and work on arts and crafts. Everyone brings lunch and the synagogue supplies the coffee and cake.

PROGRAMS AT Ys

Educational Alliance   197 East Broadway 10002 475-6200

There are elderly Jews still living on the Lower East Side, and many of them are poor, so the Alliance runs and houses several programs to help with food distribution and home care, described elsewhere. Apart from its social services, however, the Alliance has a commitment to providing educational and cultural programs to older adults, and it does this through its Group Work Services department, which seniors can join for a small fee. Activities include everything you can think of from arts and crafts, bingo and bridge lessons to Bible study, Middle Eastern dancing and crime prevention workshops. The department has its own lounge and reading room, a choral group for seniors, movie matinees, Jewish studies, self-help groups, a Yiddish corner and even a Scrabble club. Daily hot kosher lunches (sponsored by the United Jewish Council of the East Side) are served for a minimal fee. The Y's Sport-Fitness Department, which runs indoor sports programs, classes in yoga, exercise, belly dancing and self-defense also includes special programs twice a week for seniors, including therapeutic exercises for the back and other trouble spots. The Health Care Program, run in cooperation with Stern College's Nursing Program, provides screening and health education; registered nurses visit the Y weekly and do blood pressure screening and run seminars on nutrition, diabetes, heart attacks, stroke and other medical issues of concern to seniors. In addition to all these social and cultural activities, there are volunteer projects for seniors, including the Senior Companions Telephone Reassurance for the homebound, staffed by seniors. A weekly program of cultural activities includes book review discussions and concerts called P.M.—Program for the Mature, for those who have recently retired (or are now contemplating retirement). The ARP (Association of Retired Persons) is an independent self-led program for retired professionals whose activities include art and theater trips, chess, bridge and discussion of literature and world affairs. During the summer, the Alliance also has day trips for seniors (over fifty) to its Salomon Vacation Center.

Educational Alliance West
51 East 10th Street 10003   420-1150

A project of the Educational Alliance, designed to serve the Lower West Side, the Village, Soho and Tribeca (although those outside the area are encouraged to participate), this Jewish community center has a large program for seniors. "Thursday Afternoon Live" for adults "fifty plus" includes a variety of entertainment programs such as movies and music, as well as lectures and discussions on topics as varied as current events, recent books, finances and health care. There are guest speakers, discussion, refreshments and time to socialize. Once a month on Sunday there is also a less formal program: brunch with bagels and coffee, with the Sunday *Times* and playing cards available. In addition to its seniors programs, the Educational Alliance West has scheduled many courses during the day as well as evening, something that should be attractive to seniors, and these include art, literature and exercise classes (one of which is especially designed for the needs of older adults).

Brookdale Educational Center for Retired Adults
Emanu-El Midtown YM–YWHA   344 East 14th Street 10003   674-7200

This school, whose teachers are also all retired, provides a wide range of classes and activities—everything from yoga to Talmud. Not every course is Jewish in content, for in fact the Center believes that people over sixty-five have a need and the ability to learn about all sorts of things in what they consider an informal, noncompetitive setting. In addition to general courses in music, art, movement, literature, drama, current events and courses addressing the needs of older adults (NYC Housing, Wills and Estates etc.), there is a Judaica division that studies everything from "Gems of the Midrash" to "Israel Society and Politics." There are also courses in classic Yiddish literature and contemporary interpretation of Torah. Classes meet during the day.

92nd Street YM–YWHA
1395 Lexington Avenue 10128   427-6000

The 92nd Street Y has a separate Senior Adult Division (with its own membership and registration fee) that offers programs for those over sixty. The programs run Monday through Friday from 10:00 A.M. to 4:00 P.M. and include lectures, concerts, trips and regularly-scheduled classes in everything from exercise and ceramics to bridge and dressmaking. Some members of the division just come once or twice a week to attend certain classes, and others come almost every day to socialize as well. Members can use the program any way they like. The Y's Early Evening Program for Mature Adults (they meet between 5:30 and 7:00 P.M.) runs classes and workshops specifically designed for professionals and others over fifty in topics such as health, exercise and contemporary issues. Of course, in addition to these special programs run for seniors, the 92nd Street Y offers a tremendous range of educational and social activities (many of which are listed in our Adult Education section) available to anyone. Among their Personal Development courses are many that might fit the needs of seniors, such as ones on widowhood, retirement and financial planning, and some of the dance and exercise programs at the Y are geared for older adults.

The Y's Program for Singles includes specific discussion groups for singles between forty-five and sixty-five (run in cooperation with the Jewish Board of Family and Children's Services), covering topics such as mid-life transition, new social networks, and dating and sexuality. A coordinator from the Y runs social groups each Sunday afternoon for singles, with people divided into "the same age range," with a full calendar of activities including parties, trips, lectures, concerts etc.

YM–YWHA of Washington Heights and Inwood

54 Nagle Avenue 10040   569-6200/5271

When you find out that Dr. Ruth is on the board of this Jewish Community Center, you will understand why this Y really believes that life begins at sixty and is full of programs for the retired. There are many senior citizens living in the Washington Heights–Inwood section of Manhattan, and you will always see many elderly there at lunchtime when the Y's Senior Center offers kosher hot lunches. There is instruction in Spanish, French and Hebrew, as well as sculpture, painting, bridge and canasta. The Senior Center offers movies, discussions, weekly entertainment and an information and referral service for health care. In the summer there are weekly trips to the Henry Kaufmann Campgrounds. The Y also has an outreach program to the homebound elderly, described in our section on the Elderly in Need.

SENIORS' PROGRAMS AT ORGANIZATIONS

JASA–West Side Senior Center
40 West 68th Street 10023   724-3200

This senior center in the Lincoln Center area has a full cultural and educational program for those over sixty. Monday through Friday there is a full-day program that includes classes in subjects ranging from Hebrew and current events to gardening, bridge and exercise. There is no charge for these classes, which run continuously through the year, but you must register for them. Kosher breakfast and lunch is provided every day at minimal cost. Sundays at JASA include classes that are more intellectual in nature, on subjects like modern philosophy, opera, Shakespeare. There are also workshops, lectures and a performance series open to the general public. There is a modest charge for the Sunday classes and events.

JASA–Marseilles Senior Center
230 West 103rd Street 10025   663-6000

Uptown at another JASA Senior Center you can get involved in programs similar to the ones above on Monday through Friday from 9:00 A.M. to 5:00 P.M. The program here is on a smaller scale with fewer people, but there is still a very inexpensive kosher hot lunch.

JASA–SHARE   40 West 68th Street 10023   724-3200

JASA's program for older Russian immigrants is a social group that helps the newly arrived get acclimated to American culture. They do this by participating in social events together, taking trips to interesting places and learning about shopping and getting around. There is a director present on Monday, Wednesday and Friday, who also helps with things like medical forms.

National Council of Jewish Women
Katherine Engel Center for Older People
241 West 72nd Street 10023   799-7205

For a small annual membership fee, this center provides full-day recreational, education and cultural programs for older people, as well as a very inexpensive hot lunch (not kosher). There is a short waiting list to join this center, and those interested should call for a tour and an explanation of the program.

United Jewish Council of the East Side
235 East Broadway 10002   233-6037

The United Jewish Council, which mainly does outreach to the poor and frail elderly living on the Lower East Side, runs several glatt kosher luncheon clubs in the area, including one at the Educational Alliance. Some are Yiddish speaking, and all provide recreation and educational activities in addition to lunch.

CAMPS AND TRIPS FOR SENIORS

Block Vacation Program   Associated Camps   751-8580

This UJA–Federation program has two locations. At their camp in Poyntelle, Pa., men and women over sixty can go for two-week trips during the summer, where they stay in cabins, enjoy a pool and lake, and have professionals leading arts and crafts and cultural activities. The dining rooms are kosher and there are religious services. Fees are on a sliding scale. The organization maintains five hotels (four have kosher food) in Florida and seniors can vacation there for a minimum of two weeks.

Isabelle Freedman   Falls Village, Conn.   242-5586

This camp, which also offers two-week stays, has a full recreational program (lake and pool), as well as Jewish cultural programs. There is a strong crafts and dance program. *Kashrut* is observed and there is financial aid available.

Kinder Ring   Hopewell Junction, N.Y.   889-6800

This famous Yiddish camp run by Workmen's Circle also has a program for men and women over fifty-five that includes a stay of two, three, or four weeks with fees on a sliding scale. There are discussion groups, folk dancing, nature study, lake swimming and Yiddish and Jewish secular programs. *Kashrut* is not observed.

Salomon Vacation Center   Brewster, N.Y.   475-6061

Run by the Educational Alliance, this vacation camp for men and women over fifty has many activities. There is a rabbi at the camp and, in addition to two-week summer programs, there are trips during Memorial Day, Labor Day and the High Holidays. All rooms are heated and deluxe rooms have free air conditioning. *Kashrut* is observed.

Scribner Hollow Lodge   Upstate New York   533-7100

This summer vacation program for seniors run by Selfhelp includes a full program of activities. It runs in five two-week periods and has a capacity of eighty people at a time. *Kashrut* is observed.

Chapter 6
HOW WE LEARN

Perhaps there is nothing more important a Jew can do than study, for the sages believed that study led to ethical behavior. As far back as biblical times, there was a strong emphasis on communal learning, which set the Israelite people apart from other peoples, among whom learning was largely restricted to the priestly, the wealthy or royalty. The Talmud says that "a person who has knowledge has everything." Well, if we don't have knowledge in New York, it's certainly not the fault of our institutions. Where else is there a more extensive set of educational opportunities for adults who want to learn about things Jewish? For the person with no background and the Yeshiva-trained post-doctoral student, for young and old, single, married, retired, for the searcher and the well-directed, there's a course, a program, a school in Manhattan. In this chapter, we've described programs at secular and Jewish colleges, universities and institutes, as well as courses at synagogues, community facilities and organizations. We've listed conversion programs, music and dance courses, and kosher cooking classes. We've also described libraries with substantial or unusual collections. At the end of the chapter, we've added a list of those agencies and organizations that have lecture bureaus. As Hillel once said, "the rest is commentary; go and study."

COLLEGES AND UNIVERSITIES

In recent years, there has been an explosion of courses in Judaic studies and Hebrew language at universities throughout the country, and the increased interest has also improved the quality of such courses. In addition to the Jewish universities and rabbinical schools in New York, there is hardly a college or university in Manhattan that doesn't offer a course in Jewish studies or Hebrew, and many have whole departments with specialized majors as well. Some programs are for degree candidates only, but others have open enrollment for nonmatriculates. If you're interested in taking a course, call the appropriate department in the school of your choice and see what you can arrange.

THE CITY UNIVERSITY OF NEW YORK

Baruch College   155 East 24th Street 10010 725-3000

Although Baruch does not have a Jewish Studies program, it does offer Hebrew as a major, and you can always supplement your studies with courses at other branches of CUNY.

The City College
138th Street and Convent Avenue 10031 690-6741

The Department of Jewish Studies at City College offers majors in Jewish Studies and Hebrew, with a wide range of courses in history, sociology, language and literature, philosophy and mysticism, religion and nationalism. Courses include The Jew in Literature, Studies in Judaism and Christianity, The Jewish Woman, and Hasidism: Selected Texts.

Students wishing to major in or study Hebrew do so through the Department of Classical Languages and Hebrew. In addition to the Hebrew language, the department offers courses in Hebrew literature from biblical times to the present.

Hunter College   695 Park Avenue 10021   772-4000

Hunter offers an interdisciplinary major and minor in Jewish social studies that includes courses in Jewish history, literature and thought, and other courses drawn from the political science and sociology departments. Students who are interested in East European Jewish life may arrange to take courses through a reciprocal program between Hunter and the Max Weinrich Center for Advanced Jewish Studies at YIVO Institute for Jewish Research.

The Hebrew program is offered through the division of Classical and Oriental Studies. It is a comprehensive program designed to develop skills in Hebrew language and literature, as well as provide a thorough background in Jewish civilization. Courses include Hebrew language and literature from biblical to modern times, Jewish philosophy and Israeli culture. In addition to offering a major and minor in Hebrew, the department cooperates with the division of Programs in Education to provide interested Hebrew majors with courses necessary to receive State certification to teach Hebrew in junior and senior high schools in New York State.

The Graduate School of the City University of New York
33 West 42nd Street 10036 790-4395

Graduate students in history here can specialize in Jewish Studies, either on the masters or doctoral levels. In addition, the Graduate School of the City University houses the Center for Jewish Studies, which coordinates research, teaching and programs related to Jewish studies throughout the City University system. The Center encourages the development of graduate courses in Jewish studies with particular emphasis on medieval and modern Jewish history and the sociological study of Jews. It also sponsors research, public programs, publications, and is the umbrella organization for several institutes described later in this section.

COLUMBIA UNIVERSITY

Barnard College   3009 Broadway 10027   280-5262

Barnard's religion department offers a comprehensive concentration in Judaism from biblical times to the present, covering such topics as Judaism during the time of Jesus, Jewish mysticism, contemporary Jewish ethics and Talmudic literature. The department cooperates with the Jewish Studies program of Columbia in helping students develop combined, double, joint and specialized majors.

Students wishing to major in Hebrew language and literature may do so through the Department of Middle East Languages and Cultures at Columbia College.

Barnard also offers interested students the opportunity to study at the Jewish Theological Seminary of America, located two blocks to the north. Under a cooperative arrangement, students may take individual courses, spend a year's study in residence, or undertake a double major program.

Columbia College   Broadway and 116th Street
Hamilton Hall 10027   280-2521

Students interested in Judaism take courses through the Department of Religion, which offers courses in the Bible and Judaism, as well as comparative religion courses such as Religious Ethics: War and Peace in Jewish, Christian, and Islamic Thought.

Hebrew is offered by the Department of Middle East

Languages and Culture (which, by the way, also offers Akkadian, Armenian, Arabic, Bengali, Uzbek, Hindi and Indic).

Columbia University School of General Studies
Broadway and 116th Street
303 Lewisohn Hall 10027 280-3768

G.S., Columbia's Liberal Arts College for adults and students who work full time, offers a concentration in Jewish history within its history department. Those students wishing to study Yiddish do so through the linguistics department, where courses are offered in elementary, intermediate and advanced Yiddish. (In your spare time, you can also take Hausa, Hungarian, Finnish and Swahili.) Hebrew language is offered through the Department of Middle East Languages and Culture, on beginning, intermediate and advanced levels. The religion department offers courses such as Studies in Rabbinic Literature, Prophecy in Judaism and Islam, and the Meaning of Ritual in Jewish Religion.

The School of General Studies cooperates with the Jewish Theological Seminary in offering a combined program (referred to by students as the "Joint Program"), which leads to a bachelor's degree from G.S. and a Bachelor of Hebrew Literature from JTS. In addition, students who would like to spend their junior year studying Judaica and liberal arts may do so as Visiting Students in the Joint Program between Columbia and the Seminary.

Columbia University Graduate School of Arts and Sciences Broadway and 116th Street
109 Low Memorial Library 10027 280-4737

Jewish studies at the Graduate School of Arts and Sciences are coordinated through the Center for Israel and Jewish Studies (511 Fayerweather Hall, 280-2581). One of the oldest and most comprehensive programs of Jewish studies in the country, the Center brings together faculty members and students whose academic interests are primarily concerned with the study of Jewish civilization or with the state of Israel in its historical and contemporary dimensions. In addition, the Center conducts an ongoing University Seminar in which Columbia faculty and other scholars participate and establish liaison with other major Jewish scholars throughout the world. University masters and doctoral programs include concentrations in Jewish history, Hebrew language and literature, Yiddish studies and Judaism.

THE NEW SCHOOL FOR SOCIAL RESEARCH

The New School   66 West 12th Street 10011   741-5690

Courses in Jewish studies and languages at this unique educational facility may be audited, taken for credit to be applied elsewhere, or used toward obtaining a degree at the New School. Hebrew is taught by Moshe Ariel, a well-known Israeli dancer and choreographer who is also an expert in teaching Hebrew. The New School also offers a one-day intensive course in Hebrew, designed for travelers to Israel. Through the Department of Religion, you can study subjects such as Basic Judaism, The Jewish Mystical Tradition, and The Jewish Background of Christianity. There are classes in Yiddish culture and the Bible, as well.

NEW YORK UNIVERSITY

Undergraduate School of Arts and Sciences

Washington Square 10003   598-2425

Jewish Studies at NYU are housed in the Hagop Kevorkian Center for Near Eastern Studies (50 Washington Square South, 598-2411). The undergraduate school's Department of Religious Studies offers a wide range of courses in Judaism and comparative religions. Classes include Jewish-Christian Relations, Masterpieces of Jewish Literature in Translation, and Jerusalem: Holy City, Holy Places.

Hebrew (and Arabic, Persian and Turkish) is given through the Department of Near Eastern Languages and Literatures. Elementary, intermediate, and advanced Hebrew language courses are offered, as well as classes in ancient and rabbinic Jewish texts, such as the Bible, Apocrypha, Dead Sea Scrolls, Talmud and medieval Codes.

The Program of Hebrew and Judaic Studies enables students to combine interests in Jewish language, literature, history and civilization within the framework of an interdisciplinary major. Under the sponsorship of the all-University Institute for Hebrew and Judaic Studies, students take courses throughout the university.

Graduate School of Arts and Sciences

Washington Square 10003   598-2283

The Department of Near Eastern Languages and Literatures offers a course of study leading to the degrees of Master of Arts and Doctor of Philosophy, with concentrations in the ancient Near East, biblical studies, medieval Judaism, and Hebrew language.

JEWISH COLLEGES AND UNIVERSITIES

While the increase of Jewish studies programs in America's secular universities has enabled students an unprecedented opportunity to pursue an interest in things Jewish within a secular context, the growth of programs and courses in the Jewish universities has enriched opportunities at religious institutions. From their modest beginnings around the turn of the century, each of New York's Jewish institutions of learning has developed into a major center within the Jewish community, not only for the training of rabbis, but in providing undergraduate and graduate programs as well. Finally, there is life after Hebrew School. And what a life it is!

Hebrew Union College–Jewish Institute of Religion
School of Graduate Studies
1 West 4th Street 10012   674-5300

> Graduate work at HUC-JIR leads to degrees in Doctor of Hebrew Letters, Master of Arts, and Master of Sacred Music. The D.H.L. is available only to graduates of HUC's rabbinical school. The Master of Arts degree, offered by the New York School of Education of HUC-JIR is designed to educate directors of education, principals and teachers. The Master of Sacred Music is the degree given to those who have completed the four-year course in preparation for the cantorate (see below).

Institute for Professional Enrichment
22 East 28th Street 10016   683-3216

> IPE is one Orthodox answer to college. It is affiliated with Adelphi and Touro College in Manhattan, and designed specifically for yeshiva students. There are accelerated courses, most of which meet on Sundays. IPE seeks to upgrade the credentials of its students (by offering MBA's to yeshiva principals, for instance), while enabling them to study within a "Torah" environment.

The Jewish Theological Seminary of America
3080 Broadway 10027   678-8000

> *Seminary College of Jewish Studies.* The Seminary's undergraduate school offers a wide range of courses in Jewish studies, while expecting students to take a minimum of sixty credits at another college or university in order to receive a Bachelor of Arts. Many students at the Seminary College are in either a Joint Program with Columbia's School of General Studies or a Double Degree Program at Barnard College.

There is a junior year in Israel option through either the Hebrew University or another accredited Israeli university. There are dormitory facilities.

Graduate School. In addition to its specialized programs to train rabbis and cantors, JTS offers advanced degrees in Jewish Studies through the Institute of Advanced Studies in the Humanities or the Graduate School of JTS. Students may enroll in programs leading to an M.A., D.H.L. (Doctor of Hebrew Literature) and Ph.D. Consortia arrangements among the graduate school and many other universities throughout the metropolitan area enable students in doctoral programs at JTS to study elsewhere as well.

Seminary College of Jewish Music. The Seminary College of Jewish Music offers a coeducational program leading to advanced degrees in sacred music. The college trains teachers of Jewish music, choral directors, composers and research scholars.

Touro College   30 West 44th Street 10036   575-0190

Touro College, founded in 1971 and unaffiliated with a theological seminary, still sees its mission as emphasizing the relevance of Jewish civilization to Western culture. It offers a wide range of Hebrew and Judaic studies, on both the undergraduate and the graduate levels. Men and women study in separate divisions, with different programs. The men's division offers both a Talmud track and what they call the HaMaor Track, the latter for students who want to major in Jewish studies without a strong interest in the study of Talmud. The women's division also offers two tracks, an elementary and advanced program of Jewish studies. Within the Jewish studies programs, there is a specialized Certificate Program in Jewish Law and a Yeshiva–Beth Medrosh Option, the latter for students interested in pursuing their undergraduate studies within the framework of a traditional yeshiva atmosphere.

Touro College Graduate School of Jewish Studies
30 West 44th Street 10036   575-0190

Touro's graduate school offers a Master of Arts degree in Jewish Studies, primarily modern Jewish studies. A unique aspect of the graduate school is its Herzliah–Jewish Teacher's Seminary Division, which houses the Jewish People's University of the Air. This outreach program offers courses in Jewish studies over the radio and on cassettes. Although you can't get credit for these courses, they may be used as a component of a credit course. Among the twenty courses available are The Holocaust, The Jew as Myth in English and American Literature, and Shapers of Modern Jewish Thought, all taught by noted scholars of Judaica.

In addition to its regular undergraduate and graduate programs, Touro offers a Certificate and Associate degree program for newly-arrived Russian immigrants. Courses are given in English literature, American history, and the Jewish heritage.

Max Weinrich Center for Advanced Jewish Studies

YIVO Institute for Jewish Research
1048 Fifth Avenue 10028 535-6700

YIVO, a major Yiddish studies center, has an institute for graduate-level and post-doctoral students enrolled at other universities. Registration is handled by the university you attend, and credit is given for these courses, which have included Jewish folklore, Polish Jewry and Yiddish translation.

YESHIVA UNIVERSITY

Yeshiva College 500 West 185th Street 10033 960-5400

Yeshiva University segregates men and women in its undergraduate programs, and Yeshiva College is the university's college of arts and sciences for men. Both B.A. and B.S. degrees are awarded as part of a standard liberal arts program, but students must enroll in a full course of study at one of Yeshiva's Jewish studies programs listed below.

James Striar School of Jewish Studies. This program is for students pursuing an Orthodox Jewish education somewhere within the structure of Yeshiva College who have not come from Orthodox day schools (or lack the appropriate Jewish/ Hebrew background required to enter Yeshiva College). Students completing the program receive an Associate in Arts degree, and can go on to complete their bachelor's degree. As the catalog says, this program's emphasis is "more on learning 'it' than learning 'about it.'"

Isaac Breuer College of Hebraic Studies. IBC provides comprehensive programs in Hebrew language, literature and culture for students with some background in this area. It is the nation's largest center for the preparation of teachers of Hebraica, with a curriculum designed to provide a Hebrew Teacher's diploma along with a degree of Associate in Arts, Bachelor of Science and Bachelor of Arts.

Yeshiva Program–Mazer School of Talmudic Studies. For those with a strong background and interest in Talmud, this is the place to go within the university structure. It does not confer a specific degree; all courses are transferable to Yeshiva College.

Stern College for Women

245 Lexington Avenue 10016 340-7700

Named after the parents of the late Max Stern of Hartz Mountain fame, Stern College is Yeshiva University's undergraduate liberal arts college for women. The only undergraduate program not located at the main campus in Washington Heights, Stern College is a one-of-a-kind institution, the only Jewish college devoted solely to the education of women. Offering a wide range of secular and Jewish studies, Stern provides the degrees of Bachelor of Arts, Bachelor of Science and Associate in Arts, as well as the Hebrew Teacher's diploma for qualified students. There is a variety of joint undergraduate and graduate programs open to Stern women, which enable qualified students to receive B.A. and B.S. degrees as well as Masters degrees in psychology, Jewish Studies, social work and Jewish education. There are additional programs in engineering, nursing and podiatry in conjunction with Columbia and the New York College of Podiatric Medicine, as well as various programs in occupational therapy. Stern women who do not live at home are expected to live in the dormitory facility owned by the university. The Teachers Institute for Women at Stern College is for Jewish women who want to train for professions in the teaching of Hebrew language, literature and culture.

Yeshiva University Graduate Schools

Yeshiva's graduate programs in Jewish Studies and related fields are found at the Bernard Revel Graduate School, which offers graduate work in Judaic studies and Semitic languages, literatures and cultures, and confers the degrees of Master of Science, Master of Arts and Doctor of Philosophy. Also on the graduate level, the David J. Azrieli Graduate Institute of Jewish Education and Administration offers a Master of Science degree in the areas of Jewish elementary and secondary education, and confers a Specialist's Certificate and the Doctor of Education degree in administration and supervision of Jewish education.

Yeshiva University also has extensive graduate offerings in secular areas, although often allied with Jewish studies and occasionally with a sort of Jewish mission to its program. The Wurzweiler School of Social Work, for instance, requires one Judaic studies course per semester of all its students and through the Block Education Plan provides field instruction in Jewish communities throughout the world. The Benjamin N. Cardozo School of Law, a secular law school affiliated with Yeshiva University, offers several courses in Jewish law.

RABBINICAL SEMINARIES

Manhattan has three of the four major rabbinical seminaries in the United States. Only the Reconstructionist Rabbinical College, the rabbinical training school for the Reconstructionist movement, is located outside New York, in Philadelphia (although both the Reform and Conservative movements maintain campuses in other parts of the country and in Israel).

Academy for Jewish Religion
251 West 100th Street 10025   865-0600

When Stephen Wise died and the independent Jewish Institute of Religion (JIR) merged with the Reform Seminary, Hebrew Union College (HUC), some bemoaned the loss of a nondenominational rabbinical school. So began the Academy for Higher Jewish Learning, whose named has changed to the Academy for Jewish Religion, but whose purpose remains the same. Its campus has moved around over the years, and is now located at that great hotbed of Judaic pluralism, Congregation Ansche Chesed. The faculty is drawn from all over the city and beyond, and at various times has been comprised of rabbis and teachers from each of the other four seminaries. The school is extremely small, with about twelve to fifteen men and women at any given time, with a curriculum that includes Talmud, Bible, homiletics, practical rabbinics and history. Normally students are ordained at the end of a five-year program of study.

Hebrew Union College–Jewish Institute of Religion
Brookdale Center   1 West 4th Street 10012 674-5300

Hebrew Union College (HUC) was founded in 1875 as a seminary for the upstart Reform movement in America. Over one hundred years later, HUC boasts two centers for rabbinic training, in New York and Cincinnati, with campuses in Los Angeles and Jerusalem that are attended by seminarians and other students (although ordination is conferred only in New York or Cincinnati). Housed in a spanking new facility near New York University in Greenwich Village, HUC offers qualified men and women a five-year full-time program leading to a Master of Arts degree and ordination. Every student (and they are pretty serious about this) spends the first year in Israel, reflecting both the Reform movement's Zionist commitment as well as a belief that the year in Israel makes for better American rabbis. Following that year, seminary students may attend any of the three other campuses for the next two years, after which they transfer to New York or Cincinnati for their final two years. Rabbinical students at HUC choose from a wide variety of coursework during their five years, including classes in Bible, Hebrew, history, rabbinics, theology and professional development. It is particularly in this last area, from which students are required to take eight of their forty courses, that HUC has made a major contribution to the training of rabbis in the United

States, with courses offered in counseling, sensitivity training, homiletics and writing, to name just a few.

Jewish Theological Seminary of America
3080 Broadway 10027 678-8000

Straddling the borders of Morningside Heights and Harlem, JTS, or, as it is affectionately known among Conservative Jews, "the Sem," ordains male and female rabbis in a four-to-six year program, depending on the student's background. There are four progressive levels of study, including technical skills, introductory surveys, methodologies, and finally electives, professional skills and interdisciplinary courses. The Seminary's West Coast affiliate, the University of Judaism, offers a program at Levels I and II, though all ordination candidates complete their studies in New York. The study of Talmud and other rabbinic texts is given primary attention at JTS, which was founded in 1886 in order to provide the American Jewish community with rabbis trained in the United States. Unhappy with the Orthodox strangehold in areas of religious authority, but equally concerned by an increasingly assimilating Reform Jewish community, the Seminary was created for "the preservation in America of the knowledge and practice of historical Judaism." In addition to the normal (and quite heavy) coursework in the Rabbinical School, some students take courses at the Columbia University School of Social Work, with which JTS has a reciprocal relationship. Students who wish to obtain joint rabbinic and social work degrees have that option as well. A similar arrangement exists between JTS and Union Theological Seminary, which is just across the street.

Mesivtha Tifereth Jerusalem
141–7 East Broadway 10002 964-2830

MTJ, as it is known down on the Lower East Side where it is located, is a multigenerational Yeshiva, which also trains Orthodox rabbis. The school is closely associated with the late Rabbi Moshe Feinstein, a leading Orthodox figure.

Rabbi Isaac Elchanan Theological Seminary
(Affiliated with Yeshiva University)
2540 Amsterdam Avenue 10033 960-5344

Yeshiva University, founded in the same year as the Jewish Theological Seminary, started its training of rabbis in 1896. Rabbi Isaac Elchanan Theological Seminary (RIETS) was the first Orthodox rabbinical seminary in the United States. It is modeled after the traditional Yeshivot of Eastern Europe, and its students (men only), who normally come from Orthodox high schools and colleges and have extensive Jewish backgrounds, usually study for three or four years in the Semikhah (Ordination) Program. Like HUC and JTS, RIETS has a Jerusalem campus, the Caroline and Joseph S. Gruss Institute, where seminarians may spend some part of their training. In addition to the strong emphasis on rabbinics, RIETS students are extensively trained in aspects of the so-called practical rabbinate, with specially designed internships in gerontology, education, the pulpit and the needs of youth.

CANTORIAL SCHOOLS

Hebrew Union College–Jewish Institute of Religion School of Sacred Music
1 West 4th Street 10012   674-5300

The Reform movement's cantorial program takes four years to complete, at the end of which cantors are vested and receive a Masters in Sacred Music. Courses include conducting, cantillation, *nusach* (Hebrew melodies) and choral music, as well as courses in general Jewish studies. The School of Sacred Music is at present the only school in the world to vest women as cantors.

Cantors Institute of the Jewish Theological Seminary of America   3080 Broadway 10027   678-8000

The Cantors Institute, a graduate program, confers an additional degree of Bachelor of Sacred Music as well as diploma of Hazzan (Cantor). The title Cantor is restricted to men. Courses include Jewish and general music, piano and voice, and a general Jewish studies program.

Philip and Sarah Belz School of Jewish Music of Yeshiva University   500 West 185th Street 10033   960-5400

This is the cantorial school of Yeshiva University. It provides professional training for cantors and other music personnel for the Jewish community. The school awards an Associate Cantor's Certificate and Cantorial Diploma. It is restricted to men.

RESEARCH INSTITUTIONS

Leo Baeck Institute
129 East 73rd Street 10021   744-6400

Founded in 1955, Leo Baeck is a research and study center for the history of German-speaking Jewry. It has close ties to the Leo Baeck Institutes in Jerusalem and London, but only the New York institute has a comprehensive library and a large collection of archival materials. German Jewry, which produced Albert Einstein, Sigmund Freud, and Karl Marx, has long been considered one of the foremost intellectual civilizations in the world, and the Leo Baeck Institute traces its history from almost 2,000 years ago, when Jews first settled along the Rhine, to its near-total destruction in the 1940s. In addition to its library, archives and museum, the Institute sponsors public lectures and seminars, and functions as a center for research for scholars and students; it also provides scholarships for doctoral candidates and younger academics.

The Center for Jewish Studies
City University of New York
33 West 42nd Street 10036   790-4404

Located at the midtown CUNY Graduate Center, The Center for Jewish Studies coordinates the teaching and research in Jewish Studies in the City University of New York. It serves as the umbrella organization for the following four research institutes.

The Institute for Jewish Community Life. The Institute has conducted demographic studies of American Jewish communities and its findings (including one on Greater New York) have been published in various articles and monographs. A major journal in this area, *Contemporary Jewry,* is issued under the Institute's auspices. There are also public programs available for scholars, Jewish community leaders and other interested groups.

The Institute of Sephardic Studies. Established in the fall of 1985 to encourage teaching and scholarship in Sephardic civilization at CUNY, the Institute sponsors curriculum development and graduate research in the field, and offers in-service training in oral history and cultural preservation. It also works to develop public lectures and conferences.

The Jack P. Eisner Institute for Holocaust Studies. In addition to its research and publications, the Eisner Institute sponsors public lectures, conferences and in-service training for teachers. It also provides scholarships to doctoral students working in this area.

The Joseph and Ceil Mazer Institute for Research and Advanced Study in Judaica. The Mazer Institute focuses on research relating to Jewish history and literature, both in Europe and the United States. It presents public lectures, conferences and scholarly symposia, and has published a number of studies.

YIVO Institute for Jewish Research
1048 Fifth Avenue 10028   535-6700

YIVO is a member-supported, non-profit institution devoted

to the preservation of the Jewish heritage, particularly the cultural life of pre-Holocaust Eastern Europe. Founded in Vilna in 1925 and moved to New York during World War II, it is the world's leading institution in this field and its library includes the world's largest collection of Yiddish books. It also has a large photo archive, document collection, slide bank and sound archive, and is now working on a major videodisc project to make many of its photographs of life in prewar Eastern Europe more accessible to the public. In addition to being a repository for all these collections, YIVO sponsors classes, programs and exhibits. It also houses the Max Weinreich Center for Advanced Jewish Studies, for scholars enrolled at universities throughout the city.

SCHOLARSHIP OPPORTUNITIES

As tuitions go up, up, up, scholarships have been going down, down, down all over the country, in both the private and public sectors. The Jewish community does try, however, to offer both generalized and specialized scholarships to undergraduate and graduate school students. The Jewish schools provide some scholarship money for students attending their programs; for more general scholarship information, here are some resources to check.

American Zionist Youth Foundation
515 Park Avenue 10022   751-6070

AZYF has some scholarship money available for those high school seniors interested in attending college in Israel.

B'nai B'rith   823 UN Plaza 10017   490-0677

Although B'nai B'rith is no longer as actively involved on college campuses through Hillel associations as it once was, the organization retains its commitment to aid Jewish college youth through a college scholarship program.

Federation Employment and Guidance Service
510 Sixth Avenue 10011   741-7955

FEGS has some limited scholarship opportunities for students interested in pursuing vocational training.

Foundation for Future Generations
393 West End Avenue 10024   724-4556

This new group awards scholarships, grants and fellowships to students in Israel and the United States who are majoring in Jewish studies and are committed to service to the Jewish community and human society. Each award carries the name of one of the million children killed by the Nazis.

Hebrew Free Loan Society
205 East 42nd Street 10017 687-0188

The main address for individual financial aid in the Jewish community, the Hebrew Free Loan Society provides aid to college and university bound students.

Jewish Foundation for Education of Women
330 West 58th Street 10019 265-2525

This organization, housed in the Board of Jewish Education Building, gives grants and loans for undergraduate work. Applicants must be legal residents of New York City or live within a fifty-mile radius on Long Island. There is no age limit for applicants.

JWB 15 East 26th Street 10010 532-4949

Through its National Scholarship committee, JWB offers scholarships to students pursuing a masters degree program leading to a career in the Jewish community.

Memorial Foundation for Jewish Culture
15 East 26th Street 10010 679-4047

This agency provides fellowships for doctoral students in Jewish studies, as well as for others pursuing graduate studies in Jewish education.

National Foundation for Jewish Culture
122 East 42nd Street 10168 490-2280

This agency of UJA–Federation provides grants for doctoral students working in Jewish subjects, as well as advanced research grants to those working in Jewish themes of a cultural, artistic or academic nature.

Stephen Wise Free Synagogue Social Service
30 West 68th Street 10023 877-4050

This Reform synagogue has a social service department which supplies some scholarships to college-bound students.

ADULT EDUCATION

SYNAGOGUE PROGRAMS

For years, synagogues focused all their educational resources on children, assuming that adult members really didn't need substantive Jewish education programs. Well, the time eventually came to reevaluate this assumption. Years of poor Jewish education, and the large numbers of congregants who never got any Jewish education at all, have led synagogues to reconsider the concept of "Juvenile Judaism" and start taking adult education seriously. Almost every synagogue in Manhattan now has some adult educational programming, including both skills courses and others that focus on history, culture or contemporary issues, and many also sponsor adult Bar or Bat Mitzvah programs for those who missed their opportunity earlier in life. Many of the smaller Orthodox *shuls* do not have a formal adult education program, but have a Talmud or Bible study group before Shabbat morning or evening services. Be sure to check the chapter on synagogues to see which *shuls* in your neighborhood have interesting programs. Some of the more ambitious programs are described below.

Civic Center Synagogue   49 White Street 10013 966-7141

The Civic Center program is included here because of the opportunity it affords those working in downtown Manhattan to study during lunch hour. The synagogue's free lunch study is fairly loosely structured in terms of enrollment, but there's nothing lax about the content or the rabbi's interest in outreach to beginners as well as experienced learners. Classes are held every day, in subjects like Bible, Judaism and Hebrew reading. Courses are often tailored to the desires of the community. The Civic Center Synagogue also has an evening adult education program.

Congregation Ansche Chesed
251 West 100th Street 10025   865-0600

The tremendous variety of activity at Ansche Chesed, and its commitment to "spirituality, learning, social justice, egalitarianism, and tradition and change," extends to its adult education programs. In addition to providing learning experiences for people in a variety of stages of their Jewish development, Ansche Chesed has what it calls a "learning network," an informal educational system that meets in congregants' homes. There are classes in Bible, philosophy and Hebrew, and discussion groups on topics of current concern, such as dealing with death and dying, intermarriage, divorce, modern roles in fathering etc. There are also holiday workshops for adults. The faculty is drawn from a diverse group of lay and Jewish professional teachers, many of whom find teaching at this very open-ended synagogue an enjoyable experience.

Congregation Kehilath Jeshurun
125 East 85th Street 10028   427-1000

In addition to its regular two-semester course schedule, which covers topics in ancient and modern Jewish history, Jewish customs and *siddur* reading at various levels, including a ten-day crash course for beginners, Kehilath Jeshurun has many other kinds of study programs. There is daily Mishna study after morning *minyan*, Friday evening Torah study, Sunday morning Talmud *shiur* (with breakfast), and two "lunch and learn" programs. One of these, held at the synagogue and very popular among older adults, runs in four-week cycles, covering Yiddish and Yiddish folklore, music, world Jewry and fiction. The cycle repeats each month with different subtopics. The other is a midtown "lunch and Talmud" class which is held in various midtown offices.

Lincoln Square Synagogue
200 Amsterdam Avenue 10023   874-6105

Lincoln Square, along with its former rabbi Shlomo Riskin, was one of the first synagogues to concentrate on serious adult education. When Rabbi Riskin made *aliya*, Rabbi Saul Berman assumed the pulpit and took over the deanship of the Joseph Shapiro Institute of Jewish Studies. Although you get a discount if you are a member of Lincoln Square, the Institute is open—and welcoming—to all who wish to learn, at virtually every level. Courses are offered through the year (summers, too!) in Hebrew, Jewish history, Bible, rabbinic literature, Jewish law and Jewish philosophy. In the summer there is an intensive six-week Torah Institute offered for people interested in a crash course in Judaism: four full days a week (and they mean full—it starts at 7:45 A.M. with morning services, and finishes each day at 5:00 P.M.) with beginner, intermediate and advanced levels. Remember that Lincoln Square is a modern Orthodox congregation, and courses reflect that commitment, though people who attend come from a variety of backgrounds.

Society for the Advancement of Judaism
15 West 86th Street 10024   724-7000

You might expect a serious approach toward adult study from this Reconstructionist congregation, long committed to the importance of an educated Jewish community. The SAJ institute has an extensive list of course offerings each year, including lecture series, day-long courses, mini courses on various religious topics, Hebrew and synagogue skills and, interestingly enough, one of the only Arabic courses taught in a synagogue.

Sutton Place Synagogue
225 East 51st Street 10022   593-3300

The Abraham Meyer Greenstein Academy of Jewish Studies
offers courses in basic Judaism, Hebrew and history, as well as
in contemporary issues such as Jewish Medical Ethics and
Israeli Politics. Through the Center for Personal Enrichment,
a wide variety of secular courses is also available, including
subjects like How to Start a Business, Picking a Partner (for
marriage, not business!), Stress Management, and classes in
yoga, aerobics, dance and cooking. Many courses have a
definite slant toward singles and young professionals, since
Sutton Place has substantial outreach programming for these
groups. Admission to all courses at Sutton Place is open to
anyone over thirteen years of age, regardless of educational
background or membership in the synagogue (although
members receive a discount).

Wall Street Synagogue
47 Beekman Street 10038   227-7800

Yeshiva-trained investment bankers, computer analysts and
corporate lawyers have been flocking to study-sessions at this
special synagogue that serves the financial district. In addition
to groups studying Talmud, Rabbi Meyer Hager has discussed
topics such as "*Halakha* and Technology" and other matters of
interest to his Orthodox Wall Street congregants.

UNIVERSITY CONTINUING EDUCATION
PROGRAMS AND LECTURE SERIES

While many of the city's universities, both secular and Jewish,
will permit you to take a course without matriculating in a
degree program, there are some programs especially designed
for the adult seeking enrichment within a college or university
setting without necessarily receiving credit or a degree. Some
are complete courses, others a series of lectures or weekend
conferences. Below are a few such programs.

The Center for Jewish Studies
The Graduate Center, City University of New York
33 West 42nd Street 10036   790-4404

As part of the increasing research and activity in Jewish
studies throughout CUNY, the Center and its institutes
sponsor a variety of programs and lecture series for both
academic and nonacademic audiences. Topics coordinate with
research done by the institutes, and focus on sociological
issues, Holocaust studies, Sephardic studies, Jewish folklore
and ethnography.

Drisha Institute for Torah Education

122 West 76th Street   595-0307

This Institute offers high-level courses in classical Jewish texts such as Talmud, Mishna and Codes, to young Orthodox women who have finished college. Among Orthodox women, it is considered something of a milestone in this kind of education, and it draws students from all over the country.

The Jewish Heritage Series

Division of Arts, Sciences, and Humanities

School of Continuing Education at NYU

332 Shimkin Hall, Washington Square 10003   777-8000

This new series is cosponsored by NYU's School of Continuing Education and Hebrew Union College's Judaic Studies Program in the School of Education, Claiming to touch "all aspects of Jewish life—religious, historical, cultural and artistic," the program's main center (at HUC, 1 West 4th Street) offers some of the highest quality adult education in the city. Last year's classes included "The Wonderful World of Yiddish Theater," "Living with My Faith," "Jewish Parenting," beginning Hebrew and Yiddish, and "Desert Cousins: Jews and Arabs, Judaism and Islam." Faculty is drawn from the School of Education at HUC as well as from various branches of Jewish life in the New York area. It is possible to receive credit or a certificate for these courses, and a discount is offered for older adults.

Yeshiva University Center for Continuing Education

500 West 185th Street 10033   960-5206

Yeshiva's continuing ed courses, most of which meet at their Midtown Center at 245 Lexington Avenue (35th Street) include both general interest courses (some of these include certificate programs in insurance work, jewelry appraisal and real estate, as well as courses in personal finance and computer skills) and courses in Jewish study. The courses in Jewish Enrichment are very popular, and cover topics such as Jewish Medical Ethics, Religious and Ethical Issues in Jewish Business Law, and Hidden Psychological Forces in Jewish Rituals. There are also art and cooking courses, and courses meet at various times of the day, including lunch hour.

THE YM–YWHAs

Educational Alliance

197 East Broadway 10002   475-2600

For ninety-six years, the Educational Alliance has been serving the needs of the Jewish community of the Lower East Side.

Among the many other programs listed in various chapters throughout this book, the Alliance has a wide range of adult education programs, including courses in Jewish studies and history, Middle Eastern dancing and Yiddish. The Alliance's art school offers classes in painting, drawing, sculpture, ceramics and photography. Of course, you can also learn about crime prevention, art appreciation and contract bridge at the Educational Alliance, but if it's Jewish subjects you're interested in, the Jewish Culture Center has an extensive program for adults as well as children. The Jewish Family School teaches basic Jewish subjects, with parents and children learning together. The Educational Alliance and its programs are open to everyone regardless of religion, race or nationality.

Educational Alliance West
51 East 10th Street 10003 420-1150

The Educational Alliance West offers a variety of educational programs for adults, including lectures by well-known New York Jewish figures, workshops and regular courses. There is an advanced Jewish study class, as well as courses in beginner's Hebrew, Bible, Israeli politics and Jewish literature. The Y also has a choral group in cooperation with Hebrew Union College–Jewish Institute of Religion, where students learn and sing Hebrew, Yiddish and English songs of Jewish origin. In conjunction with the Jewish Theological Seminary of America, the Y offers several seminars in Jewish thought, which run for five consecutive sessions, and are taught by students and faculty of JTS. "Sunday Night Live" is another series of lectures held at the Y, where both Jewish and secular issues are discussed, again by major authors, community leaders, psychologists and journalists. There's some shmoozing, some wine and cheese, and a chance to get out of the house and forget that tomorrow is Monday.

Emanu-El Midtown YM–YWHA
344 East 14th Street 10003   674-7200

The adult education program at the Midtown Y is handled largely in conjunction with the Town and Village Synagogue down the street from the Y. There is a lecture series held annually, which brings in major Jewish figures to address contemporary issues in the Jewish community. The Jewish Study Experience at the Y offers a variety of courses in Judaica, some with such creative titles as "Freud Meets the Talmud," as well as courses in Jewish mysticism, Jewish women and other subjects of interest. Courses are open to all.

The 92nd Street YM–YWHA
1395 Lexington Avenue 10028   427-6000

Perhaps the most extensive program in the country for Jewish adult education, the Jewish Omnibus at the 92nd Street Y literally explodes with options for Jewish learning. If you want to come for a day, come for a day. If you want to come for six weeks, come for six weeks. If you want to see a film, there's a film. If its dialogue you're interested in, they've got it. Elie Wiesel, I. B. Singer, Lucy Dawidowicz have all been part of Jewish Omnibus, along with countless others who drop in at the Y to struggle with Jewish texts, sip some wine with the learned and the learners, and participate in the creation of this exciting center. Here is a summary of programs that have been offered.

Classes. Classes in the Omnibus run for nine weeks, are taught by scholars from all over the city, and cover a wide range of topics, including Jewish texts, history, philosophy and literature.

The Institutes. Jewish Omnibus Institutes are day-long intensive explorations for those who are looking for total immersion (at least for one day). The Institutes, which take place at Temple Israel at 112 East 75th Street, have covered such topics as the Jewish Woman in *Halakha,* the study of Anti-Semitism, the Literary Dimension of the Bible, and Jewish Spirituality.

Special Events. For nineteen years, Elie Wiesel has offered a four-part lecture on some Jewish text, seen in his unique way, and this special event usually sells out. There are other such series offered with special guests.

Film. Each year the Y puts on a film festival, thematically arranged and followed by a discussion. They've shown new Israeli films, Yiddish films, films dealing with the Holocaust and films about Jewish women, to name just a few.

Community Study. Each year a panel of three Manhattan rabbis comes together to explore a Jewish text. In addition to getting the flavor of different theological viewpoints, you get to watch these rabbis talk to each other, which can often be as entertaining as it is enlightening.

In addition to all this, the Y offers workshops, lectures and other courses in art and music, including Hebrew calligraphy, Israeli folkdancing and kosher cooking. Some courses are geared to personal interests rather than Jewish content, such as classes in exercise or photography. For information about course offerings, call the Y at 427-6000, ext. 162.

OTHER PROGRAMS

Academy for Jewish Studies American Jewish Committee
165 East 56th Street 10022 751-4000

So you're interested in studying something Jewish, but you can't take a course, are homebound, busy when every adult ed program is being offered, or just prefer to work by yourself? Or perhaps you're a student at a university or college with no Jewish Studies program, and you want to take a Judaica course for credit. No problem. Call the Academy For Jewish Studies, which used to be called the Academy for Jewish Study Without Walls (run by an agency with quite a few walls). You can enroll in one or more of the nine correspondence courses of the American Jewish Committee's Communal Affairs Department, including Biblical Thought, Zionism, Jewish-Christian Issues, Talmud, and Bio-Ethics. The courses have been designed by prominent scholars in the Jewish community. There are quizzes after each unit, which you mail to the Academy for evaluation. Should you wish to obtain college or university credit for the course, you need to get permission from the dean of the institution; the Academy is chartered by the State University of New York and is recommended for credit.

Agudath Israel   5 Beekman Street 10038   791-1800

Agudath Israel, an Orthodox organization with a heavy commitment to outreach and getting Jews to return to their traditional roots, has many adult study programs. Their Torah education network is geared toward Jews of all ages and different backgrounds who want to learn more. They function as a referral source for finding courses, and will provide you with information on courses available in Manhattan, as well as doing some matchmaking by arranging teachers for heavily requested classes. They also provide specialized courses, such as one recently run for nurses at Beth Israel Medical Center on nursing and *halakha,* including what nurses can and cannot do for their patients on Shabbat. For people who have some background already, Agudath Israel runs what they call their Torah Partnership, where they can match you with a study partner, private teacher or specific class. They also find teachers for the handicapped. Their lunchtime classes at Touro College on West 44th Street are geared toward experienced learners and focus on weekly *parshiot* and *Gamara.*

Leo Baeck Institute
129 East 73rd Street 10021   744-6400

Leo Baeck Institute, famous for its research on the history of German Jewry from 1700 to 1945 (it is a major resource for Jews of German or Austrian ancestry who are involved in tracing their roots back to pre-Holocaust Europe), doesn't have specific courses, but does offer monthly lectures on Thursday evening (although not the same Thursday every month, so you should call for the dates) on German-Jewish history, philosophy and culture. All lectures are open to the public free of charge.

Chabad House   210 West 101st Street   10025   864-5010

Chabad is affiliated with the Lubavitcher Hassidim, and runs classes, seminars and weekend retreats for students at Columbia and anyone else who is interested in their unique approach to Judaism. Lubavitcher Hassidim are zealous in their mission to educate Jews in the practice of Orthodox ritual, among other things. If you want to learn how to put on *tefillin* (phylacteries), you can usually find their Mitzvah Mobile stationed in front of the iron gates of Columbia University at 116th Street and Broadway, and they will be happy to teach you, provided you're Jewish and male. Women can learn how to light candles. The Chabad house also runs a weekly luncheon and study session for senior adults in the neighborhood.

Dialogue Forum Series

205 East 78th Street   10021   362-5959

Rabbi William Berkowitz runs free educational and cultural programs, usually at Town Hall or Lincoln Center, often with guest speakers.

Theodor Herzl Institute

515 Park Avenue 10022   752-0600

This Zionist adult education program is run by the World Zionist Organization. Classes are held at 515 Park Avenue and at Central Synagogue. Courses are offered Monday through Thursday mornings and afternoons, and cover a broad range of subjects, including both cultural and historical courses. More personal courses, taught with a Jewish perspective, like How to Cope with Grief, Legends Common to Judaism and Islam, and Great Jewish Figures at Times of Crisis have also been offered in previous years.

Hineni   232 West End Avenue   10023   496-1660

Perhaps you've seen her picture in *The Jewish Press*, for which she writes a column, or maybe you've caught her on cable TV. All classes at Hineni, an educational organization devoted to bringing people back to their Jewish roots, are run by the well known (in Orthodox circles anyway) Rebbitzen Esther Jungreis. Classes are held on Thursday evenings at Hineni's offices, beginning at 7:00 P.M. with prayer skills and continuing with Bible. The classes, for which there is no registration necessary and no fee charged, run all year long, and you can come to all or as many as you like. Hineni also runs several other kinds of programs, including the cable TV show, college campus events and a singles matchmaking service in Brooklyn.

Jewish Women's Resource Center
National Council of Jewish Women, New York Section
9 East 69th Street 10021 535-5900, exts. 15, 16

This center for the study and dissemination of information
about Jewish feminism and Jewish women offers courses
periodically. Sometimes the courses are related to Jewish
women, such as a course on heroines in the Bible, and at
other times they are simply courses of interest to Jewish
women; last year a Yiddish course was offered. Classes are
held both during the day and evening.

Sam and Esther Minskoff Cultural Center
164 East 64th Street 10021 737-6900

The adult education program at the Minskoff Culture Center
is cosponsored by Park East Synagogue and its ESHI Day
School, which are affiliated with the center. You needn't
belong to the synagogue or the center, but registration is
required since the courses run on a semester schedule. The
evening courses include subjects like Hebrew reading,
introduction to Talmud, Bible study, modern Jewish history
and contemporary subjects such as the Jewish Artist in the
20th Century. Several courses geared to beginners or those
returning to Jewish worship are cosponsored by Park East's
Adult Beginner's Sabbath Service and include beginner's
Hebrew reading and prayer. There is also a lecture series
dealing mainly with subjects of current interest. The Minskoff
Center has also run women's luncheon series on a variety of
Jewish philosophical topics.

Research Center of Kabbalah
200 Park Avenue, Suite 303E 10017 986-2515

Although information about the center's classes requires calling
718-805-9122, all classes are held at Congregation Emunath
Israel at 236 West 23rd Street. Basic Kabbalah (Jewish
mysticism) is taught in twenty-four sessions, and after that you
can take a course in Reincarnation that lasts just as long.
There are also lecture series that run in four sessions—a
recent one was on astrology—and for those you can pay by
the lecture. Scheduling here tends to be somewhat erratic, so
it is wise to call for information on course schedules.

Sinai Heritage Center   Empire State Building, Suite 6809
5th Avenue and 34th Street 10118 967-8060

The followers of the Grand Rabbi of Belz have set up shop on
34th Street. Way up high on the sixty-eighth floor of the
Empire State Building, the Belzer Ba'al Tshuva Movement has
created, appropriate to the site, the Sinai Heritage Center.
Designed for the uninitiated, classes are given Monday–

Thursday beginning at 5:00 P.M. (although tutorials are held at other times). They offer subjects such as Talmud, Bible, basic Judaism and *kashrut*, though it appears that the Talmud classes are open to men only. Other classes, such as Topics of Interest to Jewish Women are open only to women, while other courses are coeducational. The Center also holds special lectures from time to time, and provides counseling, presumably for those confused about their Jewish roots.

MUSIC AND DANCE PROGRAMS

Hebrew Arts School–Abraham Goodman House
129 West 67th Street 10023   362-8060

There are daytime and evening art, dance and music classes here, and not all courses have a Jewish focus (or even content), but many do pay attention to Jewish contributions to a particular art, such as a course in ensemble singing that includes medieval and renaissance music as well as Hebrew and Yiddish folk and liturgical music. Some classes deal exclusively with Jewish music, such as a Hassidic and Israeli popular song workshop, master classes in Yiddish and Hebrew art and folk songs, Ladino (Judeo-Spanish), and the art of the Cantor; others help prepare for joining choral groups. There are also courses in Israeli folk dance, darbuqa (Israeli drum), and a course called "Sacred and Secular Music of the Sephardic Jews."

Israel Folk Dance Institute
515 Park Avenue 10022   921-8050

Although an information center that does not have its own classes, this is probably the best place to call to find out where in Manhattan you can join an Israeli dance class. According to the Institute, there are no full semester classes in Manhattan; you simply go to various dance programs when you want and pay each time. Reservations are usually not necessary, and fees for all are moderate. Some classes currently available are:

92nd Street Y. This class, which meets on Wednesdays, is part of the Y's regular programming. Classes begin at 6:30 P.M. with instruction until 8:00 P.M. and continue until 11:00 with requests from students, review and just plain dancing.

Folk Dance at Columbia University. Although this program is sponsored by Columbia's Kadima, it is open to the public. Class is held on Mondays from 7:30 to 10:30 P.M. at Earl Hall. The first hour consists of instruction and new dances, followed by student requests and whatever people feel like doing.

Ethnic Art Center. At 179 Varick Street, this is a privately taught Israeli folk-dancing class conducted by a teacher who rents the space. Classes run from 7:30 to 11:00 P.M. and the fee per session is modest.

The Israel Folk Dance Institute also sells records and cassettes by mail, including some rare and hard-to-find recordings. Also available are publications, books, and their newsletter *Hora.* Call for information and a catalogue.

HEBREW AND YIDDISH COURSES

In addition to courses at universities, seminaries, Ys, and of course many synagogues, several organizations offer Hebrew and Yiddish courses at various levels.

Mordechai Anielewicz Circle
155 Fifth Avenue 10011 255-8760

This young adult group of Americans for a Progressive Israel sponsors an ulpan for those interested in learning to speak Hebrew. Call for information about times and places.

Ulpan Center   515 Park Avenue 10022   752-0600

Run by the World Zionist Organization, the Ulpan Center offers classes in Hebrew morning, afternoon and evening, for beginners, intermediate and advanced students. The method, developed in Israel, is designed to get you "conversational" in a short time, through intensive immersion in the language. Courses run by the semester here, and meet twice a week, for two hours. Special one-month courses of intensive study (fifteen hours a week) are offered during the summer.

Workmen's Circle   45 East 33rd Street 10016   889-6800

Evening and day classes, organized into two twelve-week semesters in the fall and winter, are held right at the organization headquarters. Courses are offered in Yiddish language, from beginning through advanced, and Yiddish culture.

YIVO   1048 Fifth Avenue 10028   535-6700

YIVO, the major center for Yiddish archives and research in the United States, offers all levels of Yiddish classes, including conversation. YIVO, like many educational institutions, works with the 92nd Street Y, and some of the courses are held at YIVO and others at the Y. Classes meet evenings and there are fall, spring and summer terms. YIVO also runs the Yiddish Folk Arts Institute, five days of nonstop Yiddish tradition, including classes in vocal and instrumental music, Yiddish language and East European dance, as well as films, lectures and concerts, all held at a Catskill resort that also offers sport and recreational facilities. The Uriel Weinrich Program in Yiddish, which is cosponsored by and meets at Columbia University, offers an intensive summer language program and additional enrichment activities.

The Jewish Language Club   Shalom Japan Restaurant
22 Wooster Street 10012   925-0930

Barry Farber, the WMCA talk-show host, got this great idea. Set up tables, invite people who want to speak Hebrew, Yiddish, Ladino or Arabic, and let them talk to their hearts' content. And that's just what he's done at this Soho kosher Japanese restaurant. Each Wednesday evening the restaurant closes and the doors open to the amateur linguists. The only rule? No English!

CONVERSION CLASSES

The Jewish community has come a long way since the days when a non-Jew would approach a rabbi about becoming a Jew and be told to go away. While debate still continues about the appropriateness of missionizing the "unchurched," there is a definite increase in attention to those who seek conversion. The traditional path to conversion—individualized study with a rabbi—is still available, though some rabbis hesitate to take on conversion students because of the time commitment. If you know a rabbi you think you'd like to study with, call and ask. If he or she can't help you, there are other options within a group setting.

Derekh Torah   251 West 100th Street 10025   865-1432

One of the newest and most comprehensive programs in Manhattan, Derekh Torah was begun by a group of Reconstructionist, Conservative and *havurah* Jews looking for a nondenominational course of study for potential converts, their mates or significant others, free-lance seekers and anyone else looking for an intensive introduction to Judaism, Jewish life and Jewish institutions. One of the movers behind this program is Rachel Cowen, a Jew by choice who has been a pioneer in workshops and programs for intermarried couples and other Jews by choice. Classes are small (eight to fifteen students), and run for thirty sessions, meeting in the homes of members of the class. In addition to the coursework in history, Jewish texts, theology, ethics and the like, there is a supervised Hebrew component to the program. There are also trips around the city to places of Jewish interest. One of the special features of this program is a buddy system, where each student (or couple) is matched with a Jewish family active in a particular community. Students spend some holidays and Shabbatot with their family, experiencing first-hand what it's like to live as Jews. The family might invite the student to come to a lecture or concert or movie with them as well, adding that much-needed cultural dimension to the program. Through the buddy system, Judaism is transformed from an academic course of study to a way of life. Classes are taught by rabbinical students, rabbis, and educators from all over the metropolitan area. Whenever possible, students are sponsored by rabbis in local synagogues; Derekh Torah will help you find a sponsoring rabbi. Normally, the sponsoring rabbi arranges the actual conversion at the end of the program, although Derekh Torah will help if necessary. There is now a second tier to the program for students who have completed the first course and are interested in further study.

Center for Conversion to Judaism
15 West 86th Street 10024   877-8640

One of the first members of the clergy to become interested in active conversion classes was Rabbi Stephen Lerner, a Conservative rabbi and the founder of this program. The Center for Conversion to Judaism runs very small groups (up to three couples) and individualized classes for potential converts and, where appropriate, their mates. The course of study runs about nine months, and includes a basic introduction to Judaism and Jewish life. There are holiday celebrations, tours around the city, support groups with other potential converts and Jews by choice, and two retreats a year, where people now in the program get together with former members as well as teachers in the program.

New York Federation of Reform Synagogues
838 Fifth Avenue 10021   249-1011, ext. 487

The Reform Movement has been in the forefront of outreach programs to potential Jews by choice ever since Alexander Schindler made his famous speech calling for an aggressive missionary program aimed at the "unchurched" in America. One of the chief advantages of the Reform program (sponsored by the congregational arm of the movement) is that it runs twelve courses a year, so there's only a short wait from the time you decide to take the course to the time it begins. Each course runs for twelve sessions, from 6:15 to 9:00 P.M. once a week. Classes are held in the building of the Union of American Hebrew Congregations. Classes are larger than those of the other programs described, averaging about twenty people in each class. Those contemplating conversion and involved in relationships with Jewish partners are encouraged to bring their partners to class at no charge. The course of study is pretty standard: it includes prayerbook Hebrew, history, life cycle, holidays and synagogue practices. As in the case of the other programs, you must have a sponsoring rabbi (they'll help you find one if need be) who performs the actual conversion ceremony upon the completion of the course.

KOSHER COOKING COURSES

Kosher Cooking   189 Franklin Street 10013   966-3449

Dan Lenchner and Joni Greenspan, the owners of Manna Catering, often hold kosher cooking classes in their Tribeca loft. They try to adopt current fads to meet *kashrut* standards, and have offered nouvelle kosher cuisine, as well as classes that focus on entertaining, picnic food, summer specialties and of course holiday cooking. They try to take traditional elements of Jewish cooking and give them new zest, and their High Holiday classes have included cream of carrot soup and cauliflower with pomegranate. Enrollment is limited, so call for more information.

The Kosher Cooking School
The 92nd Street YM–YWHA   1395 Lexington Avenue 10128

The Y's Kosher Cooking School features unusual international cuisines adapted to observe strict *kashrut*. Classes, which are usually about two or three sessions, are held at the Spanish-Portuguese Synagogue on the Upper West Side or other uptown synagogues. Classes recently offered were New Orleans Cajun and Creole cooking, Moroccan cooking, "The 60-Minute China Gourmet," "Passover in Israel," and a mini-series called "The Entertaining Chef," featuring international cook-ahead party menus. Of course students also get to eat the results.

LIBRARIES AND ARCHIVES

The people of the book have filled libraries everywhere with works of fiction, history, philosophy, sociology and family life, worship and holiday observance. All the public libraries in Manhattan have Jewish books in their collections; what we highlight here are special Judaica collections, of which the most significant are at universities and research centers. Borrowing is usually limited to students or people with special research grants, but many libraries are happy to let you browse or work on the premises. Others are more restrictive. In any case, call ahead to find out requirements or limitations. Many organizations also have libraries, usually maintained for the use of their staff members. If you have a particular interest and think that one of the organizations listed in this book may be able to help you, try calling to make arrangements. Although many collections are small and specialized, some are quite extensive. Many synagogues have libraries, although most are not open to the general public, and there is little enthusiasm for use by nonmembers.

SYNAGOGUE LIBRARIES

Park Avenue Synagogue
50 East 87th Street 10028 369-2600

> Park Avenue Synagogue's library consists of 67,000 volumes on subjects ranging from Jewish history and the Holocaust to popular fiction and books for young children. The library, which is open Monday through Thursday from 3:00 to 6:00 P.M. and Sunday from 9:30 A.M. to 12:30 P.M., is generally for the use of its members, but they do make exceptions.

Temple Emanu-El 1 East 65th Street 10021 744-1400

> Emanu-El's library of 23,000 volumes circulates to members only, but others are welcome to use it and it is professionally staffed. It has a large number of reference books as well as titles on the Holocaust and works of American-Jewish fiction.

UNIVERSITY LIBRARIES

Benjamin N. Cardozo School of Law of Yeshiva University 55 Fifth Avenue 10003 790-0200

> Cardozo's Chutnick Law Library is developing a research-level collection of Jewish and Israeli law. It has more than 3000 volumes that include texts and commentaries on *halakha* (Jewish law), Turkish, Islamic and English common law that has influenced Israeli law, and Israeli materials.

Columbia University
116th Street and Broadway 280-2271

> Columbia's Judaica collection, which includes about 35,000 Hebrew and Yiddish titles, as well as a large body of Jewish scholarly works, is part of the main Columbia University library. The University's Rare Book and Manuscript Library

has a distinguished Judaica collection including medieval and sixteenth-century books and more than 1000 manuscripts. There is also the Oko–Gebhardt Spinoza Collection of almost 4000 books by and about the famous Dutch Jewish philosopher. Individuals other than students, faculty, and alumni of the University must submit a written application in order to use the library. The main library is open Monday through Thursday from 9:00 A.M. to 11:00 P.M., Friday until 9:00 P.M., Saturday from 10:00 A.M. to 7:00 P.M., and Sunday from noon until 10:00 P.M. The Rare Book and Manuscript Library is open weekdays from 9:00 A.M. to 5:00 P.M.

Hebrew Union College
1 West 4th Street 10012   674-5300

The public can browse at HUC, but you must be a student here or at NYU to borrow books. There are 120,000 volumes, many in Near Eastern archaeology and philosophy. There is a special collection of modern Hebrew literature and there are children's books in Hebrew. In addition, HUC has translations of the classics into Hebrew, a collection they claim is unique in the city.

Jewish Theological Seminary
3080 Broadway 10027   678-8080

Circulation at JTS is for students only, but the library is open to the public for research as well as photocopying of materials. You can apply for a one-year membership that will give you borrowing privileges, but this is usually granted only to people doing specific research projects. The library has 250,000 titles, and is especially rich in rabbinics, including Talmud, responsa and commentaries, with a particular focus on the Middle Ages. There is a large manuscript division, and a collection of photographs, prints and illuminated documents. JTS's large microfilm library includes rabbinic manuscripts from all over the world, such as the Hebrew manuscript collection of the British Museum, the Oxford and Cambridge University libraries, and famous Hebrew collections in Paris, Vienna, Budapest, the Vatican and Madrid, to name a few. During the academic year, the library is open Sunday through Thursday until 10:00 P.M., and Friday from morning until before sundown. During school vacations the library is open until 5:00 P.M. and closed on Sundays. The library is closed Saturday, and on Jewish and legal holidays.

New York University
70 Washington Square South 10012   598-2450

NYU's Bobst Library, one of the largest open-stack libraries in the nation, has a large number of volumes in Judaica and Hebraica, though there is no specialized collection.

New York University School of Law–Gruss Collection
40 Washington Square South 10012 598-2454

Since 1984 the law school library has been assembling a special
collection relevant to the school's Chair of Talmudic Civil Law.
Works include commentaries on legal passages in the Bible,
codes of Jewish law and commentaries on them, and an
extensive responsa collection (responses of rabbinical authorities
to legal questions). As of December 1985, there were 3500
volumes, about eighty percent of them in Hebrew, and journals
in Hebrew and English.

Stern College 245 Lexington Avenue 10016 340-7700

Stern College, the women's division of Yeshiva University, has its
own library, and its 90,000 volumes are a mix of general books
and Judaica. Anyone can browse, but borrowing is for students
and alumnae of Stern only, and there are no outside
memberships offered.

Touro College 30 West 44th Street 10036 575-0190

Touro College's library contains 140,000 books and microfilm, of
which 40,000 volumes are in Judaica (some titles in Yiddish and
Hebrew). In addition, the library has more than 700
professional journals, many of them in fields of Jewish
education, history and culture.

Yeshiva University 500 West 185th Street 10033 960-5400

The Hebraica-Judaica library, a division of the Gottesman
Library, has 125,000 books, 1000 manuscripts, and bound
periodicals, journals, and microfilm. The collection focuses on
Near and Middle Eastern literature, modern Hebrew literature,
literature of the biblical and rabbinic periods, and Jewish history.
The library is open to the public for reference and browsing,
but only students of Yeshiva can borrow books. Hours are
Sunday from noon to 10:45 P.M., Monday through Wednesday
from 9:00 A.M. to 12:30 A.M., Thursday until 11:45 P.M., and
Friday until 12:30 P.M.

ORGANIZATIONS, INSTITUTES AND COMMUNITY CENTERS

American Jewish Committee
165 East 56th Street 10022 751-4000

The Committee's Blaustein library has 35,000 volumes, as well
as many pamphlets, with an especially large number of titles
on anti-Semitism. There are also many books on civil rights,
Jewish community organization, contemporary Jewish
problems and interreligious relations. The Oral History
library, an ongoing project documenting the American-Jewish

experience in the twentieth century, has over 600 taped interviews and transcripts. It is open to educators and scholars by appointment.

Americans for a Progressive Israel–Hashomer Inc.
150 Fifth Avenue 10011   255-8760

The library here, which is open by appointment, has 5000 books and fifty bound periodicals about Jewish history and sociology, Zionism, socialism, and the kibbutz and youth movements in Israel.

Anti-Defamation League of B'nai B'rith
823 United Nations Plaza 10017   490-2525

The library here has about 5000 books, 10,000 catalogued pamphlets and microfilm, most in the areas of civil rights, human relations, anti-Semitism and political extremism (there is quite a large collection of anti-Semitic periodicals). The library is open by appointment.

Leo Baeck Institute
129 East 73rd Street 10021   744-6400

This noncirculating library is open to the public and has 60,000 volumes. Since Leo Baeck is a research center for the history of German-speaking Jewry, its library is rich in this field. In addition to rare items like early sixteenth-century writings, there are first editions of Moses Mendelssohn and other prominent writers, and books salvaged from famous Jewish libraries destroyed by the Nazis. There is also a large collection of periodicals dating from the eighteenth century to the present. The Leo Baeck Archives include thousands of family, business and community records of German Jewry for the past 200 years, and more than 30,000 photographs recording European Jewish family life, indispensable to scholars and genealogists.

Board of Jewish Education
426 West 58th Street 10019   245-8200

Since the BJE works to help Jewish educators improve the quality of Jewish education, much of their noncirculating 18,000 volume research library is in that field. There is material on education in the United States and Israel, on elementary and secondary day schools, doctoral theses in education, and material on curriculum planning. There is a comprehensive Holocaust section, as well as a selection of classics in Yiddish. About fifty percent of the library is in Hebrew.

Council of Jewish Federations
730 Broadway 10003   475-5000

The Council has books, pamphlets, reports and speeches in the area of Jewish social welfare and Jewish community organization. The library is open to the public.

Educational Alliance
195 East Broadway 10002   475-6200

The library here has more than 1000 books for all ages, as well as periodicals and Israeli newspapers.

Federation Employment and Guidance Service
114 Fifth Avenue 10011   741-7110

The FEGS library has 2500 books on educational guidance, vocational rehabilitation and occupational information. In addition, it has catalogues of schools and colleges, information about scholarships, and thousands of clippings, reports, pamphlets and journals about the labor market and other subjects related to employment.

Jewish Braille Institute
110 East 30th Street 10016   889-2525

The braille and large-type library here has more than 90,000 volumes in English and Hebrew (mostly English). The bulk of the collection is in religion and history, but there are also novels and biographies. The cassette library, which is growing by leaps and bounds, includes tapes in English, Hebrew, Yiddish, German and Russian. Use of the library is free of charge for the blind, visually impaired and physically handicapped and is by appointment.

National Jewish Archive of Broadcasting
The Jewish Museum   1109 Fifth Avenue 10128   860-1889

This new and growing archive of radio and television programs includes close to 2000 programs with Jewish content. There are documentaries, interviews, tapes from "The Eternal Light," and plays produced for PBS. Everything from major networks is here including popular shows such as "The Goldbergs," "Rhoda," and "Saturday Night Live." Virtually anything with Jewish content or interest is being catalogued here. There are also tapes made outside the United States, including the most complete videotape available of the Eichmann trial in 1961. Selected programs are screened throughout the year as part of the museum's programming. The archives are open to qualified scholars and researchers by appointment.

Jewish Women's Resource Center
National Council of Jewish Women, New York Section
9 East 69th Street 10021 535-5900

This unconventional library consists of published works on the Jewish woman, and a collection of unpublished work documenting Jewish issues related to the women's movement. There are dissertations on the position of Jewish women, birth ceremonies developed for welcoming girls into the covenant, egalitarian *ketubot*, Rosh Hodesh (new moon) ceremonies for women, feminist Passover Haggadot, and materials on other rituals being developed to integrate women into traditional Jewish experiences in a new way.

New York Public Library–Judaica Collection
Fifth Avenue and 42nd Street 930-0601

With an entrance on the south side of 42nd Street, the New York Public Library's Judaica Collection is well known, and its 200,000 titles are on a variety of subjects. Rare Hebrew texts include forty incunabula and early kabbalistic and ethical tracts. Since it is located in the Main Branch, which is a noncirculating research library, no books can be borrowed. The collection is open to the public, and librarians are quite helpful. Hours for the collection are Monday, Wednesday, Friday and Saturday from 10:00 A.M. to 6:00 P.M., Tuesday until 9:00 P.M.

92nd Street YM–YWHA
1395 Lexington Avenue 427-6000, ext. 137

The library here is open to all for browsing, but you need to be a member to borrow books. Library membership is $20 a year, or comes as a bonus if you are enrolled in any Y course. The collection is not exclusively Judaica (they have a children's library also) but out of their total collection of 35,000 volumes, many are Judaica. The Archives division of the library, which is open by appointment, has tape recordings of events held at the Y, as well as written and photographic material on the history of the Y.

World Zionist Organization
515 Park Avenue 10022 753-2167

As you might expect, the emphasis is on the history of Zionism, and there are 75,000 volumes here, as well as newspapers, photographs and other archival material. This is not a circulating library but is open to the public.

YIVO Institute for Jewish Research
1048 Fifth Avenue 10028 535-6700

A leading institution for the study of East European Jewish

history and culture, YIVO's library has 300,000 volumes, including the world's largest collection of Yiddish books. There are also large collections in Eastern European and American Jewish history, and Yiddish folklore. The reading room is open to the public and there is no membership fee. The archives at YIVO hold 100,000 photographs (16,000 of them of pre-Holocaust Europe), 4000 art and ceremonial objects, and 22 million documents about the life of East European Jews and their descendants, including genealogy listings and a collection of documents from over 800 *landsmanshaften* (mutual aid societies formed by immigrants from particular geographical areas in Eastern Europe).

MUSIC LIBRARIES

Hebrew Arts School
129 West 67th Street 10023   362-8060

The Birnbaum Music Library at Abraham Goodman House, which is scheduled to open at the end of this year, will have some rare Jewish music manuscripts, as well as texts, records and cassettes and literature from the Renaissance right up through the twentieth century. They plan to have extensive material on living Israeli composers.

Jewish Theological Seminary   3080 Broadway 10025 678-8080

The seminary's library has a large music section; the Cantors Institute reprints cantorial and Jewish materials not easily obtainable, and there is a collection of tapes of authentic folk materials from the Middle East. There are 1400 albums of classical music and 1000 Jewish records including some rare recordings.

New York Public Library–Performing Arts Center at Lincoln Center   111 Amsterdam Avenue 10023   870-1650

The Jewish Music Library at the Lincoln Center Performing Arts division has about 4000 records, and there are also materials available in the Jewish Division at the 42nd Street Library.

Martin Steinberg Center–American Jewish Congress
15 East 84th Street 10028   879-4500

The library at the Martin Steinberg Center for the arts includes klezmer and Ladino records and cassettes, publications on Jewish music, and records of Moroccan synagogue music.

YIVO   1048 Fifth Ave. 10028   535-6700, ext. 34

The Max and Frieda Weinstein Archive of YIVO Sound Recordings has 6000 recordings from the end of the nineteenth century to the present. It spans vocal and instrumental music, including cantorial music, Yiddish musicals, klezmer music, art and choral music, political songs and children's songs, and even includes dramatic readings and comedy skits. The archives are also rich in sheet music, manuscripts, scores, program notes and correspondence. They have also recently catalogued several major music collections, including those of composers Lazar Weiner and Shmuel Bugatch, and the manuscripts, recordings and papers of bandleader Al Glaser. The archive and its listening facility are open by appointment.

SPEAKERS' BUREAUS

Many agencies and organizations are delighted to send representatives to synagogues, community centers and other groups to speak on their work or more general Jewish subjects. The following groups told us they had Speakers' Bureaus; for more information about each organization see the index.

Agudath Israel of America
5 Beekman Street 10038   791-1800

America-Israel Friendship League
134 East 39th Street 10016   213-8630

American Associates, Ben-Gurion University of the Negev
342 Madison Avenue, Suite 1923 10173   687-7721

American Committee for Israel Peace Center
345 East 46th Street Suite 208 10017   972-5907

American Council for Judaism
298 Fifth Avenue 10001   947-8878

American Friends of Haifa University
206 Fifth Avenue 10010   696-4022

American Friends of the Anne Frank Center
135 East 55th Street 10022   759-2080

American Friends of the Hebrew University
11 East 69th Street 10021   472-9800

American Friends of the Jerusalem Mental Health Center—Ezrath Nashim
10 East 40th Street Room 2701 10016   725-8175

American Jewish Alternatives to Zionism
133 East 73rd Street Suite 404 10021   628-2727

American Jewish Public Relations Society
234 Fifth Avenue 10001   697-5895

American ORT Federation
817 Broadway 10003   677-4400

American Society for Jewish Music
155 Fifth Avenue 10010   533-2601

American Society for Technion
271 Madison Avenue 10016   889-2050

American Society of Sephardic Studies
500 West 185th Street 10033   960-5235

American–Israeli Civil Liberties Coalition, Inc.
15 East 26th Street 10010   696-9603

Americans for Progressive Israel
150 Fifth Avenue Suite 911 10011   255-8760

Americans for a Safe Israel
147 East 76th Street 10021   988-2121

Anti-Defamation League of B'nai B'rith
823 United Nations Plaza 10017   490-2525

Association of Reform Zionists of America
838 Fifth Avenue 10021   249-0100

B'nai B'rith Career & Counseling Services
823 United Nations Plaza 10017   490-0677

B'nai B'rith, District No. 1
823 United Nations Plaza 10017   490-2525

Bnai Zion
136 East 39th Street 10016   725-1211

Board of Jewish Education of Greater New York
426 West 58th Street 10019   245-8200

Brith Milah Board of New York
10 East 73rd Street 10021   879-8415

Chamah
78 Pearl Street 10004   943-9690

Coalition to Free Soviet Jews
8 West 40th Street 10018   354-1316

Federation of Reconstructionist Congregations and Havurot
270 West 89th Street 10024   496-2960

The Gesher Foundation
421 Seventh Avenue #905 10001   564-0338

Group Project for Holocaust Survivors and their Children
345 East 80th Street, #31J 10021   737-8524

Hadassah, The Women's Zionist Organization of America, Inc.
50 West 58th Street 10019   355-7900

HIAS
200 Park Avenue South 10003   674-6800

Hineni
232 West End Avenue 10023   496-1660

Histadruth Ivrith of America
1841 Broadway 10023   581-5151

Holocaust Survivors Memorial Foundation
350 Fifth Avenue Suite 3508 10118   594-8765

International Network of Children of Jewish Holocaust Survivors, Inc.
1 Park Avenue Suite 1900 10016

Israel Cancer Research Fund
1290 Sixth Avenue Room 270 10104   969-9800

Israel Tennis Centers Association
133 East 58th Street Suite 407 10022   308-7266

JWB (Jewish Welfare Board)
15 East 26th Street 10010   532-4949

Jerusalem Institutions for the Blind–Keren-Or, Inc.
1133 Broadway 10010   255-1180

Jewish Community Relations Council of New York, Inc.
111 West 40th Street 10018   221-1535

Jewish Cultural Clubs and Societies
1133 Broadway, Suite 1024 10010   675-8854

Jewish Defense Organization
134 West 32nd Street, 1602 10001   239-0447

Jewish Educators Assembly
15 East 26th Street 10010   532-4949

Jewish National Fund
33 East 67th Street 10021   737-7441

Jewish National Fund of America
42 East 69th Street 10021   879-9300

Jewish Women's Resource Center, JCJW
9 East 69th Street 10021   535-5900

Labor Zionist Alliance, Inc.
275 Seventh Avenue 10001   989-0300

League for Yiddish
200 West 72nd Street 10023   787-6675

National Association of Jewish Vocational Services
386 Park Avenue South, Suite 301 10016   685-8355

National Conference on Soviet Jewry
10 East 40th Street 10016   679-6122

National Jewish Community Relations Advisory Council
443 Park Avenue South 10016   684-6950

New Israel Fund
111 West 40th Street Suite 26000 10018   302-0066

New Jewish Agenda
149 Church Street #2N 10007

New Jewish Agenda of Manhattan
c/o Bender, 41 West 87th Street #1F 10024   595-0214

New York City Holocaust Memorial Commission
111 West 40th Street 10018 221-1573

New York Federation of Reform Synagogues
838 Fifth Avenue 10021 249-0100

North American Conference on Ethiopian Jewry
200 Amsterdam Avenue 10023 595-1759

Rabbinical Alliance of America
156 Fifth Avenue 10010 242-6420

Research Center of Kabbalah
200 Park Avenue Suite 303E 10017 986-2515

Second Generation
350 Fifth Avenue Suite 3508 10018 594-8765

Simon Wiesenthal Center
342 Madison Avenue 10017 370-0320

State of Israel Bonds
730 Broadway 10003 677-9650

Task Force on Missionaries and Cults (JCRC of NY)
111 West 40th Street 10018 221-1535

Thanks for Scandinavia
745 Fifth Avenue 486-8600

UJA-Federation of Jewish Philanthropies of Greater New York
130 East 59th Street 10022 980-1000

Union of Orthodox Jewish Congregations of America
45 West 36th Street 10018 563-4000

United Israel World Union, Inc.
1123 Broadway #723 10010 688-7557

United Jewish Appeal, National Office
99 Park Avenue 10016 818-9100

United Synagogue of America
155 Fifth Avenue 10010 533-7800

Women's League for Israel, Inc.
515 Park Avenue 10022 838-1997

Women's American ORT
315 Park Avenue South 10010 505-7700

World Conference of Jewish Communal Service
15 East 26th Street 10010 532-2526

Chapter 7
HOW WE CREATE: NEW YORK'S JEWISH CULTURAL RESOURCES

A city with *two* Jewish museums? A city where you are as likely to see a klezmer concert advertised in the local newspaper as a concert by Billy Joel? A city where you can see a Yiddish film on the same avenue that has some of its most exclusive boutiques, or buy a Jewish newspaper at its bus and train stations? Such a city has to be the Jewish cultural capital of the world!

From the 92nd Street Y to Yonah Schimmel, from the crowded bookstores on the Lower East Side to the Yiddish theater on Second Avenue, from the teeming garment center to the publishing company started by two Jews (Max Simon and Lincoln Schuster)—all this and a radio station that "speaks your language." New York has it all, and we've listed more here than even its Jewish mayor could show you. Enjoy, enjoy.

MUSEUMS AND COLLECTIONS

Leo Baeck Institute
129 East 73rd Street 10021 744-6400

The art collection here, like everything at Leo Baeck, serves to enhance the cultural legacy of German-speaking Jewry. There are ninety paintings and several thousand drawings, and every year the institute mounts two or three exhibitions of material from its collections.

Board of Jewish Education
426 West 58th Street 10019   245-8200

Since this is the major coordinating body of both day schools and synagogue religious schools, the exhibits in the small gallery here are often collections of the works of teachers or students in Jewish schools throughout the city. Gallery hours are from Sunday through Thursday, 11:00 A.M. to 4:00 P.M. and admission is free.

Hebrew Union College–Jewish Institute of Religion
1 West 4th Street 10012   674-5300

Exhibits rotate, and always have an interesting historical focus. A recent one was of *mizrach* plaques dating from the eighteenth century.

The Jewish Museum   1109 Fifth Avenue 10028   860-1888

What began with a donation to Jewish Theological Seminary of his library and a number of Jewish ritual objects by Judge Mayer Sulzberger is now, of course, the largest museum in America devoted to the collecting and preserving of Jewish art and artifacts. Since 1904 when the donation was made as a way of suggesting that there ought to be a Jewish museum, the collection has grown in leaps and bounds, and following World War II it took the place it so richly deserves (thanks to the donation of the Warburg mansion) on Museum Mile with New York City's other outstanding collections. As with most major museums, shows change constantly here, and reflect Jewish art and culture for thousands of years; you are as likely in one visit to see an eighteenth-century Hanukkah lamp, as a relic from ancient Israel or a 1982 lithograph of Jews in America. Among the outstanding shows in recent years was "The Precious Legacy," featuring treasures from Czechoslovakia, and it is these recent exhibitions that have now—along with recent publicity for Museum Mile—created standing-room only crowds for the museum. Since the Jewish Museum was established by Jewish Theological Seminary, it has a strong commitment to education as well as to preserving Jewish culture. Its education department offers school programs and special tours, as well as Family Workshops that focus on holidays, traditions and crafts. There are also lectures, guest speakers, films and concerts that promote Jewish cultural learning. At the museum's Tobe Pascher Workshop, artists create original ceremonial objects and conduct classes for both amateur and professional craftsmen.

The Jewish Museum is open Monday–Thursday from noon until 5:00 P.M., Sunday from noon until 6:00 P.M., and is closed Friday, Saturday, major Jewish holidays and most legal holidays.

Union of American Hebrew Congregations
838 Fifth Avenue 10021 249-0100

The House of Living Judaism exhibits sculptures, paintings, and other artwork by contemporary Jewish artists. Hours vary.

Yeshiva University Museum
2520 Amsterdam Avenue 10033 960-5390

In addition to scale models of historic synagogues, and the popular one of the shtetl, the museum contains ceremonial objects and clothes, manuscripts, books and photographs, and hosts major shows, which have included one on Ashkenazic culture (ten centuries of Jewish life in Germany) and one on room environments for the Jewish holidays. There is of course much educational outreach here, with workshops, tours, lunchtime programs, family events and teacher-education programs. The museum is open Tuesday through Thursday from 11:00 A.M. to 5:00 P.M., and Sunday from noon to 6:00 P.M.

Yivo Institute for Jewish Research
1048 Fifth Avenue 10028 535-6700

The YIVO Institute has the richest resources for Yiddish culture and the heritage of East European Jews, and in addition to its public educational programs and extensive library (described in the section on Libraries and Archives) there are often small exhibits of photographs representing life in Eastern Europe before the Holocaust. One recent exhibit was of photographs and other items gathered from the many *landsmanshaften* (societies formed by people from the same towns in Europe to help them start life over here and maintain ties to their roots) that flourished in the United States. Hours of exhibits are Monday through Friday from 9:30 A.M. to 4:30 P.M.

GALLERIES

Abraham Goodman House–Hebrew Arts School
129 West 67th Street 10023 362-8060

It is not surprising that the building that houses the Hebrew

Arts school also has a small gallery. The displays here vary, and often feature lesser-known Israeli artists. The gallery is open Monday through Thursday from noon to 6:00 P.M., Sunday from 9:00 A.M. to 1:00 P.M., and occasionally during concerts, so that patrons can browse during intermission.

Bezazel Art Gallery 11 Essex Street 10002 228-5982

This art gallery, on the same street as many of the Lower East Side's Judaica shops, has a large inventory of prints, lithographs and paintings. It is the main representative of the noted Israeli artist Ebgi.

Educational Alliance

197 East Broadway 10002 475-6200

The community gallery at the Alliance exhibits mostly the works of local artists, so not all shows are on Jewish themes. They do have occasional Jewish exhibits, and during Passover each year there is one in remembrance of the Holocaust. The gallery is open Sunday through Thursday from 9:00 A.M. to 10:00 P.M. (except Tuesday when it opens at 3:00 P.M.) and Friday until 6:00 P.M.

Emanu-El Midtown Y

344 East 14th Street 10003 674-6200

The second floor photo gallery shows the works of both well-known photographers and new talent.

Gallery Israel, Ltd. 56 East 11th Street 10003 505-2505

Sharing space with the Great Judaica Bookstore and Art Gallery (which also sells fine art), Gallery Israel shows the works of Israeli artists Ivan Schwabel, Yaakov Boussidan, Malla Carl, and Yoram Raanan, and the sculptor Aharon Bezalel. It also exhibits woodcuts, tapestries, and photographs, and sells handcrafted Judaica in several media. The gallery is open Sunday from 11:00 A.M. to 7:00 P.M., Monday through Thursday from 10:00 A.M. to 6:00 P.M., and Friday until sundown.

92nd Street YM–YWHA

1395 Lexington Avenue 10028 427-6000

The gallery here is adjacent to the concert hall, and you can spend intermission studying the latest exhibit (you'll wind up looking at it anyway if you wait on the long and very slow line for the bar in the same room). The exhibits are usually one-person shows of paintings and photographs by professionals, and there are good biographies and explanations of the work to accompany them. Some work is for sale. Gallery hours are irregular but usually coincide with concerts or other events that draw a crowd.

Omanut Art Center   118 East 25th Street   460-8700

Although Omanut sees itself as a wholesaler of Israeli art, it is happy to sell to individual collectors. The gallery's owner, Meir Levin, sells primarily to other New York galleries, and he specializes in Israeli artists, many of them seldom represented elsewhere. Omanut represents more than 60 Israeli artists, including Agam, and works are from all schools and at all price ranges.

Sotheby's   1334 York Avenue 10021   606-7000

About twice a year, this famous auction house has a major Judaica auction, and it is worth a visit just to see the items and the people who come to bid for them. Prices for most items, of course, are quite high, so if you are interested in bidding on something here, be sure you know what you're doing. There is plenty of advanced advertising and opportunity to examine the collection (some items come from synagogues or wealthy private collectors) several days before the auction and study the catalogue descriptions of the items as well as the estimated prices. The price of rare Judaica goes up all the time. We recently attended a Sotheby auction and saw spice boxes going for thousands and a rare nineteenth-century English traveling Torah, complete with embroidered mantle and tin traveling case, go for more than $50,000. The auctions usually include rare books and manuscripts, paintings, and art and ceremonial objects.

ART AND GIFT SHOPS

There are gift shops to buy a *Kiddush* cup for a baby or a *mezuzah* for a friend who has just moved, and there are shops where gifts cost several hundred dollars—or even several thousand—and might be for yourself. Many of the shops we list in this section cater to collectors and their prices are on the high side. Visit them if you have a serious interest in Judaica and are willing to invest in fine antique or reproduction items, or are interested in collecting the work of contemporary Israeli artists. Most specialize in ritual items, and many are the exclusive dealers for individual artists.

Atikoth, Inc.   16 East 71st Street 10021   570-2591

Once you squeeze through the doorway into the crowded little shop of Atikoth, you will find many unusual items, most of which have a history, which the shop's owner, Gloria Abrams, will be happy to share with you. Most of the items come from the collection of Dr. Solomon Yovely, a noted scholar who was influential in forming many of the great collections in this country, including those of the Jewish Museum and the B'nai B'rith building. The unusual items include Torah wimples and Sephardic Hanukkah lamps (some of which go back to the sixteenth century).

A & Y Sofre Stam   47 Essex Street 10002   254-1400

The sign on the door says "we rent *chuppahs*," and there are many other religious articles here too, from antique *Havdalah* sets to illuminated papers and manuscripts. The store is owned by scribes, and in addition to repairing Torahs and *tefillin* they will also prepare hand-calligraphed *ketubot*. Modern religious supplies are also sold.

Ben Ari Arts   11 Avenue A 10003   677-4730

Ben Ari has extensive selections for both home and synagogue, including candlesticks, menorot, seder plates, *Kiddush* cups, and plaques. Styles here range from very traditional to modern (Wolpert-style menorot), and although silver dominates the showcases, there is also a nice group of ceramic objects. There are also paintings, prints and artistic *ketubot*.

Grand Sterling Silver
345 Grand Street 10002   674-6450

Grand sells nothing but silver (most of it sterling hollowware) and has a large selection of *Kiddush* cups and ritual objects, as well as tea sets.

The Hecker Corporation
605 Fifth Avenue 10017   593-2424

The Hecker Corporation, which specializes in silver ritual objects, is the sole agent for Ludwig Wolpert, whose work is shown at the Jewish Museum. They also have exclusives on the works of Ario Fier, Shavi Carmel, Adi, and Moshe Ophir, and they deal with these artists at Israel prices. Hecker also features some of the finest reproductions of eighteenth-century Judaica, originals of which were lost in the holocaust. Brass objects include versions of well-known Wolpert Hanukkah lamps. There are fine reproductions of antique spice boxes, etrog boxes and small items for the home, as well as ritual objects for the synagogue. Most of the items are silver, and prices are what you might expect, although there are *mezuzot* for as little as $10. Hecker also has some unusual items, like medieval wedding rings, silver reproduction gregger and a silver dreidel. Hecker will also make dedication plaques for synagogues.

In The Spirit   460 East 79th Street, Suite 9B   861-5222

The quality (and prices!) of some of the items at this studio-gallery are about as high as the Upper East Side apartment house in which it is located. In The Spirit is owned by Brenda Bernstein, who also manages the gallery, and Shirley Kagen, who designs most of the Judaica sold here. Menorot, *Kiddush* cups, candlesticks, and seder plates adorn the shelves of the gallery, in designs that are both contemporary and ancient. They see themselves as creating "new art for old traditions," and you will see some unusual items here. Where else can one buy a hand-laced handkerchief specifically designed to be held by bride and groom as they are lifted in separate chairs at their wedding reception? In The Spirit also represents some major artists in the Jewish world. Prices start at approximately $200; a few items are less. The gallery is open by appointment only.

Israel Government Coins and Medals
350 Fifth Avenue 10018   560-0690

The Israeli government issues commemorative coins and medals that are sold all over the world. Mailings inform potential buyers (medals are often used as UJA–Federation and Israel Bond awards), who might otherwise not know about the limited and infrequent mintings of coins. To get on their mailing list write directly to this office.

Jewish Museum Gift Shop
1109 Fifth Avenue 10028   860-1895

The Museum Shop carries a full line of Jewish ceremonial objects of all prices, but here are some of the most striking: work by members of the Tobe Pascher workshop, including menorot designed by Ludwig Wolpert, items by his daughter Chava Wolpert Richard, silver-plated candlesticks from the Hadany Workshop in Israel, as well as a Shabbat candelabra by the potter Irene Helitzer and porcelain *Havdalah* set handpainted by Gloria Nelson with 22k-gold highlights. These are just some of the items shown here, and they can run into the hundreds of dollars. Among less expensive objects are some designed by Helitzer, Birenbaum, Penzer and other artists, as well as attractive ritual objects in ceramic and metals. In addition, the shop carries graphics—designed exclusively for it by artists like Agam, Barnet, Bakin, D'Arcangelo, Chaim Gross and Luise Kaish to name a few—posters of past museum exhibits and less expensive posters. *Ketubot* in a variety of designs are available, including an egalitarian one, with text in both Hebrew and English, that is reasonably priced, and others ranging in price, including a limited edition one for $125. There is a good selection of art and photography books including catalogues from major Judaica museum shows around the country, as well as a nice assortment of general interest Jewish books. There are greeting cards and note paper with Jewish themes and a small selection of records, tapes, children's toys and craft items. The shop is open the same hours as the museum, Monday through Thursday from noon to 5:00 P.M., Tuesday until 8:00 P.M., and Sunday from 11:00 A.M. to 6:00 P.M. It accepts all major credit cards.

Moriah Art Crafts   699 Madison Avenue 10021   751-7090

Moriah caters to collectors, and you will find a variety of unusual items (although you will also find antique and reproduction *Kiddush* cups and menorot). At Moriah, prices vary widely, and objects are selected for their unusual qualities; we saw a heavily-carved Polish wooden omer counter as well as some very interesting Persian *ketubot*. Although most of the collection consists of ritual objects, there are also some interesting paintings.

Parks and Stock, Ltd.   67 West 73rd Street 10023 877-2480

Paul Parks's specialty is photography with powerful Judaic imagery, and he represents such well knowns as Laurence Salzmann and Roman Vishniac, as well as Frederic Brenner, Steven Bamberg and Felix Bonfils. (He is also an agent for Shalom of Safed, whose posters seem to be everywhere and who is becoming a household presence in Jewish families.) Many of the photographers have traveled to far-off Jewish communities to photograph these vanishing civilizations. Salzmann and Vishniac have photographed Eastern European Jews, Brenner the Jews of India, Ethiopia and other exotic places, as well as the Hassidim of Jerusalem. Bamberg has done some interesting studies of Hassidim in Brooklyn, as well as of senior citizens in Miami Beach. Parks has expanded into the area of vintage Jewish photography and will be happy to show you nineteenth- and early twentieth-century images of East European Jews or Manhattan. Photographs start at about $350.

Emanuel Weisberg   45 Essex Street 10002   674-1770

Selling to both individuals and synagogues, Weisberg carries many antique items including olivewood candlesticks, *Kiddush* cups, and wooden menorot. Many small gifts are available here, as well as Torah covers, new *Kiddush* cups, other ritual items and some books.

BOOKSTORES

Many general publishers publish books of Jewish interest, and you will often be able to find these at neighborhood bookstores, at the many large bookstores along Fifth Avenue from 42nd Street to 57th Street or in department stores. But many titles and all Hebrew texts are a different story. For a really good selection of Jewish books, from popular fiction and books abut holiday celebration to prayerbooks and Yiddish and Hebrew texts, you must go right to a Jewish bookstore. Jewish bookstores are an odd breed; many seem to have a stronger commitment to carrying books to suit all tastes than to merchandising their wares. As a result, you may often have to climb over stacks of books to find what you're looking for; better yet, ask for what you want, since the owners know their stock well. Since many of these stores also carry records, magazines and religious objects, as well as artwork and jewelry, we have tried to indicate what each stocks.

Bloch Publishing Co.   19 West 21st Street   10010   989-9104

Bloch Publishing is New York's oldest Jewish publisher. They carry only their own books, which include prayerbooks, kosher cookbooks, some children's books and other titles. They recently have reduced their space and stock, but they will try to fill phone requests for books they do not have, as well as out-of-print books. Much of their business is phone and mail order, both to individuals and congregations, but they are also open for browsers Monday through Friday from 9:30 A.M. to 4:00 P.M. They do not accept credit cards.

Central Yiddish Culture Organization

25 East 21st Street 3rd floor   10010   505-8305

Open Monday through Thursday from 9:00 A.M. to 5:00 P.M., this store carries Yiddish textbooks, as well as children's books, magazines and records. No credit cards are accepted.

S. Goldman-Otzar Hasefarim

33 Canal Street   10002   674-1707

Goldman's is a fairly traditional Orthodox bookstore, and although they do carry some recent popular fiction as well as children's books, most of the stock here is prayerbooks and Hebrew texts. There is also a small selection of records, tapes, games and Orthodox magazines. They consider themselves the primary outlet for Soncino Press and Judaica Press books. Goldman's is open Monday through Thursday from 9:30 A.M. to 6:00 P.M., Friday until 3:00 P.M. and Sunday from 10:00 A.M. to 6:00 P.M.

H & M Books and Gifts

46 Hester Street   10002   475-1977

This shop on Hester Street carries Hebrew texts, popular books, paperbacks and children's books in Jewish thought, as well as Hebrew magazines, records, tapes and games. H & M (which is also a skullcap manufacturer) also carries all types of religious articles including *tallitot* and *keepot* in a variety of styles and fabrics and gift items for the home, such as challah covers and silverplated *Kiddush* and *Havdalah* sets. There is also silver and plated jewelry including chains with Jewish symbols. H & M also sells *ketubot* ranging from very plain for $1 to printed designs for moderate prices. The store is open from Sunday through Thursday from 10:30 A.M. to 6:00 P.M. and Fridays until 1:00 P.M. It accepts checks but no credit cards.

Israeli Gifts   575 Seventh Avenue 10018   391-4928

There are not many Jewish bookstores outside the Lower East Side, and this one in the middle of the garment district is handy. It carries Hebrew texts, translations, Bibles and prayerbooks, as well as paperback books and children's books. It also sells many gift items, including ritual items for the home, religious articles, hand-crafted jewelry, and sterling silver and 14k-gold wedding rings with inscriptions. They seem to specialize in handmade plaques as well, and artistic *ketubot* are on sale here starting at $100. Israeli Gifts is open weekdays from 9:30 A.M. to 6:00 P.M. and accepts American Express, Visa and Mastercard.

Gur-Ary Israeli Trade Books
49 Canal Street 10002   226-0820

The window is crowded with books, children's games and craft items. Inside there is a selection of books for all ages, and many other Judaica items including puzzles, Hebrew alphabet stencils, Jewish cookie cutters, gifts and craft items like kits for crocheted *keepot*. Gur-Ary is open on Sunday from 10:00 A.M. to 5:00 P.M., Monday through Thursday from 9:00 A.M. to 5:30 P.M., and Friday until 1:45 P.M. It accepts checks but no credit cards.

J. Levine   58 Eldridge Street 10002   966-4460

5 West 30th Street 10001   695-6888

It's exciting to see a Jewish bookstore with the range of merchandise that J. Levine has (especially since the loss of Behrman House to New Jersey last year). Although there are many ritual items for sale here (including handwoven *tallitot*) as well as artwork, the stock of books is extensive, with one of the largest selections of recently published popular Jewish books. You will find traditional Hebrew texts here but also the latest Jewish-subject books by major publishers, as well as a large selection of paperbacks and children's books. There is a good selection of sheet music, records, tapes, games and craft items. J. Levine also carries seventy-five different *ketubot*, standard and artistic, ranging in price from $5 to $500. The new Midtown store, though smaller, has a representative sampling of what is downtown. Both stores are open Sunday through Wednesday from 9:00 A.M. to 5:30 P.M., Thursday until 7:00 P.M. and Friday until 2:00 P.M. and accept all major credit cards.

Philip Feldheim, Inc. 96 East Broadway 10002 925-3180

Philip Feldheim specializes in out-of-print Judaica, and is open Monday through Thursday from 3:00 to 5:00 P.M., Friday from 11:00 A.M. to 1:00 P.M., and Sunday from 11:00 A.M. to 4:00 P.M.

Judaica Emporium 3062–70 Broadway 10027 864-6501

A recent addition to the area around the Jewish Theological Seminary, this small bookstore carries many textbooks and traditional books. There are a few recent titles too, and a small case of gift items including *mezuzot*, *Kiddush* cups and other ritual items. There are games and toys, records and tapes. Judaica Emporium, which is open Monday through Thursday from 9:30 A.M. to 7:00 P.M., and Friday until 3:30 P.M., accepts Mastercard and Visa.

Sefer Israel Inc. 156 Fifth Avenue 10010 929-6411

This bookstore carries Hebrew texts, school text books, children's books and some popular and paperback books. It is open Monday through Friday from 9:00 A.M. to 5:00 P.M.

Shaller's Bookstore
2555 Amsterdam Avenue 10033 928-2140

Shaller's, across from Yeshiva University, provides a great deal of service to students, and carries Hebrew and other textbooks they need. It also has a selection of children's books, books by Jewish publishers, and recent books of Jewish interest. They carry a few magazines, cassettes for children and cantorial and Yiddish tapes. Shaller's sells *tefillin*, and an assortment of *keepot* and *tallitot*. They sell standard *ketubot* and can arrange with one of the rabbis at Yeshiva to have one inscribed (up to $350). You can order large-type prayerbooks here as well. Shaller's is open Monday through Thursday from 11:00 A.M. to 8:00 P.M. and Sunday from 11:00 A.M. to 7:00 P.M. Credit cards are not accepted.

Shilo Publishing 70 Canal Street 10002 925-3468

Though primarily a publisher (they have been publishing textbooks for Hebrew schools and universities since 1914), Shilo will sell to the public. They have no regular hours however, so you should call first. No credit cards are accepted.

Louis Stavsky 147 Essex Street 10002 674-1289

Louis Stavsky carries a nicely-arranged and very large

assortment of Hebrew texts, popular and paperback Judaica books, cookbooks, school texts and children's books, but according to an article sent to us by the store, music is one of the things for which they are best known. Their extensive supply of albums by voices that will never be heard again live includes sets by Yosselle Rosenblatt (often considered the greatest cantor ever), Zawel Kwartin, Pierre Pinchik, Moishe Oysher, and many other legends. They have a catalogue of cantorial music and will fill mail orders; you can also call the store for information. Stavisky also carries less esoteric records and cassettes, including children's records, as well as sheet music. They have games, ritual items, costume jewelry, Torah covers, Bar and Bat Mitzvah sets, and *ketubot,* ranging from standard to colorful artistic ones at $350.

The Great Judaica Bookstore and Art Gallery
56 East 11th Street 10003   505-2505

This bookstore and art gallery, known also as Steimatzky's, carries Hebrew texts, popular fiction and Judaica, school texts, children's books, newspapers, magazines, records, tapes and games. It also operates a gift shop that carries sterling silver and gold jewelry, paintings, lithographs, sculpture, tapestries, photographs and artistic *ketubot.* The shop is open Sunday through Thursday from 10:00 A.M. to 6:00 P.M., and Friday from 10:00 A.M. to 4:00 P.M. It accepts all major credit cards.

Transcontinental Music Publications
838 Fifth Avenue 10021   249-0100

If you're looking for Jewish art music, works arranged for choir, orchestra, or solo voice, this is the place to visit. Affiliated with The Union of American Hebrew Congregations, Transcontinental Music Publications is the largest publisher and distributor of Jewish music in the world.

West Side Judaica   2404 Broadway 10024   362-7846

This seems to be the only real Judaica bookshop on the Upper West Side, something we find shocking in a neighborhood undergoing such a renascence of Jewish life (although there are many other bookstores with a decent stock of Judaica in the area). There is a pretty complete stock of books here, including Hebrew texts, popular and paperback books, children's books and text books. West Side Judaica has games and toys, craft items, records and tapes, and a good selection of Jewish sheet music. The store also carries jewelry, gift items and religious supplies including *tefillin,* menorot, *mezuzot, keepot,* and *tallitot.* It carries both standard and artistic *ketubot* from $2 up to about $200. The store is open Sunday through Thursday, from 10:00 A.M. to 7:00 P.M. and Friday until 3:00 P.M.

JUDAICA SHOPS

Rabbi Eisenbach Store
49 Essex Street 10002 674-8840

Rabbi Eisenbach is a scribe who, in addition to repairing Torahs, also does Torah appraisal, checks *tefillin* while you wait, and sells *mezuzot*, *tefillin* and other religious articles.

Israel Wholesale Import Corp.
21 Essex Street 10002 228-1661

This is another store that seems to do as much business in items for weddings and Bar or Bat Mitzvahs as books. They carry Hebrew texts, popular books, used books, children's books and games, as well as records and tapes. They also carry religious objects—including *keepot, tefillin, mezuzot*—and items for the home. They manufacture their own *tallitot* in wool, silk and rayon. They advertise that they specialize in "novelties for fundraising campaigns" and do imprinting of *keepot* and other items. They carry both standard *ketubot,* starting at $5, and handmade *ketubot* on paper or parchment in a range of prices up to $200. Israel Wholesale Import Corp. is open from 9:00 A.M. to 6:00 P.M. and accepts Visa and Mastercard.

Ergo Manufacturing 29 Canal Street 10002

Brass menorot and napkin holders crowd the window of this shop that specializes in ritual objects imported from Israel.

Miriam Embroidery 48 Canal Street 10002 925-9272

This company specializes in embroidered Torah covers and *tallit* bags, but has other religious items as well.

Weinfeld's Skullcaps 19 Essex Street 10002 254-9260

In the window hang *tallitot* in all colors; inside are stacks and stacks of boxes. The sign in the window says, "If you don't see what you want, ask for it," and we're sure that if it's a ritual item they'll have it somewhere.

Yeshiva University Museum Gift Shop
2520 Amsterdam Avenue 10033 960-5390

The museum's gift shop is small, but includes some nice silver, brass and ceramic ritual objects. There are modern silver *Havdalah* sets, interesting menorot, and pretty ceramic *Kiddush* cups. There is a case of nice Near Eastern reproduction jewelry and attractive *mezuzot*. You can also buy posters, puzzles, children's books and catalogs from past exhibits at the museum. Hours are Sunday from noon to 6:00 P.M., and Tuesday–Thursday from 10:30 A.M. to 5:00 P.M.

Z & A Kol Torah Inc.

13 Essex Street 10002   267-8370

The gift selection here includes some nice ceramic challah platters and *Kiddush* cups. There are also embroidered challah covers, Bar and Bat Mitzvah sets, *tallitot* and artistic *ketubot*. The store is open Sunday through Thursday from 10:00 A.M. to 5:30 P.M.

Zion Talis Mfg. Co. Inc.

48 Eldridge Street 10002 925-8558

Zion Talis claims to be the largest manufacturer of *tallitot* in the world, and they also carry *tallis* and *tefillin* bags, *keepot* and other religious items for home and synagogue. Although they are best known for these items, Zion Talis also carries a supply of popular and paperback Jewish books, including fiction, and used books and children's books. They have records, tapes, games, craft items and jewelry, as well as oil paintings and lithographs. They carry both standard and artistic *ketubot*, ranging from $3 up to approximately $600. Zion Talis is open Sunday through Thursday from 8:30 A.M. to 5:30 P.M. and Friday until 1:00 P.M., and accepts Visa and Mastercard.

SYNAGOGUE GIFT SHOPS

Hours change frequently, so call for information.

Central Synagogue
123 East 55th Street 10022   838-5122

Civic Center Synagogue
49 White Street 10013   966-7141

Congregation Habonim
44 West 66th Street 10023   787-5347

Congregation Kehilath Jeshurun
125 East 85th Street 10028   427-1000

Congregation Rodeph Sholom
7 West 83rd Street 10024   362-8800

Congregation Shearith Israel
8 West 70th Street 10023   873-0300

East 55th Street Conservative Synagogue
308 East 55th Street 10022   752-1200

East End Temple
398 Second Ave. 10010   254-8518

Ft. Tryon Jewish Center
524 Ft. Washington Avenue 10033   795-1391

Hebrew Tabernacle Congregation
551 Ft. Washington Avenue 10033   568-8304

Mt. Sinai Jewish Center
135 Bennett Avenue 10040   928-9870

Park Avenue Synagogue
50 East 87th Street 10028   369-2600

Park East Synagogue
163 East 67th Street 10021   737-6900

Stephen Wise Free Synagogue
30 West 68th Street 10023   877-4050

Sutton Place Synagogue
225 East 51st Street 10022   593-3300

Temple Emanu-El
1 East 65th Street 10021   744-1400

Temple Israel of the City of New York
112 East 75th Street 10021   249-5000

Temple Shaaray Tefila
250 East 79th Street 10021   535-7597

Village Temple
33 East 12th Street 10003   674-2340

ARTISTS

Artists in New York whose work reflects Jewish themes include painters, weavers, sculptors, ceramicists, calligraphers, paper cutters, quilters, silversmiths and many others. Some of them show their work at galleries and museums listed in this chapter, and many accept commissions. An important resource for artists all over the country working with Jewish themes is the Martin Steinberg Center of the American Jewish Congress, 15 East 84th Street (879-4500), which publishes a list of artists as well as the *Jewish Arts Newsletter* listing upcoming events.

Ita Aber *162 West 83rd Street, 877-2071,* whose work has gained international fame, works in textiles and focuses primarily on the restoration of synagogue materials and creating new ark curtains. Aside from this she considers herself a "feminist artist working with ancient Jewish men's and women's symbols." (Aber also does secular feminist pieces.) Her embroidery and appliqué work has been shown in museums and her studio is open to visitors. In addition she teaches workshops and gives individual instruction.

Shoshana Averbach *c/o I. J. Averbach, 350 Central Park West, 10025, 663-6886* is a calligrapher who designs birth and wedding announcements, invitations, cards and envelopes. She also designs *ketubot,* some with a small amount of illumination, and will do the calligraphy for any text that you bring her. Prices begin at about $150.

Judith Brown *64 Jane Street, 10014, 691-1113,* whose work appears in synagogues, museums (including the Jewish Museum and the Museum of Modern Art in New York), and private collections, as well as in universities and corporations, creates Judaica for individual collectors as well as large buyers. Most of the Judaica she has done for synagogues has been in brass, but she can work in other materials (such as steel, silver, and bronze), and the prices for such objects as menorot and *Kiddush* cups can range from approximately $500 into the thousands, for larger items and commissioned work.

Lee Bearson *317 West 87th Street #9D, 10024, 874-3531* has specialized in *ketubot* using classic illumination, including raised gold-lettering and designs in gouache in styles ranging from intricate Islamic-influenced patterns to contemporary. She also does calligraphy and graphic design in Hebrew motifs and works closely with clients designing Bar and Bat Mitzvah and wedding invitations as well as award plaques and greeting cards. Prices depend on the complexity of the design.

Dina Bursztyn *947 Amsterdam Ave. #4B, 749-6723* is a ceramic artist whose one-of-a-kind handbuilt and glazed work has a whimsical quality (we especially like her hanukiot with the New York skyline on it). She makes Hanukkah menorot, seder plates, Shabbat candlesticks and other ritual items that range in price from $30 to $500.

Ruth Devorah *D'Vora Designs, 240 Central Park South, Suite 5Q, 10019, 582-6148* designs soft sculpture when she is not working as a cantor. Her Mogen Dovids, which can be hung on doorknobs or used as crib decorations, have been extremely popular at craft fairs and Hanukkah gift shops and she has now added baby bibs with other motifs including a *chai.* Items come in assorted calico prints and can be ordered by mail or phone for reasonable prices.

Ruth Dunkell's paintings can be seen at the *Dalia Tawil Gallery,* which functions as her agent *(112 East 7th Street, 10009, 477-0861).* Her paintings of Judaica are contemporary, simple likenesses of ritual objects such as Torahs, yads, and Hanukkah lamps. Prices range from $350 to $1500.

Lydie Egosi, whose work can be seen by appointment *(220 East 57th Street, 826-7075)*, was already an accomplished oil painter when she made her first trip to Israel in 1968. Already committed to expressing Judaic themes in art (she grew up in Paris in an assimilated family and only became intensely connected after marrying a Polish-born Israeli who had fought in the 1948 War of Independence), she was inspired by the design and color of contemporary Israeli textiles, and felt that the Judaic themes she was exploring would lend themselves well to appliqué. She has been at the forefront of a revival of interest in the use of fabric in ritual art, and has created many complex tapestries that function as Torah mantles, ark curtains, and decorative wall hangings. She has had many shows throughout the country and her work hangs in many synagogue sanctuaries; in addition, she has an art gallery in Sag Harbor, N.Y., where she and her husband Charles have been instrumental in a revival of active Jewish life among its summer residents.

Edith Fishel *1192 Park Avenue, 10028, 289-9548* is a sculptor and ceramicist who has taught at the 92nd Street Y, and whose works have been sold at museum shops throughout the country and featured in books and magazines. All her work—which includes menorot, seder plates, charity boxes, spice boxes, *mezuzot,* and other ritual items, as well as whimsical items like porcelain hamentashen and pairs of napkin rings made like wedding rings—is one-of-a-kind stoneware or porcelain, hand-decorated and kiln-fired. Each item is individually priced and she will accept commissions.

Pauline Fisher *845 West End Avenue, 10025, 222-0260*, who has taught needlework design at the Jewish Museum and Yeshiva Museum, creates a variety of ritual items, including *tallit* bags, Torah covers, and challah covers. She works on canvas with wool, silk and metallic thread, and with precious materials. Some of her work has been in helping synagogue sisterhoods create Torah covers—designing, organizing, and teaching members how to do the work.

Sharon Frankel *812 West 181st Street, 10033, 923-6736* uses calligraphy and illumination in a variety of ways to create custom-designed *ketubot* for weddings and anniversaries. Prices start at about $300 and there are many styles, designs, and colors available. In addition Ms. Frankel has a line of greeting cards for the New Year, festivals, births, weddings and Bar or Bat Mitzvah, available as individual cards or in bulk by mail.

Wendy Friedman *23 East 10th Street, 10003, 598-0393* no longer takes on commissions for individual *ketubot* and birth announcements (whose intricate designs in gouache took about 100 hours to create), but she continues to do work for museums and synagogues. Since each piece is totally different, she cannot quote prices. Ms. Friedman plans to create more printed certificates in addition to the full-color egalitarian marriage contract that she designed using the imagery of the covenant tablet surrounded by creation motifs. It is sold at the Jewish Museum for $10.

Jay Greenspan *P.O. Box 914, Cathedral Station 10025, 496-5399 or 663-7993* does calligraphy and illumination. His *ketubot* are all very different, ranging from traditional styles to very contemporary work, and he will do *ketubot* on real parchment. Greenspan also designs posters, certificates, book plates and other decorations, and does papercutting. He is also available to do Bar or Bat Mitzvah and wedding invitations. As a scribe, Greenspan repairs Torahs and teaches calligraphy at several schools and Ys in Manhattan.

Kei January *567 Fort Washington Avenue, 10033, 304-0538* is a lithographer whose classic Jewish themes reflect the spirit of fine book illustration. She does not accept commissions, but you can call to see her work.

Susie Kessler *270 West 89th Street, 6th floor, 496-5399* specializes in machine appliqué and quilting. Her designs range from baby bibs (some are custom made with the baby's Hebrew name) and challah covers to one-of-a-kind velvet appliquéd wall hangings. We also saw an ultrasuede cut fabric (similar to papercutting) and a Torah breastplate that had been commissioned (with the Torah portion included in the design) as a synagogue donation in honor of a Bar Mitzvah. Prices range from $8 for small items up to $250, and the work can be seen by appointment.

David Klass *136 West 24th Street, 10011, 243-7633* is a sculptor who works on commission, and has created works of Judaica for synagogues and institutions. Each contemporary piece is hand made and his metal work uses traditional methods of blacksmithing, coppersmithing and the lost-wax technique of metal casting. His very original-looking menorot are copper and brass and they range from small versions for the home to five-foot high versions for synagogues and Jewish centers. Klass also designs Trees of Life for synagogues.

Benjamin Levy *317 West 89th Street, 10024, 362-2493* was born in Tel Aviv and studied in Israel, Paris and New York. His paintings are in permanent collections of the Jewish Museum in New York, the Miami Museum of Modern Art, the Tel Aviv Museum, the Skirball Museum in Los Angeles and the Hirshhorn Museum in Washington, D.C. Levy works in oil and watercolor and also does silk screens, posters and etchings. Much of his work has been inspired by old family pictures and shows a distinct Yemenite influence. Prices for his oil paintings begin around $3000. His work can be seen at his home.

Abraham Menashe's *306 East 5th Street 10003, 254-2754* photographs are in the collection of the Metropolitan Museum of Art and his work has appeared in many magazines as well as two books. His striking images often focus on the triumph of the handicapped; their spiritual quality has given him a reputation as a fine Jewish photographer.

Claire Tovah Mendelson *499 Ft. Washington Avenue, 6M, 928-2732,* who does calligraphy and illumination, has been designing *ketubot* for more than fifteen years and has a range of styles and motifs from traditional to contemporary. Many of the *ketubot* we saw have an old world, traditional feeling, some with gold leaf. She uses Middle Eastern art styles and Jewish symbolism. *Ketuba* prices begin at about $325. Mendelson also designs awards, baby announcements, and wedding and Bar and Bat Mitzvah invitations. She also produces a very attractive line of Jewish greeting cards.

Ernest Moeller *200 Bennett Avenue, 10040, 923-7423* is a wimple-maker. What is a wimple? In Eastern European tradition the swaddling cloth from a baby boy's *bris* was often embroidered with his name and then donated to the *shul* in his honor, to be used as a tie to wrap around a Torah scroll. Mr. Moeller continues this tradition, of course using fabric chosen by the client in place of swaddling cloth. He doesn't have set designs, but rather allows his imagination to create personalized wimples. Prices start at $75, not including the cost of the fabric.

HOW WE CREATE **131**

Harold Rabinowitz is a fellow of the *Tobe Pascher Workshop* at the *Jewish Museum (860-1864)*. He teaches Industrial Arts, has exhibited his contemporary silver candlesticks, wedding rings, and other Judaica in museums throughout the country, and his works appear in many synagogues as well as private collections. Prices are available on request.

Chava Wolpert Richard *Tobe Pascher Workshop, Jewish Museum, 860-1864* is the daughter of Ludwig Y. Wolpert, whose name is a household word among collectors of Judaica. She is, of course, an artist in her own right, and in addition to her semi-abstract painting she designs contemporary Jewish ceremonial objects. Her seder plate, which sells for $60 in a limited edition signed and numbered, is popular, and she has also created a limited-edition honey and apple set for the New Year at the same price. Ms. Richard also makes gold and silver Judaic jewelry at prices ranging from $12 up to $400, as well as wine bottle stoppers and decanter labels inscribed *"l'chayim."* By the way, you can also buy menorot designed by Ludwig Wolpert and executed by his students at the Tobe Pascher Workshop by calling or writing to Ms. Richard at the Museum.

Rona Rones *607 West End Avenue, 10024, 873-5276* is a weaver who combines her artistic talent and religious commitment by weaving *tallitot* and challah covers. Her work is done with fine, white wool, and stripes can be selected from approximately twenty colors. The *tallitot* are of course made with kosher *tzitzit*, and the collar *(atarah)* is also hand woven and can include an embroidered name; matching bags are woven on request. Custom orders take three to six weeks, but there is also a large selection for immediate delivery. *Tallit* prices range from $95 to $175 (matching bag approximately $40) and the challah covers are $25. Orders are taken by phone or mail.

Dan Rous *200 West 90th Street, 6B, 877-9719* is a quilter and designer who creates wallhangings and *chuppahs* on commission. *Chuppahs* are quite elaborate (they can take from six to eight months to make) and cost between $1000 and $2000. They use traditional motifs such as pomegranates, antelopes, turtle doves and verses from the *Song of Songs*. Since Rous is a cantor he can "perform the wedding and do the canopy too."

Sidney Simon *929-0554*, both painter and sculptor, has been doing all the artwork for the Jewish Chapel at West Point, but his work has spanned different faiths as well as different media, and he has done large pieces for churches and public buildings as well as synagogues. His paintings and sculpture have been exhibited in museums and galleries all over the United States as well as in Europe, Australia and Japan.

Bonnie Srolovitz *1045 Fifth Avenue, Suite 14B, 10028, 988-0779* designed the 6'6" Hanukkah menorot that were displayed in the World Trade Center in 1981, and she has recreated this very contemporary design in solid brass in small scale for the home. Each piece is signed and numbered in a limited edition and sells for $1300. She is now developing a line of Judaica items with the same contemporary look, and she showed us a Mogen Dovid paperweight in chrome that sells for $18. She can be called for information and prices.

Frederick Terna *The Reece Galleries, 24 West 57th Street, 10019, 533-5830* not only paints in Judaic themes, but devotes a great deal of time to lectures on Jewish art, ranging from surveys like "3,000 Years in Sixty Minutes" to lectures on synagogue architecture, or a study of the binding of Isaac represented in art throughout the centuries. His work is strongly influenced by his life—born in Vienna and educated in Prague, he spent three-and-a-half years in German concentration camps, studying art in Paris after his release—and his work appears in private and public collections including the Smithsonian and the Yad Vashem Museum in Israel.

Betsy Teutsch *866-5448* creates one-of-a-kind *ketubot* on rag paper with india ink, gouache and gold leaf. She does both traditional and egalitarian *ketubot* in a variety of shapes and calligraphic styles. Prices begin around $300. She sells limited-edition serigraphs, and designs baby announcements, Bar or Bat Mitzvah and wedding invitations, certificates and other calligraphed items.

Karyl Weicher's *P.O. Box 1967, Cathedral Station, 10025, 866-2970* papercuts, all of which reflect biblical and ceremonial Jewish motifs, have a very nice rounded quality. Some have been reproduced as cards, but most are made to commemorate holidays and family events. Her baby-naming papercuts are individually done—no stencils are used—and each is marked with the baby's name (in English or Hebrew) as well as the birth date. Since most papercuts are framed and hung on the wall (one Jewish custom is the *mizrach*—a papercut hung on the eastern wall of a home or synagogue to indicate the direction of the Western Wall), all of Ms. Weicher's work is done with handmade paper mounted with acid-free rice paste, essential to preservation.

ENTERTAINERS

Singers, dancers, mimes, clowns, storytellers, all Jewish and with a variety of expressions of their Jewishness—you'll never be bored. Prices vary widely according to audience size, length of performance and other arrangements, so it is best to ask right away for a general range. So many of these performers work in more than one area that it became impossible to divide them by type; you'll have to read through the list to find what you want. Maybe you'll change your mind and hire a mime or a Yiddish ventriloquist for your wedding.

Two good sources for entertainers working in Jewish themes are the JWB Lecture Bureau (532-4949) and the UJA–Federation Directory of Performing Artists, called *In the Jewish Tradition* (980-1000).

Alhambra *c/o Isabelle Ganz, 418 Central Park West #39, 10025, 749-2084.* The use of authentic instruments helps this trio capture the music of the Judeo-Spanish and Middle Eastern traditions. They mix sacred and secular music, and perform folk music originating from Morocco all the way to Armenia.

Moshe Ariel Dance Company *c/o JWB Lecture Bureau, 15 East 26th Street, 539-4949.* Born in the Middle East, Ariel performed with the Inbal Dance Theater of Israel before coming to study and work in the United States. Dances are based on interpretations of the Bible, life in the Diaspora, and the rebuilding of Israel. The company has also received raves for its Yemenite dance and Israeli folk dances. Ariel is available for lectures and demonstrations.

Shoshana Averbach *c/o I. J. Averbach, 350 Central Park West, 10025, 663-6886,* who is also a calligrapher, sings in Hebrew, Yiddish, Ladino and English, accompanying herself on piano or guitar. She also plays the flute. Averbach has taught music at Hebrew schools in the metropolitan area and has performed at community centers and organizations. She sings traditional songs and also writes some music herself.

Susan Belling *230 Central Park West, 10024, 873-8235.* This soprano performs both lieder and Broadway show tunes, but she can create a recital that is one hundred percent Jewish in content too. She has performed at Abraham Goodman House and the Jewish Museum, and her repertoire includes Yiddish, Ladino and Israeli songs as well as liturgical music and works by modern Jewish composers.

Carla Boscoe *421 Hudson Street, #318, 10014, 929-7356.* A cantorial student at Hebrew Union College, Carla Boscoe's repertory includes songs in Czech, Hebrew, Polish and Spanish, as well as opera, folk and Broadway tunes.

Billie Brenan *322 West 57th Street, 30B, 10019, 765-5448.* What can we say about an entertainer who also serves lunch? Billie Brenan's one-woman show is a "comedy in Yiddish and English," the (mostly) hilarious retelling of her life, including her experiences as an immigrant Jewish child. And during the whole thing, she says, "I come on stage with the ingredients for making blintzes, make them on stage while performing my show, then serve them to the audience at the conclusion."

Marianna Brodey *649 East 14th Street, Apt. 8C, 10009, 533-6788.* This soprano puts together concerts depicting Jewish life by combining song and story, and also gives recitals with guitar. Some of her programs include "The Jewish Woman in Song," "Mediterranean Holiday," which includes Judeo-Spanish ballads of the Middle East, and specialized programs such as "Sing-along Freilachs," Yiddish theatre songs and children's songs. In addition to performing, Ms. Brodey has taught workshops in New York. She has no preference about audience size but prefers performing for the "middle to golden age" set.

Stanley Burns *315 Eighth Ave., 10001, 807-1110.* The "Magical Ven-thrill-o-quist" entertains both adults and children with a comedy routine that has a "smattering" of Jewish humor. His performances for children include Jewish holiday material and Judaic folklore.

Roberta Caplan *110 East End Avenue, #7E, 10028, 734-5062.* A solo artist who has also performed with dance companies in the U.S. and Israel, Roberta Caplan combines elements of folk dance with her extensive classical and modern dance background. Her repertoire includes "Rachel Hannah" (the story of an immigrant) and "Sabbath Spirit." In addition to performing solo and teaching, Ms. Caplan is director of a dance trio called "Rakdaneem," which performs dances on Jewish themes.

Miriam Eisenstein *268 West 91st Street, #3A, 10024, 724-1042.* Storyteller Miriam Eisenstein performs Yiddish classics (with translation) and stories by Sholom Aleichem, and she talks about the lives of the Eastern European Jews that the stories reflect. She performs these dramatic narrations for all age groups, but is very popular with seniors.

David Ellin *50 West 97th Street, 14F, 10025, 222-8989.* David Ellin's credits include performances on Broadway, Off-Broadway and in regional theater as well as appearances in major films. He sings to his own piano or guitar accompaniment and his one-man shows include American, Yiddish and Israeli folk songs and humorous and theatrical monologues.

Cori Ellison *314 West 56th Street, #4A, 10019, 307-0350.* A soprano whose repertory includes traditional and cantorial Jewish music, Yiddish theater songs, as well as the works of international composers, Cori Ellison tailors her recitals to the interests of her audiences. She performs both formal concerts and informal dialogues.

Rita Falbel *23 West 68th Street, 10023, 873-3129.* Born in Vienna into a musical family, Rita Falbel's first songs were German lieder and Yiddish and Hebrew folk tunes. Her professional career has taken her to Europe and the Middle East and her songs—in seven languages—span the continents, but her performances, which include guitar accompaniment, have strong Jewish content. She also has children's programs and does workshops.

Mary Feinsinger *99 East 4th Street, #5C, 674-1194* is on the staff of the 92nd Street Y and the Hebrew Arts School where she gives master classes in Yiddish and Hebrew song (she also does cantorial work at Central Synagogue), so her concerts of Hebrew, Yiddish and Ladino music can also be adapted for workshops. She can also deliver a mixture of Jewish music and opera and show material.

Felix Fibich *50 West 97th Street, #14V, 865-3935.* Born and raised in Poland, Felix Fibich is an actor, director, choreographer, dancer and authority on Jewish dance. His program is a combination of dance performance and lecture and ranges from the excitement of Polish Hassidim, to the oriental nature of Yemenite and Bukharian Jews, and the dance of modern Israel.

Carol Freeman *53 Downing Street, 10014, 255-7890* is a performer, researcher and teacher of traditional Yiddish folksongs. Her repertoire includes some rarely heard nineteenth-century ballads as well as better known folk songs, and in concert each song is preceded by an explanation of its history in Eastern European Jewish life. Freeman, who has performed at festivals, concert halls, synagogues, universities and community centers throughout the United States, also sings in Ladino and several Eastern European languages.

Isabelle Ganz *418 Central Park West #39, 10025, 749-2084,* a prize-winning mezzo-soprano who teaches at the Abraham Goodman House and also serves as the cantor of the Rossmoor Jewish Congregation in New Jersey, is just as comfortable singing folk music. She performs a variety of programs and accompanies herself on guitar, harp and drum doing Sephardic songs in Ladino, Hassidic songs in Yiddish and Hebrew, and modern Israeli songs in Hebrew, English, Ladino and Yiddish. She has also formed a trio called Alhambra that specializes in Judeo-Spanish music.

Sima Gorezkaya *457 West 57th Street, Apt. 811, 10019, 246-5742.* The ensemble of Sima Gorezkaya (she has worked in the musical theater in Kiev, with the Ukranian Philharmonic and the Israeli National Opera), Slava Ovetsky (violin), and Vladimir Zaitsev (piano) sings in Russian, Ukranian, Hebrew and Yiddish, and can vary the content according to the interest of the audience. They bill themselves as an "all-occasion ensemble" with the emphasis on weddings, Bar and Bat Mitzvahs, parties and receptions.

Hannabelle & The Clown Company *840-1234.* Although we found out that Hanabelle really lives in Brooklyn, we couldn't resist listing her—after all, there aren't that many clowns working in Jewish themes, and Hanabelle is so popular that she is often booked for appearances at the Jewish Museum. Although we all know that a clown transcends cultural and ethnic barriers, Hanabelle does performances centered on Jewish holidays and her Judaic content has been particularly satisfying to Jewish educators.

The Heritage Chamber Orchestra *270 West 89th Street, 10024.* Although this group performs all kinds of music written for chamber groups, its primary focus is the research, programming and performance of music of Jewish content. Last season they performed at Alice Tully Hall, featuring the work of Leonard Bernstein, Paul Ben-Haim and Ernest Bloch.

Jewish Players Caravan *410 East 6th Street, 10009, 869-6971.* Martin Ewenstein's group performs in Yiddish and/or English, and their productions on Jewish themes, such as "Chumesh Lider," and "King Solomon and Shalmai the Cobbler" can be understood by everyone. They have performed at Jewish institutions all over New York to great delight.

Tibor and Stella Herdan *528 West 111th Street, Apt. 25, 10025, 864-1351.* Singing stars Tibor Herdan and Stella Richmond perform in Yiddish and Hebrew, Hungarian and Roumanian, and sing cantorial music and folk songs as well as selections from opera and musicals. They have appeared throughout the United States for major Jewish organizations.

Just Imagine! *262 Elizabeth Street, #7, 10012, 226-5077.* Laine Barton's group combines mime, movement, masks and music and there are performances for both children and adult audiences. Their work for Jewish audiences uses violin to evoke traditional European Jewish flavors. Their pieces include "Shabbat Shalom," "Guess Who is Coming to *Shul*," and "One Penny, No Change" (about the New Year). Performances vary according to the age group and there is often improvisation and audience participation. Laine Barton also runs classes and workshops in pantomime, theater and mask making.

Betty Klein *145 East 92nd Street, 10028, 876-0437* sings folksongs in Hebrew, Yiddish, Ladino and Russian—as well as in Spanish, and Irish brogue. She accompanies herself on piano and guitar and has entertained Jewish audiences throughout the metropolitan area.

Klez-meyd-lekh *c/o Rebecca Miller, 222-5507* is the only all-woman klezmer band in New York (and probably anywhere else). Their authenticity of style comes from a passionate interest in the music and a search for material that reaches even obscure works. They use violin, accordion, guitar, piano, wind instruments and voice to recreate the sounds of Eastern Europe, and they will also sing Israeli songs.

Linda Kundell *210 West 89th Street, 10024, 877-2798.* A classically trained soprano who has had performances in many New York concert halls, Linda Kundell has varied programs of songs on Jewish themes and by Jewish composers. Performances are tailored to the audience and include Yiddish and Hebrew songs.

Linda Kunkin Duo *84 East 7th Street, 10003, 982-7968.* Accompanied by Vlad West on piano, Linda Kunkin sings beautiful music in Yiddish, Hebrew, Ukrainian, Russian, Polish and English for dinner parties, corporate events, gallery openings and other occasions.

Elliot Levine *50 Morton Street, 10014, 255-8114,* who has performed on Broadway in everything from Shakespeare to "Finian's Rainbow," has put together a one-man show called "From Sholom Aleichem With Love." He got the idea after playing the role of Mendele in a 1962 revival of "The World of Sholom Aleichem" and did extensive research into the writings, biographies, and photographs of the "Jewish Mark Twain." He has performed the show for more than fifteen years to sparkling reviews, and he travels all over the country—for which he requires in addition to his fee and expenses "dressing room and good lighting."

Libaynu Theatre Dance Co. *57 West 90th Street, 10024, 580-3327.* Dafna Soltes' creation, "Blessed Is The Heart," inspired by the life and tragic death of the Hungarian Jewish heroine Hannah Senesh (who was killed trying to rescue Allied officers in Nazi-held Hungary), is a one-woman show and is so popular that the letter from her manager said they are already scheduling performances through the end of 1987. The daughter of a rabbi and a Hebrew-school teacher, Soltes combines the one hour and fifteen-minute performance with a question and answer period if requested. She also offers workshops for teenagers, college students and adults as a follow-up to the play, including participation in discussion, movement, vocalization and creative reading around the emotional issues of the Holocaust.

Naomi Mindlin *215 West 91st Street, #51, 10024, 724-3276.* Some of Naomi Mindlin's contemporary solo work, in particular "Ani Maamin: I Believe," is based on Jewish themes. She usually does not incorporate an explanation of Jewish content into the performances, but does discuss the sources of a piece before or after its performance.

David Montefiore *Eric Semon Associates, Inc., 111 West 57th Street, 10019, 765-1310.* Tenor David Montefiore's father was First Cantor of the United Kingdom, and with that musical background he turned to the study of opera after moving to the United States. He has appeared in major operatic roles and in oratorio performances all over the world, and has won acclaim as Yosl in "The Jewish Gypsy" on the Yiddish stage in 1983 and for his recent appearance in "A Match Made in Heaven." When he is not on tour he is available for solo concerts where the Jewish content can be up to 100%.

Sasha Nanus *95 Horatio Street, #220, 10014, 736-1100.* The program created by mime Sasha Nanus moves the audience from the Garden of Eden through the shtetls of Europe to a day in the life of a female soldier in the Israeli army. Her range is guaranteed to delight audiences of all ages.

Wendy Osserman Dance Company *115 West 27th Street, 11th fl., 10001, 807-0386.* Wendy Osserman's abstract choreography has been called painterly by one reviewer. Her work includes dances on Jewish themes. Her dance company was formed in 1976 to present original dance works in collaboration with composers, poets, musicians, actors and visual artists. There are mini-performances, longer programs, workshops and lecture-demonstrations.

Peninnah Schram *525 West End Avenue, 10024, 787-0626.* Traditions, wisdom and values have been transmitted from generation to generation in many of the world's cultures through storytelling. As a theater major, Schram began producing plays for adults and children and then became a professional storyteller, no doubt using some of the stories she heard from her parents who told her Talmudic and Midrashic tales as well as Jewish folk stories. She has various programs of stories, for children and adults, and has held storytelling workshops at major Jewish organizations and educational centers in New York. She has also recorded stories on albums and cassettes which she sells through her company, Pom Records, at the same address.

MEDIA

There are more than a dozen Jewish publishers in Manhattan (and more in Brooklyn) who publish everything from Hebrew prayerbooks and Yiddish texts to children's books and popular works. As for magazines, we've counted more than eighty-five Jewish magazines published out of Manhattan, but of course many are scholarly journals, organization magazines (such as *UJA Quarterly*) and trade magazines (such as *Jewish Funeral Directors Magazine*) that do not publish articles or contain information about events in New York—or even discuss issues related to the New York Jewish community. Newspapers, radio and television, however, do keep a watch on the changing New York scene, so we will list them in some detail.

NEWSPAPERS

Local newspapers are a good way to find out what's happening in New York during any given week, and of course Jewish newspapers are a rich mine of information about everything from what's on in Yiddish theater to how to find a date (as well as how to understand the Torah portion for the week). Finding a Jewish newspaper in Manhattan, even one that is published here (many come from Orthodox areas of Brooklyn), can be a bit tricky. The best place uptown to find a Manhattan edition of *Jewish Week* (they publish editions for other boroughs and the advertising and listings are sometimes different) is at the newsstand at 72nd Street and Broadway outside the entrance to the subway. Larger newsstands tend to carry more Jewish newspapers (although we've had little success in the Port Authority bus terminal), and, if you ask, many vendors will recommend the nearest possibility. You might also want to call the newspaper's office and ask where you can get a newsstand copy. We are listing here only those newspapers that focus on New York and what goes on around town.

Algemeiner Journal   404 Park Avenue South,   689-3390
This Yiddish language weekly is related to the Lubavitcher

movement, but it is an independent newspaper with no particular political leanings. It carries news stories, addresses itself to current issues, and lists happenings in New York City as well as running theater reviews, book reviews and human interest stories.

Aufbau   2121 Broadway   873-7400

This German-language Jewish bi-weekly newspaper was founded by German Jews in 1951 and publishes all types of articles from politics to literature, including events in New York and things of special interest to its German-Jewish readers.

Israel Shelanu   258-8696

Although this Hebrew weekly is actually published in Brooklyn, it does have a Manhattan phone and lists places to go and things to do in New York. It also publishes interviews with prominent New Yorkers and has articles about city life.

Jewish Daily Forward   45 East 33rd Street   889-8200

It would be hard not to include this famous Yiddish Labor-oriented weekly among our newspaper listings, although its coverage of New York happenings is not extensive. The paper has an English section and covers news of New York as well as the rest of the world.

Jewish Journal   1841 Broadway, Room 315   265-3274

This independent English-language weekly covers news in the New York metropolitan area as well as Israel, and has a large around town section that covers happenings, classes, shows and events in New York.

The Jewish Week   1 Park Avenue   686-2320

For Jewish events around New York, this is probably the most complete source you will find. Published by UJA–Federation, the articles reflect their positions on events, but the listings here cover everything from art gallery openings to radio and TV programs for the week. There are reviews of new plays, announcements of cultural events, a calendar of events and coverage of community news. In addition, there is substantial coverage of singles events. There are several editions of *Jewish Week,* including ones for Manhattan, Brooklyn, Queens, LI, Westchester and New Jersey, and although many of the features and listings are the same, the advertising and some of the calendar listings reflect the region, so be sure to check the front of the paper to see which one you are getting—for some reason we haven't yet figured out, many of the uptown newsstands carry the Queens edition of the paper.

Morgen Freiheit   43 West 24th Street   255-7661

Many of the readers of this independent Yiddish weekly work in the garment trade. The paper still retains some of the flavor of its Labor movement origins (what Yiddish paper doesn't?) and it includes news about events in the New York area, including a cultural page. There is a four-page English supplement that can be purchased separately, with somewhat different content, although some of the articles are translated from the Yiddish.

West Side Jewish News   210 West 91st Street   496-0401

Published three times a year by the West Side Jewish Community Council, this paper contains Jewish news of interest to those living on the Upper West Side, as well as a community calendar, notices of events, and neighborhood advertising. Members of the WSJCC also receive other mailings.

Yiddisher Kamfer   275 Seventh Avenue   675-7808

This Yiddish Labor-Zionist paper features news from Israel, Canada and Mexico as well as New York, and includes listings of events in New York.

RADIO AND TV STATIONS

Since New York has such a large Jewish population, many radio and television stations include some Jewish programming (besides dramatizations of Holocaust stories or other Jewish historical events), either among the Sunday morning religious programming or at particular times of the year (like Hanukkah programs in December). What we are listing here are radio and TV stations that have almost exclusive Jewish programming, or regularly-run Jewish programs on other stations.

WEVD-FM (97.9) The "station that speaks your language" broadcasts everything from prayer services to tips on making matzo balls, interview shows, news of Jewish cultural events and of course Jewish music of all kinds—Yiddish, Hebrew, Russian, Ladino, Israeli. This is truly *the* Jewish radio station in New York, and even the ads are glatt. Every afternoon you can hear the popular "Jewish Home Show" where there are usually guests dealing with issues in modern Jewish-American life. The Art Raymond show, something of an institution at this point, features Israeli, Yiddish and American-Jewish music, all introduced and enhanced by Raymond.

WFAS-FM (104) AM (1230) The "Message of Israel" airs each Sunday morning from 7:00 to 7:15 A.M.,reaching over 100 cities across the country. Speakers, usually rabbis, deal with contemporary issues and problems.

WFDU-FM (89.1) This station at Fairleigh Dickinson University in Teaneck, N.J., sponsors "Sounds of a People" each Sunday morning between 11:00 A.M. and 12:30 P.M.

WFMU-FM (91.1) This station is sponsored by Upsala College and there is substantial Hebrew-Jewish programming. "Morning Chizuk," produced by the Agudath Israel Orthodox organization, airs Monday through Thursday mornings at 7:30 and includes Torah discussion, explanations of laws and customs, and rabbinic narratives.

WHBI-FM (105.9) A variety of Jewish programming, including Uncle Yossie for children and Torah study for adults.

WMCA-AM (570) Every afternoon at 4:00 you can hear Barry Farber's "Live from Israel" program.

WNBC-AM (660) Every Sunday morning, between 7:30 and 8:00 A.M., you can listen to "The "Eternal Light." Sponsored by the Jewish Theological Seminary of America, this program features dramatic presentations, music and speakers dealing with contemporary issues.

WNYC-AM (830) **FM** (93.9) *Jewish People's University of the Air.* This educational outreach program sponsored by Touro College and its Herzliah Jewish Teachers Seminary Division runs on Sunday morning (6:30 A.M.) on WNYC-AM and Sunday afternoon and evening on WEVD-FM (98). The recorded courses, also available on cassettes, are given by members of the faculty of Touro and other universities, and include Jewish history and literature, as well as contemporary Jewish issues. The courses cannot be used as credit toward a degree, but they may be used as part of a credit course, and they are not only used by other universities and organizations in the United States, but also by the U.S. Armed Services, as well as the blind and handicapped. Some of the courses are "The American Jewish Experience," "The Jewish Woman in History and Literature," "Sephardic and Oriental Jewry," "Shapers of Modern Jewish Thought," and "Highlights of Modern Hebrew Literature." You can write to Touro College for a free brochure (Jewish People's University of the Air, 30 West 44th Street, 10036.

WNYM-AM (1330) In addition to other Jewish programming, WNYM has begun broadcasting the New York area's only evening Jewish news program. Other Jewish programming runs from Monday through Thursday from 9:00 P.M. to the wee hours, and Friday, Saturday and Sunday beginning at 10:00 P.M. until the early hours of the morning, and includes news programs, study sessions, political programs, entertainment and even a Russian-language cultural program sponsored by Project Chamah.

WQXR-AM (1560) FM (96.3) On Friday afternoons at 5:30 you can hear part of the services from Temple Emanu-El.

WSOU-FM (89.5) Broadcasting out of Seton Hall University in South Orange, New Jersey, host Charlie Bernhart holds forth on Thursdays, from 6:00 to 7:00 P.M. on "The Jewish Hour."

WVOX-AM (1460) This station broadcasts Shabbat services at 9:00 A.M. each Saturday.

National Jewish Television (cable) runs a variety of programs including international news, reviews of Jewish books, and the "Hineni Show"—Torah study with the famous Rebbitzen Jungreis.

Manhattan Cable runs Torah study programs on a variety of topics dealing with family life (including information about dealing with problems and disabilities), sponsored by the Jewish Board of Family and Children's Services, and interview programs.

WNBC airs *First Estate,* a long-standing spot for Jewish issues among TV's heavy Sunday morning Christian programming, is a talk show with guests, and is produced with the cooperation of the NY Board of Rabbis. The Board of Rabbis is also involved in the production of "Point of View" on WOR-TV.

AUDIOVISUAL MATERIALS

Most Jewish educators rely on the Jewish Media Service of the JWB for film rental, as well as the Board of Jewish Education, but there are many other places, both research institutions and commercial ventures, where one can obtain slides, film strips, 8 and 16mm films and other materials. Prices vary widely and one should ask questions about delivery, restrictions on use, length of rental time, and what kinds of fees are charged—depending on policies toward synagogues, *havurot,* study groups or individuals. Since these materials are quite expensive, many places require a deposit or guaranteed payment with a credit card.

ADL of B'nai B'rith A/V
823 United Nations Plaza 10017   480-2525
(contact: Linda Miller)

> Serving individuals as well as institutions, this department of B'nai B'rith rents 16mm films, and has videocassettes for purchase. They have over 300 films on such subjects as the nature of prejudice and discrimination, the Holocaust, Israel, Jewish-Christian relations, anti-Semitism and Soviet Jewry. Rental fees range from $20 to $80 and three weeks notice is required (they will mail the material two weeks in advance by parcel post). Only mail requests will be accepted.

Almi Cinema   1585 Broadway 10036   315-8660

> Almi rents to schools, synagogues and individuals. You should allow plenty of time for shipping when you call to reserve a film, although if you are in a rush they will make special arrangements for an additional fee. Almi's films include the popular *Image Before My Eyes, As If It Were Yesterday,* a film documenting the work of Belgians to save Jewish children during the Holocaust, *Hester Street, The Sorrow and the Pity,* and *The Garden of the Finzi-Continis.* The first two are also available for purchase as videocassettes.

Board of Jewish Education
426 West 58th Street 10019 245-8200

> BJE's Media Center has a lending service available to Jewish educators and communal workers; it includes all kinds of materials for schools, and informal education programs for all age groups. In order to rent films you must represent a Jewish school, synagogue, Y, community center or youth group that is a member of BJE's Media Center.

First Run Features   153 Waverly Place 10014   243-0600

> This film company, cofounded by film director Maxi Cohen whose work has been shown at the Jewish Museum, rents several Jewish films and videos including *Kaddish, Joe and Maxi* (about Cohen's relationship with her father, this is a portrait of both generational differences and a family's difficulty in coping with death and dying) and *Routes of Exile,* a story of the history of Moroccan Jews that explores the idea of Jewish-Arab coexistence.

Jewish Educational Video
489 Third Avenue 10016   683-1522

This company produces and distributes videotapes on a variety of Jewish subjects, many of them entertainment vehicles such as *Lights,* an animated Hanukka special, and *Shalom Express.* In addition to providing the Jewish community with educational and entertaining products, they are also in the market for new "properties" and will help produce and distribute the work of filmmakers with whom they negotiate a contract.

Jewish Media Service, JWB
15 East 26th Street 10010   532-4949

As part of JWB, an organization that supports and advises Jewish community centers and institutions, many of JMS's services (workshops, consultations etc.) are geared for community groups and professionals. They do, however, run a nonprofit media distribution service and their catalogue, which is available for a small fee, includes a wide range of feature films, short films, videotapes and educational materials.

National Council of Young Israel
3 West 16th Street 10011   929-1525

Young Israel's Torah Tape Library has over 1600 recordings, including lectures about Talmud, the Bible, Jewish law and philosophy, and holidays. Tapes are available to the public free for listening on the premises, and may be borrowed by obtaining a membership card for a nominal fee. For an additional fee you may become a mail member (this involves deposits and postage fees).

Phoenix Films   470 Park Avenue South 10016   684-5910

Phoenix Films has an entire catalogue of film and video material for Jewish studies, and among the many listings are *Children in the Holocaust, From Out of the Ashes, In Dark Places: Remembering the Holocaust,* and *The Jewish Wife.* Materials are available for sale and rental to individuals and organizations.

Simon Wiesenthal Center
342 Madison Avenue 10017   370-0320

This famous center for Holocaust studies has two ninety-minute films available for purchase or rental, *Wallenberg* and *Genocide.*

YIVO Institute for Jewish Research
1048 Fifth Avenue 10028   535-6700, ext. 32

The Slide Bank, a project of YIVO's Max Weinreich Center for Advanced Jewish Studies, is a lending collection for slide presentations on all aspects of Jewish life, from religious observance to cultural history. To use the service, you phone the Slide Bank and make an appointment during which staff members will help you search the card catalog (arranged by subject, city and photographer) to make an appropriate selection of up to fifty slides. There is a modest fee for use, and in-city users are expected to return slides within one week. (The Slide Bank can be used by anyone throughout the United States, with all arrangements made by mail.) A *partial* list of subjects for which presentations can be put together includes everything from *Kristallnacht*, Yiddish theater, immigration, trade unions, Torahs and "mountain Jews," to etrog containers, *mikvaot* and chicken pluckers. The Institute is now working on a videodisc project that will make even more of its photographs available to users, who someday will also be able to become subscribers to a series of periodic videodisc releases.

In addition to the Slide Bank, YIVO (which put together the footage to create the film *Image Before My Eyes*) has a library of rare film that is made available to scholars and researchers.

PRESS AGENCIES

Black Media Project   16 East 85th Street 10028   879-4577
This organization is a clearinghouse for information about Black-Jewish relations, and puts together stories for both Black and Jewish newspapers. The organization began with foundation funding but is now working by itself to syndicate news and noteworthy events that will promote improved relations.

Jewish Telegraphic Agency
165 West 46th Street 10036   575-9370
JTA is an international agency dedicated to disseminating news and information of interest to the Jewish community. Its main headquarters are in New York but it has bureaus in Washington, Paris and Jerusalem and stringers throughout the world supplying Jewish news to Jewish newspapers across the country.

THEATER

You don't understand Yiddish? Never mind, it doesn't matter. When we were children growing up in the fifties, our parents often spoke Yiddish at the dinner table to have secret communications, and although we didn't understand all the words, we knew exactly what they were saying. It's not much different in the Yiddish revivals today, in which, as one reviewer recently put it, only three things are needed: "A pair of young lovers kept apart by avaricious or stubborn parents, a marriage at the end with everyone happy, and much dancing with hands on hips." And what grand entertainment it all is! This is, of course, an oversimplification, for in its heyday, Yiddish theater in America included serious drama, both original works and translations of Shakespeare, Chekhov, Ibsen and other great playwrights, as well as musical comedies. Many great actors of stage and screen got their start in the Yiddish theater. Yiddish theater was so much a part of New York culture that recently the owner of the Second Avenue Deli at 10th Street put Hollywood-style stars into the sidewalk outside the restaurant to remind people (and tell the young) just how famous those stars of the Yiddish stage were. Today in addition to Yiddish musicals you can see serious plays depicting Jewish immigrant life and the struggles of World War II refugees as well as plays exploring contemporary issues in Jewish identity. Here are the major theater companies; of course, plays open in different locations and often move from theater to theater depending on reviews and audiences.

American Jewish Theatre 92nd Street YM–YWHA
1395 Lexington Avenue 10128 427-4410

> There is always a real range here in the course of a season, from old time Yiddish theater to contemporary plays. Recent productions here have included *The Rachel Plays*, set in East Side tenements in 1939, *Jesse's Land*, a drama about a refugee determined to start a new life in rural Connecticut after World War II, and *The Jewish Kid*, a humorous story of adolescence in Hoboken in the 1940s. In addition, the American Jewish Theater has initiated the Deborah Project, a program involving such famous women writers as Cynthia Ozick, Anne Roiphe, Shirley Lauro and Wendy Wasserstein, that seeks to encourage women writers to explore their Jewish identity through theater. They present readings of new works as well as one-act plays. As part of its regular program, the American Jewish Theater also sponsors play readings (free of charge) and postperformance discussions of new productions.

Folksbiene Playhouse
123 East 55th Street 10022 755-2231

> This theater is supported by the Yiddish fraternal group, The Workmen's Circle. There are several plays a year here in

Yiddish, including the recent production of *Broome Street America,* and *A Play for the Devil.*

Jewish Repertory Theatre
344 East 14th Street 10003   674-7200

The Jewish Repertory at the Emanu-El Midtown Y usually features recent English-language plays focusing on the Jewish experience. They produce five plays each season and offer both subscriptions and single-performance tickets. You can call the box office after 2:00 P.M. at 505-2667.

CULTURAL EVENTS AT Ys, ORGANIZATIONS AND INSTITUTIONS

American Society for Jewish Music
155 Fifth Avenue 10010   533-2601

This organization, whose purpose is to raise the standards of composition and performance in Jewish liturgical and secular music, encourages research and publishes a scholarly journal. It also seeks to promote music by sponsoring performances, especially of new and rarely heard music. Four times a year it presents free programs of cantorial, instrumental and solo vocal music that sometimes include lectures. All concerts are free.

Educational Alliance
197 East Broadway 10002   475-6200

In addition to all its educational and social service activities, the Educational Alliance's Center for Cultural Arts has several programs, including dramatic workshops, panel discussions involving artists, and "Sundays at Three," a monthly program of discussions, forums, recitals and informal theater presentations. The Jewish Family Life Institute has programs for the entire family including holiday celebrations, *Shabbaton,* outings and the Y's annual Lower East Side Jewish Festival Street Fair. The Alliance's Joseph and Ceil Mazer Theater has concerts, plays, dance recitals, opera and film series.

Emanu-El Midtown YM–YWHA
344 East 14th Street 10003   674-7200

In addition to all its arts programming, the Midtown Y sponsors the Jewish Repertory Theatre at its Milton Weil Auditorium, which is described in our theater section. Its Dance Center, an outgrowth of its dance education programs, brings presentations to the community at reasonable prices, and its music school sponsors free lunchtime chamber music concerts. The Y also has begun "14 East," an informal club and coffee house open every Sunday with musical and dramatic performances.

Hebrew Arts School–Abraham Goodman House
129 West 67th Street 10023 362-8719

The Merkin Concert Hall at Abraham Goodman House has a distinguished record for presenting fine chamber music, particularly for giving exposure to lesser-known groups and unusual works, including early music performed on original instruments. Many of the concerts here are not necessarily Jewish in focus, but its Heritage Concerts of Jewish Music feature some unusual offerings including eighteenth- and nineteenth-century European music such as Offenbach's "Esther," Jewish music from Russian, Middle Eastern and Ladino traditions, as well as works by contemporary Jewish composers. The Hebrew Arts School and the Tarbuth Foundation also present afternoon concerts combining Jewish art and history, with historical presentations, music and even refreshments to match, and recent offerings have included "Jews of the Orient: China, Japan and India" and·"Sanhedrin in Paris: Napoleon and The Jews." In addition, The Ann Goodman Recital Hall presents free twilight concerts of Jewish music.

Hebrew Union College–Jewish Institute of Religion
Brookdale Center 1 West 4th Street 10012 674-5300

The Institute sponsors a community program called "Sunday Afternoon at the College" that includes concerts of Jewish music, both classical and folk, and a lecture series on a variety of Jewish topics.

The Jewish Museum   1109 Fifth Avenue 10128 860-1888

Programming here often coordinates with current exhibits and may include music, film and panel discussions (for example, last year during the "Jews of India" exhibit there were several programs with Indian music, film and lectures on Jewish culture in India). The National Jewish Archive of Broadcasting, which is part of the museum, offers screenings from its large collection of television videotapes, and the shows are usually planned to·tie in with current exhibits or are part of a series built around a theme. The screenings are on Sunday afternoons and are free with museum admission. In addition, the Jewish Museum has family programs with both hands-on activities and shows.

League for Yiddish
200 West 72nd Street 10023 231-7905

In addition to its mission to raise contributions for Yiddish cultural organizations, the League for Yiddish has also sponsored readings by young Yiddish writers.

National Foundation for Jewish Culture
122 East 42nd Street, Suite 1512 10168   490-2280

This is a national organization whose main role is overseeing a number of UJA–Federation-funded cultural organizations such as Leo Baeck Institute, YIVO, and the Congress for Jewish Culture. In addition to this mission and "the preservation of the historical and cultural treasures of the Jewish community," the National Foundation for Jewish Culture has sponsored specific programs in New York, such as a National Jewish Folklore Conference, a Jewish Ethnic Music Festival, and a Jewish Theater Conference and Festival.

92nd Street YM–YWHA
1395 Lexington Avenue 10128   427-6000

The activities here are so many, they are difficult to describe. In addition to all the workshops in the arts, and the Yiddish culture festival of music and film, and Jewish film programs of the Jewish Omnibus described in our Adult Education section, and the American Jewish Theater described in this culture chapter, there are many concerts in the fine hall here, including performances of Jewish opera. In addition, the Y's library now has a new program called "The Oral Tradition," Jewish stories for adults told by master storytellers; these include Hassidic, Sephardic, and Oriental folktales told by a variety of performers specializing in this area. The Y has a major lecture series (some of which is part of the Jewish Omnibus) that includes famous politicians, economists, writers, critics, artists and important figures in the humanities. There are also several film programs in addition to those that are part of the Jewish Omnibus and Yiddish Film Festival, and these usually combine viewing the film with discussion led by a guest speaker. The Y also has a new program of family concerts on Sunday afternoons, designed to give children a first taste of classical music.

The Martin Steinberg Center   American Jewish Congress
15 East 84th Street 10028   879-4500

The Martin Steinberg Center, which houses the National Jewish Artisans Guild and the National Council on Art in Jewish Life, is an organization that supports artists throughout the country working in Jewish themes, but they also sponsor some cultural events in New York, including exhibits of members' work, conferences, films, arts festivals and holiday celebrations.

Yeshiva University Museum
2520 Amsterdam Avenue 10033   960-5390

The Yeshiva University Museum runs programs during weekday

lunch hours and Sunday afternoons. The weekday programs are for adults and include speakers, special tours, slide shows and musical presentations, most of which are designed around current exhibits. You bring your own lunch and the museum provides beverages and dessert. On Sunday, many of the programs (although not all) are billed as Family Workshops, and are geared to holiday activities that include baking, art projects and films. Also on Sunday there are documentary film programs and dramatic presentations for adults.

YIVO Institute for Jewish Research
1048 Fifth Avenue 10028   535-6700

YIVO, the center for Yiddish and Jewish Studies, sponsors a variety of cultural events during the year, including "The Golden Peacock: Yiddish Literature in Performance" (which can be booked for communities throughout the country). There is a lecture series that brings in prominent speakers on topics of Jewish cultural interest, and other periodic cultural programs. Last year YIVO also sponsored an "annotated" walk through the Yiddish Theatre District on Second Avenue.

YM–YWHA of Washington Heights and Inwood
54 Nagle Avenue 10040   569-6200

The Washington Heights Y has a Sunday Concert Series, featuring well-known chamber groups and musicians. In addition, there is a Sunday afternoon Jewish and Yiddish film festival. The Y also has other cultural events, most of them specifically programmed for the Senior Center and its Russian membership.

TOURS OF JEWISH NEW YORK

Ethnicity is in, so many tour companies now run tours to the Lower East Side as part of their offerings. What could be more culturally enriching than a tour of one of the synagogues of the Lower East Side (even if it's now a Chinese laundry) or Ellis Island? Many Jewish organizations and synagogues also sponsor occasional tours as fund-raisers or educational events, but we are listing here the regularly-run tours that seem particularly interesting.

92nd Street YM–YWHA
1395 Lexington Avenue 10128   427-6000

The Tours Department of the 92nd Street Y has a complete program of tours at regularly-scheduled dates (there is a complete brochure) that includes both walking tours and bus tours, as well as specialty tours like "Walking Gourmet." Not all tours are based on Jewish themes (there are tours of Tammany Hall and field walks in Queens) but many are. Some recent tours have included "The Great Sukkot of the West Side," Jewish Williamsburg, "Gourmet Lower East Side," and a bus tour called "The Jewish Farmer of New Jersey" that visited the sites of the original Jewish farm colonies of southern New Jersey.

Project Ezra Tours
197 East Broadway 10002   982-3700

You will see the original building of the *Jewish Daily Forward* (which has moved uptown), the major Yiddish newspaper that was read by millions at the turn of the century, Essex Street, where Hassidim run stores that sell electrical appliances and repair Torahs worth thousands of dollars. Although the Jewish population of the Lower East Side is nothing compared to what it was, the stores and synagogues (at least the synagogue buildings) are still there, and a visit to this area is an important tie to our heritage. The guides are volunteers who accept groups of up to twenty. Project Ezra is an organization that serves the Jewish elderly of the Lower East Side and provides substantial services, and all fees for tours go directly to the project. They will also provide speakers complete with slides.

United Jewish Council of the East Side, Inc.
235 East Broadway 10002   233-6037

This nonprofit community organization also operates programs for senior citizens, as well as the homebound and Russian immigrants. Their walking tour of the Lower East Side includes landmark buildings like the Bialystoker Synagogue, *shteebels* along East Broadway and New York's oldest *mikvah*. It also tries to show people how the neighborhood continues to be a vibrant center for the more than 30,000 Jews who still live there. Tours are arranged for all kinds of groups and they will also come to any group with a slide show.

Chapter 8
HOW WE BELONG

Mordecai M. Kaplan, one of the foremost Jewish thinkers of the twentieth century, once wrote that to be a Jew means first belonging to the group. Everything else, whether it is behavior or belief, follows from a person's commitment to the people. In New York, with its many agencies, organizations, and its large population of Jews, we sometimes have trouble finding a place for ourselves within the context of a smaller unit. The groups described in this chapter—synagogues and *havurot* (worship and study groups), as well as fraternal and women's organizations—all attempt to provide New York's Jews with a sense of belonging, a sense of community, as well as a place to worship.

In what follows, we have described almost one hundred synagogues and *havurot*, as well as organizations primarily focused upon smaller groups. Many of the groups described in our final chapter, "The Larger Picture," are also membership organizations, providing opportunities for participation through educational, social or cultural activities.

SYNAGOGUES

In 1984, the *American Jewish Year Book* (American Jewish Committee) reported that Manhattan had the lowest level of synagogue affiliation in the New York area, with fewer than two in five families belonging to a synagogue. Clearly, many New Yorkers attend synagogue functions or support them in other ways without necessarily affiliating, because at last count there were over one hundred synagogues in Manhattan, alive and well and reaching out in some cases to those unaffiliated Jews in their neighborhoods. Last year alone saw the birth or rebirth of two major Manhattan synagogues, literally across the street from one another on Manhattan's Upper West Side. The Lower East Side, once home to the city's most dynamic synagogues only to find itself largely abandoned as Jews moved uptown, still has an active Jewish community, and has recently experienced renewed interest in some of its synagogue structures and facilities. Traditional synagogues throughout Manhattan have begun to reach out to those seeking community, by offering beginners' services to the uninitiated. In Conservative, Reconstructionist and Reform synagogues, programs for intermarried couples are multiplying as the liberal community tries to provide meaningful Jewish experiences to families neglected in the past. Speaking of groups traditionally ignored by the Jewish community, singles are being wooed by many area synagogues, in direct response to the large number of Jewish singles in Manhattan and their articulated need for some connection to the organized Jewish community.

Jews join particular synagogues for a variety of reasons. A primary one is location, which is why the list that follows has been organized according to Manhattan neighborhoods. But there are other important concerns, such as movement affiliation or ideological commitment. Your choice of a synagogue might be determined by its programs for children, singles, marrieds or seniors; its educational resources; its social programs; its religious programming, including worship style and frequency; or its social service facilities. In the listings below, we have indicated which congregations have such programs.

Many of Manhattan's synagogues are affiliated with one (or more) of the four major movements in American Jewry, each of which has offices in Manhattan. Regional offices of the Conservative, Reconstructionist, Reform and Orthodox movements provide member synagogues with educational, religious, youth, administrative and other aids and programs. For more information concerning programs and resources of the various movements call or write:

Federation of Reconstructionist Congregations and Havurot   *Reconstructionist*
270 West 89th Street 10024   496-2960

National Council of Young Israel
3 West 16th Street   929-1525

New York Federation of Reform Synagogues   *Reform*
838 Fifth Avenue 10021   249-0100

Union of Orthodox Jewish Congregations of America
Orthodox   45 West 36th Street 10018   563-4000

United Synagogue   *Conservative*
155 Fifth Avenue 10010   533-7800

Please note that many Orthodox congregations are only loosely affiliated, or perhaps not affiliated at all, with any national institution. Other synagogues may call themselves Conservative or Reform but not be officially under the rubric of those institutions. They use such designations to indicate general philosophy and worship styles. We have indicated in our listings the way each congregation views itself; this does not necessarily reflect official movement affiliation

LOWER MANHATTAN

It is perhaps hard to believe that Lower Manhattan, now the city's financial district, was once home to Manhattan's first Jewish settlers. A plaque near Battery Park marks the founding in 1654 of the first Jewish community in North America. The first synagogue, Shearith Israel, now on the Upper West Side, had its original home at 26 South William Street. Today, a garage has taken its place. Apart from the synagogues listed here, there are many offices scattered throughout the financial district that have morning and afternoon services for regular daveners and people reciting Kaddish. For a list of these *minyanim,* which change frequently, call Agudath Israel, 5 Beekman Street (791-1800).

Chatham Jewish Center   *Conservative*
217 Park Row 10038   233-0428

> This is a very small group that meets for late Friday night services and holidays. It's a neighborhood *shul,* fairly private, with many of its members slowly retiring and moving to Florida.

Civic Center Synagogue *Orthodox*
49 White Street 10013 966-7141

In addition to its fairly large membership, the Civic Center has more than a thousand nonmember supporters who live in other parts of New York City and its suburbs, but who come during the day for prework (7:30 A.M.) shaharit services, noontime and afterwork mincha services, to say Yiskor and Kaddish, and to attend lunchtime adult education programs. In 1968 the synagogue won an award for its outstanding architecture (it is shaped like a candle), but what is more unusual is the number of programs it offers in a synagogue located in an area of office buildings: there is a primary school program on Sundays, a Hebrew religious school on Thursday afternoon, adult education in the evening (in addition to the lunchtime program), a *minyan* club with elected officers, a sisterhood, and the Educational Alliance hopes to start a nursery school there. There is also a gift shop open every day. Who says synagogues thrive only in residential areas?

Wall Street Synagogue *Unaffiliated*
47 Beekman Street 10038 227-7800

Although the Wall Street Synagogue does not have a strong Shabbat program and has no school, for those who work on Wall Street and are interested in a daily *minyan,* it offers a warm and *hamish* atmosphere. It calls itself a traditional synagogue with no particular affiliation, but its service is closer to Orthodox than any other branch (although it seems more inclusive of women than most Orthodox *shuls*). There are no real facilities; in fact the synagogue has a banquet hall but no kitchen. Although there is no formal adult education program, financial types often spend lunch hour studying Talmud with the rabbi, and there are many informal study programs as well as speakers. The synagogue publishes a magazine called *Synagogue Light.*

LOWER EAST SIDE

Almost every Jew who reads this book or lives in Manhattan (or for that matter anywhere in the United States) has a relative, knows someone, or *is* someone whose first days on these shores included living on the Lower East Side. And although many Jews left the neighborhood, either to go uptown or out of Manhattan, there are still about 35,000 Jews living, working, and praying here. Despite the frequent characterization of the Lower East Side as a place with eight elderly Jewish men looking to kidnap one or two others for a *minyan,* the community maintains more active *shuls* than any other neighborhood in Manhattan, and more bookstores, food places and social service facilities answering the needs of the local Jewish community. In this section, we describe first the large, full service, or architecturally noteworthy synagogues. Then we've listed the *shteeblach* we located—smaller facilities, sometimes just a rented room, but with programs that often include learning groups and social functions, in addition to daily services. Many of these *shteeblach* have no phone, so if you'd like to daven there, you'll just have to go on Shabbat morning, or early in the morning or late in the afternoon during the week.

Adas L'Israel Meseritz *Orthodox*
415 East 6th Street 10013

> Designed in the Italian style, the sanctuary is all white, long and narrow, and quite pretty. There is a fairly active program, with men's and women's groups as well as daily and Shabbat services. The building itself was built in 1910.

B'nai Jacob Anshe Brezen *Orthodox*
180 Stanton Street 10002

> People who read Paul Cowan's book, *An Orphan in History,* remember this synagogue's rabbi Joseph Singer, who had a profound effect on Cowan's return to Judaism. In addition to daily worship services, this synagogue has been aided by Project Ezra in operating a soup kitchen for neighborhood people. Rabbi Singer also maintains accounts with local merchants, so that members in need may get food without embarrassment.

Bialystoker Synagogue *Orthodox*
7 Willet Street 10002   475-0165

> Housed in a federal, state and city landmark building, the Bialystoker Synagogue is one of the largest and most beautiful of the Lower East Side synagogues. It has a hand-carved ark, dating from 1904, and magnificent murals. Worship services are held each day, morning and evening, as well as on Shabbat.

Community Synagogue Center *Orthodox*
325 East 6th Street 10003   473-3665

> Although this synagogue has a sanctuary that seats 600 and indicates that it has a large congregation, its location is one that most Jews have long since abandoned (although the rehabilitation of the East Village may soon change all that).

There are daily services here, but virtually no other activity—
no school, clubs, youth or seniors groups, adult education, or
anything to suggest a very active *shul*.

Congregation Beth Hamedrash Hagadol   *Orthodox*
60 Norfolk Street 10002   674-3330

This is the oldest Russian synagogue in the United States,
founded in 1852. Housed in a former church, there are
services here daily, in the morning and evening, as well as on
Shabbat.

Congregation B'nai Jeshurun Anshe Lubz   *Orthodox*
12–14 Eldridge Street 10002

Known as the Eldridge Street Synagogue, this building has
recently become a national landmark and is now undergoing
restoration, almost 110 years after it was built. It was the first
Lower East Side synagogue that was actually built as a
synagogue. When restoration is completed, the sanctuary will
become a museum.

Congregation Mogen Avraham   *Orthodox*
87 Attorney Street

A friend told us that ten years ago when he went to daven
here, in looking for the bathroom he was directed outside—to
an outhouse. How things have changed! The sanctuary has
been modernized (bathroom facilities added), and despite the
deterioration of the neighborhood has a daily and Shabbat
minyan.

Downtown Talmud Torah Synagogue   *Orthodox*
142 Broome Street 10013

A congregation meets here at the Beth Jacob School, which is
a Yeshiva for girls. Services are held daily, in the morning and
evening, as well as on Shabbat.

East Side Torah Center   *Orthodox*
313 Henry Street 10002 473-5078

A friend described the inside of this synagogue as similar to that
of any synagogue on Long Island, which makes it unusual down
here. It is quite beautiful and has stained-glass windows. There
used to be a school, which no longer exists, but the synagogue is
active, with programs for the holidays, learning groups, and
daily and Shabbat services.

First Roumanian American Congregation   *Orthodox*
89–95 Rivington Street 10002   673-2835

Perhaps the largest synagogue on the Lower East Side, and one
of the most beautiful, this synagogue was home to some of the
most famous cantors in the world, including Jan Peerce and

Richard Tucker. There are daily services, in the morning and evening, as well as on Shabbat.

Mesivtha Tifereth Jerusalem *Orthodox*
145 East Broadway 10002 964-2830

There is a daily *minyan* here at this, one of the last remaining Lower East Side Yeshivot. The large and impressive building has a school that educates people of all ages, from nursery school through postgraduate work, including rabbinical studies.

United Hebrew Community of New York–Adath Israel of New York *Orthodox* 201 East Broadway 10002 674-3580

If you listen to the Art Raymond show on WEVD, you have heard this place mentioned frequently, because it prints and distributes a Hebrew calendar free to anyone who asks for it. The primary activity here is providing death benefits, funeral arrangements and cemetery plots for its members. There are regular services, and during the High Holy days they welcome all who wish to come.

Young Israel of Manhattan *Orthodox*
225–229 East Broadway 10002 732-0966

Located in the middle of "Shteeble Row," and surrounded by *shuls*, this was the first Young Israel synagogue in the world, founded as a more open, accepting Orthodox community. They recently renovated and modernized the large sanctuary. There are educational, social and cultural programs here, as well as daily and Shabbat services.

SHTEEBLACH

Many of these *shteeblach* are named for the towns in Europe their members left behind, and the style of worship, prayerbook and melodies reflect what they remember from their home towns. A good number of these are located on "Shteeble Row," between numbers 225 and 285 East Broadway. Occasionally you'll find two *shuls* with the same address; they're both there, sharing the small space between them.

Bais Hamedrash Chassidei Belz
255 East Broadway 227-6145

Chevra Austria-Hungary Anshei Sfard
239 East Broadway 349-0089

Chevra Bechurim Bnei Menashe Ahauas Achim
225 East Broadway

Chevra B'nai Ischak Chasidei Boyon
247 East Broadway

Chevra Mishkan Israel Anshe Zetel
135 East Broadway

Congregation Adas B'nai Israel
257 East Broadway

Congregation Adat Israel
203 East Broadway

Congregation Agudath Israel Youth
233 East Broadway

Congregation Anshe Tashkanveh
241 East Broadway

Congregation Beth Hachasidim de Polen
233 East Broadway

Congregation Chasam Sopher
8 Clinton Street   777-5140

Congregation Erste Lutowisker
262 Delancey Street   982-0007

Congregation Etz Chaim Anshe Volozin
209 Madison Street

Congregation Massas Benjamin Anshe Podhajce
108 East 1st Street

GREENWICH VILLAGE, SOHO, CHELSEA, GRAMERCY PARK

This area of Manhattan, wedged between the Financial District
of Lower Manhattan and the Midtown business area, is comprised of what often seem like distinct villages. The synagogues
here are as distinct as each area, each with its own characteristics,
and you will find quite a bit of variety—especially in parts of the
Village that have been going through changes in recent years.

The Brotherhood Synagogue (Congregation Beth Achim)
Conservative   28 Gramercy Park South 10003   674-5750

The Brotherhood Synagogue, founded in 1954 with the idea
of "making brotherhood a reality," originally shared a church
building in the West Village, but in 1974 the congregation
acquired the crumbling landmark Friends Meeting House on
Gramercy Park. In restoring the structure for its own use
great efforts have been made to preserve this beautiful
Italianate 1859 building, and the surrounding courtyards have
been transformed, one into a memorial to victims of the
Holocaust (as well as members of the synagogue who have
died), another into a re-creation of a biblical garden. It is said
that during the nineteenth century the Quakers used part of

the building as a school for poor New York children who were given a hot breakfast along with their education, that other parts served the pre-Civil War underground railroad to shelter and feed fugitive slaves, and that in 1905 the Travelers Aid society was formed here to help needy travelers. The tradition continues today, for the Brotherhood Synagogue provides one of New York's shelters for the homeless. The congregation has always been committed to serve the local community (they run a number of cultural programs), and is also active in helping Jewish immigrants in New York and Jews in other communities in the world—they sent the first Torah to the Jews of Ethiopia and have helped Jews in India, Mexico, Singapore and the Bahamas. The synagogue has a full religious school program, adult education (including a "lunch and learn" program on Thursdays), and also had the one of the first education programs for developmentally disabled children and adults.

Congregation Beth Simchat Torah *Unaffiliated*
57 Bethune Street 10014   929-9498

New York's only gay and lesbian congregation is also one of its fastest-growing ones. Although the synagogue has no rabbi at this time, it boasts 650 members as well as approximately 1500 unaffiliated (nondues-paying) members. Beth Simchat Torah has services every Friday night, and Saturday morning services once a month. As you might expect from a pioneering congregation, Beth Simchat Torah has none of the traditional synagogue trappings or groups defined along traditional lines. All its activities are egalitarian (no separate sisterhood or men's club for example) and this includes worship services as well, where not only is participation egalitarian but all prayers are "degenderized." There is a variety of adult ed courses and adult Bar and Bat Mitzvahs are encouraged. In keeping with its welcoming atmosphere, there is no charge for attending High Holiday services here and its community room is available to nonmembers free of charge. There is no school at this time, but as the congregation develops, so will its programs.

Congregation Emunath Israel *Orthodox*
236 West 23rd Street 10011   675-2819

This traditional Orthodox synagogue has about 300 members, many of whom are older adults. There are an active sisterhood and adult education programs in addition to three daily *minyanim* and Shabbat services. Its library is open to the public and its school program also includes a Sunday nursery-primary program for children three to six.

Congregation Talmud Torah Adereth El *Orthodox*
135 East 29th Street 10010 685-0241

This lovely little synagogue has a small membership and offers daily as well as Shabbat services. It is frequented by members of the Stern College community, both students and faculty, as well as students from NYU Medical Center. It has a small banquet hall, but has no other real facilities, and a sisterhood is its only adult program. There is no school in this congregation.

Congregation Tel-Aviv *Unaffiliated*
27 East 20th Street 10010 475-7081

Although this small synagogue has few programs or facilities and no school, they are quite eager to attract young people and offer what probably are the lowest membership dues in New York (and probably the United States). This desire to attract more members (especially those who cannot afford the usual tariff for affiliation) is bolstered by their attitude at worship services, for although the congregation considers its services traditional, participation by women is the norm here. At this time, services are held only Friday evenings because of the difficulty of finding a Saturday morning *minyan*, but they are hoping to offer a full Shabbat program. They do have a regular adult ed program that is available to nonmembers.

Conservative Synagogue of Fifth Avenue *Conservative*
11 East 11th Street 10003 929-6954

Located in a townhouse with a garden in the Village, this Conservative synagogue has Friday night and Saturday morning services and fairly traditional programs including a sisterhood, *havurot*, adult education program, and two to three-day-a-week school for ages six to thirteen.

East End Temple *Reform*
398 Second Avenue 10010 254-8518

This synagogue, which draws its membership from the Peter Cooper/Stuyvesant Town/Gramercy Park/Kips Bay community, sees itself as a "family oriented" congregation, even though it is located in an area heavily populated by singles. They are in a transitional phase, planning to have a new membership drive as well as the development of new programs, which they hope will extend to the community as well as their membership. They have both Friday night and Saturday morning services, as well as some Friday night family services and activities. Their sanctuary and banquet facilities are small (again, this may change) but they do have a gift shop and a number of programs including a men's club, sisterhood, and groups for teens, young marrieds and singles. Their school runs from ages ten to fourteen and they are beginning a post-B'nai Mitzvah program. There is an adult education program available to nonmembers.

Tifereth Israel–Town and Village Synagogue
Conservative   334 East 14th Street 10003   677-8090

This synagogue on the border of the East Village has taken on little of the character of that neighborhood (at least as we remember it from the late sixties). It does, however, consider itself fairly innovative within a traditional Conservative framework, with an egalitarian service and informal ambience. Children are welcome and encouraged to attend. It has services Friday night and Saturday morning, as well as services Monday and Thursday, when the Torah is read, and Sunday mornings. In addition there is a junior congregation on Saturday morning. There is an adult education program as well as a sisterhood and young marrieds group. It has both primary and pre-B'nai Mitzvah programs and teen groups affiliated with Kadima and USY.

Village Temple   *Reform*
33 East 12th Street 10003 674-2340

Although it is in the heart of the Village, this Reform synagogue operates more like a small-town family synagogue than you would expect. Its programs are traditional by any standards, and it does little community outreach, preferring as little contact with outsiders as possible. Although its high school youth group (affiliated with NFTY) is open to nonmembers, its adult education program is not, and none of its facilities are available for rental by nonmembers. It does have a gift shop open weekdays and before services Friday night. It has both Friday night and Saturday Shabbat services, and once a month there is a Friday evening family service. Its school program includes B'nai Mitzvah training as well as confirmation classes for thirteen to sixteen year olds.

Young Israel of Fifth Avenue   *Orthodox*
3 West 16th Street 10011   929-1525

Another of the three Young Israel synagogues in Manhattan, this is a medium-sized community that holds daily and Shabbat services, with a lot of communal singing and participation. There are Jewish studies classes during the week. There are also men's and women's groups.

MIDTOWN

Business is business, but most religious Jews attend daily *minyan,* and many of Midtown's synagogues (although not all) are in business just for that purpose. They have large congregations of people who work in the area, and offer early morning prework, lunchtime, and postwork *minyanim*. Some of them have especially convenient times for those who need to recite Kaddish. A few of them have lunchtime study programs as well, but most of them do not have extensive social programming, since their members usually hold membership in another *shul* closer to home where they are involved with their families. In addition to the Midtown synagogues we list, there are many *minyanim* that gather in offices, and often these operate on a rotating basis. To obtain a *minyan* map for this area, call or write to Agudath Israel, 5 Beekman Street, 10038 (791-1800).

Central Synagogue *Reform*
652 Lexington Avenue 10022 838-5122

Considered by many to be more progressive than its uptown equivalent, Temple Emanu-El, Central Synagogue is large by Midtown standards (or any, for that matter, since the congregation numbers 1400 and occupies substantial space, including a large community house across the street). It offers a tremendous number of facilities and programs, including a library, gift shop and museum open weekdays from 9:00 A.M. to 5:00 P.M. There are worship services here every morning and evening as well as on Shabbat. In addition to its after-school religious programs, Central Synagogue has a fulltime weekday nursery school. Everything here is very well run, and there is a full range of programs including a men's club, sisterhood, youth groups (eight to fifteen) and groups for singles, young marrieds, and senior citizens. Its adult education program includes semester-long courses in beginning and intermediate Hebrew, conversational Yiddish, Mishna, Jewish music and even choir preparation. In addition, the Community House is used by other organizations that sponsor adult programs (see section on Adult Education).

Congregation Beth Israel West Side Jewish Center
Orthodox 347 West 34th Street 10001 279-0016

This Orthodox *shul* in the heart of Midtown serves both the business community that surrounds it and the neighborhood. Although there is no religious school for children, there are several study groups for adults, meeting during the week and on Shabbat afternoon, mostly dealing with Jewish texts. The synagogue is of moderate size, although like other Midtown congregations it has a large number of unaffiliated "friends," who work in the neighborhood and support the community, even though they belong to a synagogue where they reside.

One service that the congregation provides is a *bikur cholim* society, which is comprised of members of the *shul* who visit people (both members and nonmembers) in the hospital. Worship takes place every morning (two *minyanim*, at 6:45 and 7:45 A.M.) and evening; there is also a 1:30 P.M. mincha service. Services on Shabbat are held at sundown on Fridays and on Saturday morning and afternoon. Currently, a junior congregation is being planned. The facility is used by several Jewish groups, including Parparim, a Jewish dance group.

East 55th Street Conservative Synagogue   *Conservative*
308 East 55th Street 10022   752-1200

This is fairly main line Conservative, with traditional daily and Shabbat services, as well as a men's club and sisterhood. There are no youth, singles or seniors groups, and no facilities or banquet hall, although the synagogue does have an adult ed program. One friend told us that the *Kiddush* after Shabbat morning services here is one of the best in town!

Ezrath Israel   *Orthodox*
339 West 47th Street 10036   245-6975

Known as the Actor's Synagogue, Ezrath Israel was home to some of America's best-known Jewish actors, producers, directors and others in the entertainment industry. Although there aren't many there these days, you can see caricatures of some of them hanging on the walls. Daily *minyanim* are held at 8:00 A.M. and 5:30 P.M., and there are Shabbat services as well.

Fur Center Synagogue   *Orthodox*
230 West 29th Street 10001   594-9480

This is really a *minyan* for people who work in the area, although there are Shabbat services in addition to daily services. There are no facilities (other than a banquet room which is available for rental on Sunday afternoons) and no programs for its members.

Garment Center Congregation   *Orthodox*
205 West 40th Street 10018   391-6966

This is also a very small synagogue, in spite of the fact that it lists a dues-paying congregation of 500 and an additional 5000 nonpaying affiliates. Daily services, including Shabbat, attract those who work in the garment district, and when Yiskor is said, attendance is very high (often requiring repeat services to accommodate everyone). There is a sisterhood and the congregation owns cemetery plots.

Maimonides Temple   *Unaffiliated*
P.O. Box 20374 10017   722-6984

Since many congregations, even in Manhattan, have a distinct "couples" or family orientation, this new synagogue dedicated to filling the religious and social needs of New York's singles should continue to be a big hit. In addition to helping those New Yorkers who already want a synagogue that more directly meets their needs, the synagogue is attempting to reach the substantial number of young professionals who leave their hometowns to pursue careers in the Big Apple and have no idea where to go to be with other Jews. In addition to High Holiday services, which were held last year at the International Center at United Nations Plaza, the congregation currently meets once a month for a combination dinner, *Oneg Shabbat* and Friday night service at the United Engineering Center at 345 East 47th Street (at First Avenue) which several hundred attend each time. There is singing during the kosher-style dinner, and the group enlarges as more join for the coffee hour which is followed by the service. The congregation has a "liberal Reform orientation" and uses the Reform prayerbook and liturgy. There are no membership dues, but reservations for the dinner or *Oneg* (with a different contribution for each) are required.

Metropolitan Synagogue of New York   *Reform*
10 Park Avenue 10016   679-8580

This synagogue, which is located at 40 East 35th Street (although the synagogue offices are around the corner), has large facilities and shares a building with the Community Church. It has been known for its magnificent liturgical music during services. Many programs are in the planning stages, including a preschool program centering on the Jewish holidays. There are both singles and young married groups, as well as an adult education program, and there is a religious school. Services are on Friday evenings and Saturday morning.

Millinery Center Synagogue   *Unaffiliated*
1025 Sixth Avenue 10018   921-1580

This is essentially a synagogue for people working in the fashion industry. It is located in a small building, and there are no programs other than its daily, Friday evening and Saturday morning services, but it has "done a very good job for about fifty years" serving its community—its 1000 members have weekday worship services available not only in the early morning and late afternoon but at lunchtime as well.

Radio City Synagogue   *Orthodox*
30 West 47th Street, Suite 305 10020   819-0839

This is another Midtown synagogue designed to serve the working community of its neighborhood, in this case the diamond and jewelry district. It provides an opportunity for many, who might be unable to attend services at home because of their work schedule, to say Yiskor and Kaddish, and will even duplicate services so that the more than 500 members (and an additional 2000 on their mailing list) can be accommodated. There are no real facilities or programs here, and no school, but there is a daily *minyan* in the afternoon and evening, and an adult education program that attracts many professionals, and is available to nonmembers.

Sutton Place Synagogue   *Conservative*
225 East 51st Street 10022   593-3300

This very large congregation, in addition to daily and Shabbat services, has a real commitment to community outreach, with several education programs and specialized groups. Its services and school are pretty traditional and it also offers a B'nai Mitzvah program and youth groups. As part of its commitment to education, Sutton Place offers both a beginner's service and junior congregation on Saturday morning. Their Abraham Meyer Greenstein Academy of Jewish Studies has a large faculty and includes not only Jewish studies and skills courses, but courses in business and personal enrichment such as computer literacy, stress management and exercise. Many of the courses are geared for singles, since Sutton Place has strong programming for this group; their singles *havurah,* which has a separate membership fee, provides separate singles-only services as well as *Shabbaton* and social events designed just for this group (some divided into specific age groups as well). Members of the *havurah* are also entitled to participate in certain synagogue activities without additional membership. In addition to its large facilities that include banquet halls and meeting rooms and a gift shop, Sutton Place has the traditional men's club and sisterhood groups.

UPPER EAST SIDE

New York's silk-stocking district has some of the most influential financial and political figures in the city, so it is not unusual to find some of them speaking or giving workshops at synagogues in this area. Many of the congregations here are large, with substantial programming and religious schools—and of course, this is where you will find the synagogue that formed the basis for *Our Crowd.*

Congregation Kehilath Jeshurun   *Orthodox*
125 East 85th Street 10028   427-1000, ext. 264

A synagogue that has an active day school is usually a

synagogue where there is a lot going on, and this is certainly true of Kehilath Jeshurun, considered by some the most progressive Orthodox institution on the East Side. In addition to its regular daily worship services, morning and evening, there are Shabbat morning services for toddlers, primary schoolers, elementary school children and teens, and for those who wish to participate but who are unfamiliar with the service. If you want a large Orthodox synagogue jam-packed with activities, this is it—a men's club, sisterhood, singles group, couples club, youth group, and programs for seniors. In addition to a regular evening adult education program with semester-long courses in Hebrew, modern Jewish history, *siddur* reading and customs, Kehilath Jeshurun runs a "lunch and learn" program with topics rotating on a four-week cycle. Its gift shop is considered one of the best synagogue shops in Manhattan, and the synagogue's extensive recreational facilities are available to members of the congregation. Kehilath Jeshurun is affiliated with Ramaz, a traditional Jewish Day School, which starts at nursery school and continues through the high school level and is open to nonmembers of the synagogue. It has extensive recreational facilities, which are available to members of the congregation.

Congregation Orach Chaim *Orthodox*
1459 Lexington Avenue 10128   722-6566

This small neighborhood synagogue, which claims to have the oldest *chevra kaddisha* (burial society) in New York City, holds daily services every morning and evening, as well as at sundown on Friday, and on Saturday both morning and evening. It has an adult education program and an active sisterhood. Both because of its commitment to *bikur cholim* (visiting the sick) and its proximity to Mount Sinai Hospital and other local hospitals, members frequently put up out-of-town guests who are visiting hospital patients.

Fifth Avenue Synagogue *Orthodox*
5 East 62nd Street 10021   838-2122

The Fifth Avenue Synagogue is one of the foremost Orthodox synagogues in Manhattan. Its first rabbi, Israel Jakobowitz, is now chief rabbi of London. There are services every morning and evening, as well as Friday at sundown and on Saturday morning and evening. It has a men's club and sisterhood, as well as a young marrieds' group. At the time of this writing, it was just beginning a program for singles. All of these groups are open to nonmembers of the congregation. Although there is no formal adult education program, there is a class held for members of the congregation prior to services. There is an educational program for children, beginning at the age of six and continuing through high school.

Park Avenue Synagogue   *Conservative*
50 East 87th Street 10128   369-2600

An East Side landmark, proud of its commitment to Jewish art, with stained-glass windows, sculpture, lithographs and paintings throughout the building, Park Avenue Synagogue is the largest Conservative congregation in this area, and it is high church indeed. There is usually an organ and choir at its Shabbat services and there are services every morning and evening, with the first Friday evening of each month set aside for Family Services, and the last Friday evening each month set aside for late night services. Park Avenue has an extensive Hebrew school program and one of the best Hebrew high schools in Manhattan, and it offers many programs for children, beginning with an early childhood center, religious school from age five through high school, teen youth groups, and a junior congregation every Shabbat morning. Adults need not feel slighted, for Park Avenue has a men's club, sisterhood, as well as three singles groups, a group for young marrieds and one for senior citizens. There are a library and gift shop, as well as a museum, all of which are open to the public. The synagogue also has a commitment to the neighborhood poor through a food pantry.

Park East Synagogue   *Orthodox*
163 East 67th Street 10021   737-6900

This is another large synagogue with its own day school, and it has good programming and facilities. Its rabbi is committed to community outreach, and is very active in issues related to oppression of Jews and others. Park East Synagogue holds services each morning and evening through the week and on the Sabbath. In addition, there is a beginners service each Saturday morning and a junior congregation. There is a library for use by members, a gift shop open to the public, and a gym, which is available to nonmembers for a charge. This is a full-service synagogue, with a men's club, sisterhood and youth group, all of which are open to nonmembers. Its singles programs are very good. Educational resources include a weekday nursery school, starting at age two-and-a-half, the ESHI day school through the eighth grade, and an after-school program for students from age six through high school.

Temple Emanu-El   *Reform*
1 East 65th Street 10021   744-1400

If you've ever tuned in to WQXR after work on Friday evening, you've already had a taste of services at Temple Emanu-El. This monumental synagogue facing Central Park is the Congregation that inspired Stephen Birmingham's *Our Crowd*, the history of New York's wealthy German-Jewish population. It is still one of the largest synagogues in Manhattan, and the virtual center of

New York's Reform movement, some of whose offices are across the street. This is "classical" Reform at its highest. There is a story that when the old Union prayerbook was going out of print, in order to avoid being forced to use a new version, Emanu-El had a special edition of the old version printed to store away so that they would never have to use the new version when copies of the prayerbook wore out. There are daily evening services here, as well as Friday evening and Saturday morning services. There is a library and gift shop, both of which are open to the public. This is a full-service synagogue, with a men's club, sisterhood, singles, seniors and youth groups. In addition, it maintains the Emanu-El Old Age Center. All of these programs are open to nonmembers of the congregation. In addition to a full adult education program, the Temple operates a weekday Nursery School for children two-and-a-half to five (open to nonmembers) and an after-school religious school for students ages five to fourteen.

Temple Israel of the City of New York   *Reform*
112 East 75th Street 10021   249-5000

The founding of this congregation in East Harlem in 1870, when Harlem was a suburb of New York, was considered quite radical. At that time the major synagogues were all located below 50th Street, most of them all the way downtown. According to accounts of the synagogue's history, the shopkeepers living on Third Avenue near 125th Street would have had to travel two hours (which indeed they would not) on Shabbat to attend services elsewhere in Manhattan. So Temple Israel—called at its founding "Congregation Hand-in-Hand"—was begun over a printing shop, and soon moved to larger quarters. In the next 100 years it moved many more times, first west, and then downtown, following the Jewish population until it found its present home on the Upper East Side about twenty years ago. Along the way it left behind some pretty formidable edifices, and its new building is quite modern. Temple Israel holds services every Friday evening (once a month, late), and Saturday morning. There are occasional Saturday afternoon services and Friday evening Family Services. There are a library and gift shop, both of which are open to the public. The congregation has an afternoon religious school and a high school program, a men's club, sisterhood, singles group and youth group. There is a weekday nursery school for children two-and-a-half to five (open to nonmembers).

Temple Shaaray Tefila   *Reform*
250 East 79th Street 10021   535-8008

Shaaray Tefila is a large synagogue built by remodeling a movie theater. There are services each Friday evening and Saturday morning, and the synagogue has a library, gift shop and museum, all of which are open to the public. The congregation offers sisterhood, singles, seniors and youth groups and maintains a Soup Kitchen for neighborhood poor people. In addition to an adult education program, Shaaray Tefila has a nursery coop and an after-school religious-school program.

Temple of Universal Judaism (Congregation Daat Elohim) *Unaffiliated* 1010 Park Avenue 10021 535-0187

The Temple of Universal Judaism is not affiliated with any movement, although it seems to consider its service closer to Reform than anything else. This synagogue, which is housed in a church, may have the largest number of mixed-married couples on its roster, and is committed to outreach to such couples. There are services here most Friday evenings and major holidays, and the synagogue may form a religious school soon, but for the time being there are no education programs here and no other programs in spite of a moderate membership and a fairly large facility.

Yorkville Synagogue *Orthodox* 352 East 78th Street 10021 249-0766

Nestled between other East Side brownstones, the Yorkville Synagogue fits right into the neighborhood, at least architecturally. This congregation serves a traditional community, though its brand of Orthodoxy is fairly modern and intellectual (its rabbi is a professor at Yeshiva University's Law School). There is a daily morning and evening *minyan* here, as well as worship services on Shabbat.

UPPER WEST SIDE

When the dust from the revolution settled, the Upper West Side was transformed into a Disneyland of gourmet restaurants and designer boutiques. Years ago this neighborhood was a traditional family one, and the area was crowded with small synagogues. Most of them are still here—some flourishing, others functioning as *shteeblach*. In addition, the influx of young business people has brought new life to some synagogues in this area, and several new ones to life, and many have now begun programs to attract the young, the singles and two-career families with young children. The problem here isn't finding a synagogue; it's which one to choose.

Commandment Keepers Ethiopian Hebrew Congregation
Unaffiliated 1 West 123rd Street 10027

This unique congregation is the only Black *shul* in Manhattan, its members tracing their origins back to Ethiopia and Solomon and Sheba. There are regular Shabbat morning services here, with an interesting blend of Orthodox and southern Black davening.

Congregation Ansche Chesed *Conservative*
251 West 100th Street 10025 865-0600

The smorgasbord that is the Upper West Side has no better example than Ansche Chesed. One of the most talked-about synagogues in Manhattan, Ansche Chesed ushered in the renewal of active synagogue life on the Upper West Side by offering the "me generation" and nonestablishment sixties types a synagogue with more choices than they had ever dreamed about. Worship services are held here each morning and evening, and on Shabbat there are at least four different *minyanim,* each with its own style (we should add that women participate equally in all of them), as well as an adult beginner's service and a children's service. Even during the High Holidays, Ansche Chesed offers several choices of services ranging from what they call "classical sanctuary service" to informal *havurah*-style services.

Ansche Chesed has *havurot* (fellowship groups) as well, and a Learning Network offering semester courses on a wide range of Jewish topics (including one called "All-purpose Jewish Singing"). There are always workshops, with speakers invited from all over the city, and there is also a monthly "intergenerational" brunch-discussion group. The synagogue's Havurah Schools meet weekly to offer an after-school Jewish educational program for students ages five to thirteen, and Yaldenu, a professional Jewish day care center for children eighteen to thirty months old, offers full-time and part-time care. Project Dorot, a social action project to aid elderly Jews in the neighborhood, has its center at Ansche Chesed. If you love the Upper West Side and lots of activity, this is the place!

Congregation Bina *Unaffiliated*
600 West End Avenue 10024 873-4261

A unique group in Manhattan, Congregation Bina serves the religious, cultural and charitable needs of the Jews of India who are residing in the United States. The congregation also works toward fostering and preserving the ancient traditions, customs, music and folklore of the Jews of India. Worship services are held on the High Holidays, and holiday celebrations take place throughout the year at members' homes. Plans are underway to build a synagogue.

Congregation B'nai Jeshurun *Conservative*
257 West 88th Street 10024 787-7600

B'nai Jeshurun, the oldest Ashkenazic synagogue in New York City (founded in 1825), was once a mainstay of the Jewish Upper West Side scene, but in recent years suffered a major decline. It is now reorganizing and experiencing a renewal as part of the overall growth in the area's active Jewish community. It plans to continue its strong connection with the Conservative movement, and because of its need to attract dynamic membership from the Upper West Side community, its services, which are held each Friday evening and Saturday morning, are egalitarian, as will be its new organizational policies. There are plans for a school, adult education, home study groups, youth groups and senior citizen groups. Included in its plans are cooperative activities with other groups at the Lindenbaum Jewish Center around the corner.

Congregation Habonim *Reform*
44 West 66th Street 10023 787-5347

Located in the Lincoln Center area, Habonim was the bastion of fairly tradition-minded German Jews who were late arrivals to this country. It began after the classical Reform movement was established, and was founded more on the model of a liberal Conservative synagogue. Habonim, which holds services Friday evenings and Saturday mornings (four times a year there is a special Friday evening family service), has a large older population and is a comfortable place for Reform Jews seeking a more traditional atmosphere. The sanctuary has stained-glass windows representing the various stages in life, as well as biblical symbols. There are a men's club, sisterhood, seniors group, and a combined singles–young marrieds group, all open to nonmembers. There is an after-school religious program beginning with second grade and continuing up through confirmation. The synagogue also has a gift shop.

Congregation Kehilath Jacob *Orthodox*
305 West 79th Street 10024 580-2391

This is considered one of the city's "best bets" for a truly *freylach* Simchat Torah. Congregation Kehilath Jacob was the synagogue of Rabbi Carlebach, and his noted son Shlomo—as the awning out front declares—has now held the pulpit for many years.

Congregation Ohab Zedek *Orthodox*
118 West 95th Street 10025 749-5150

Originally located in Harlem, when there was a substantial Jewish population there and the famous Yossele Rosenblatt served as cantor, in 1926 Ohab Zedek moved downtown with its congregants. There is still a daily morning and evening *minyan* as well as one on Friday evening, Saturday morning and evening, in one of the Upper West Side's loveliest sanctuaries. There is an after-school religious school, a post–Bar Mitzvah program, and adult education classes which are taught by the rabbi. There are both men's and women's clubs and a preteen youth group that meets Saturdays and during holidays. The synagogue supports a *chevra kaddisha* (burial group) as well. A West Side singles group also meets at the synagogue.

Congregation Ramath Orah   *Orthodox*
550 West 110th Street 10025   222-2470

This synagogue has a daily *minyan* morning and afternoon, as well as Shabbat services. There is no school connected with the synagogue, but there is an active sisterhood that also plans some social service programs.

Congregation Rodeph Sholom   *Reform*
7 West 83rd Street 10024   362-8800

Rodeph Sholom is considered the most "classical" of the West Side Reform synagogues, and its day school was the first Reform day school in the United States. It has one of the most highly regarded nursery schools in Manhattan, which attracts new members to its congregation, since the school programs are open to members only. Services are held Friday evenings and Saturday mornings, and twice a month there are Friday family services. Rodeph Sholom has no real adult education courses, but it does have speakers once a month, and in most years it runs an adult Bar and Bat Mitzvah program beginning in the fall and culminating in a group B'nai Mitzvah after six or seven months of study. The synagogue's men's club, sisterhood, singles, young marrieds, senior citizens and youth groups are all open to nonmembers. Strongly committed to the neighborhood, the synagogue participates in programs to house homeless people, collect food for the needy, and service the elderly (through Project Dorot). It also maintains an interfaith program with churches in Harlem. In addition to its day school, Rodeph Sholom runs after-school religious school beginning at age eight and continuing through B'nai Mitzvah and confirmation. The synagogue has a gift shop as well as a museum.

Congregation Shaare Zedek   *Conservative*
212 West 93rd Street 10025   874-7005

This congregation is suffering from a lack of membership, although they have a heavy endowment and are hoping that a new rabbi will bring about a revival. They have no school and few programs or services other than a men's club and sisterhood, although their enormous and quite beautiful sanctuary (it holds 1000) does have daily services and services on Saturday morning. The building is over 100 years old.

Congregation Shearith Israel   *Orthodox*   8 West 70th Street 10023   873-0300

Shearith Israel (also known as the Spanish and Portuguese Synagogue), the oldest congregation in the United States, is the center of New York's Sephardic community. Many of its customs show strong influences of the British Sephardic tradition as well, and its sanctuary (with some of the original Colonial fixtures moved from downtown) and services are extremely formal. All its music is different from that of other synagogues, and this is the best (and only) place in Manhattan to learn first-hand about the Sephardic tradition. There are services every day at Shearith Israel and once a month a youth service. This synagogue is *the* place to be on Tisha B'av, when the entire sanctuary is draped in black cloth and lit only by candles. Shearith Israel has a religious school and post–B'nai Mitzvah programs through high school, including a youth group. The rabbis here are very scholarly and there are good adult education courses focusing on the differences between Sephardic and Ashkenazic culture. In addition, the synagogue has a men's club, sisterhood, young marrieds–professionals group, and a weekly senior citizen's group. There is some cooperation with the 92nd Street Y, which runs a program for toddlers that meets at the synagogue as well as some social service programs.

The Jewish Center   *Orthodox*
131 West 86th Street 10024   724-2700

The Jewish Center, which is a synagogue and not a Jewish center, is slightly more staid than Lincoln Square, but it is a powerful Orthodox presence on the Upper West Side, with a substantial number of younger Jews as members. The Jewish Center was actually founded by Mordecai Kaplan, the founder of the Reconstructionist movement; he later left because of his heterodox views and founded the first Reconstructionist synagogue a block away. There are services at the Jewish Center each evening during the week, as well as Saturday morning and evening, and a junior congregation meets each Saturday morning. Groups include a sisterhood, young marrieds, singles, and youth groups for all ages, who no doubt jam the synagogue's rather substantial recreational facilities that include a gym and pool.

Lincoln Square Synagogue   *Orthodox*
200 Amsterdam Avenue 10023   874-6105

This is considered the hippest Orthodox synagogue on the Upper West Side (if not all of Manhattan), and many of its members are young professionals whose quest for the yuppie ideal has not at all diminished their commitment to Orthodox Judaism (or their interest in meeting like-minded singles, which is why the synagogue also functions as a social center for this part of the membership). Lincoln Square has one of the strongest education programs in the city—they claim that "we're Orthodox, but there's nothing orthodox about the way we teach our heritage"—and the varieties of programs certainly seem to bear this out. There is a nursery school with full and half-day programs, a large Hebrew school with Bar and Bat Mitzvah program, as well as a Hebrew High School. The adult education program at Lincoln Square, the Joseph Shapiro Institute, has language, literature and history courses at all levels as well as courses in Jewish law and thought (see section on Adult Education); there is also its intensive summer Torah institute, again geared to different levels of educational experience. In keeping with its reputation for superb outreach programming, Lincoln Square is famous for its learner's *minyan* on Saturday mornings. There is also a youth *minyan* on Saturday morning, along with the synagogue's normal daily worship service schedule. Lincoln Square does not have traditional men's club or sisterhood, but there are a singles group, youth groups, and a senior citizen's group. They are hoping to increase their programming for seniors by opening a weekday Senior Center that will not only provide recreation and entertainment but also kosher lunches.

Old Broadway Synagogue

Orthodox   15 Old Broadway 10027

If you think that Old Broadway is near Wall Street, you're wrong. It is on the edge of Harlem, which had a flourishing Jewish population in the early years of this century. This synagogue, having suffered from the mass exodus downtown, has been revitalized, and it is a warm and spirited congregation where some of the students from Jewish Theological Seminary hang out. Given its population, the synagogue has a pretty observant character, but its proximity to the exciting intellectual center of JTS, Columbia and Barnard, makes its membership pretty unusual.

Society for the Advancement of Judaism

Reconstructionist   15 West 86th Street 10024   724-7000

The SAJ, as it is known to Upper West Siders, was the first Reconstructionist synagogue in the United States, founded by Mordecai Kaplan in 1922. The first synagogue to promote the equality of women in education as well as ritual, it also served as the forum for Kaplan's new ideas about American Judaism. It maintains an extensive library, and has both an after-school religious school and post–B'nai Mitzvah program, as well as adult education programs and lecture series covering subjects in Hebrew and Yiddish culture as well as Reconstructionism. The SAJ has a sisterhood and a youth group affiliated with Young

Judea. It holds its services on Saturday morning.

Stephen Wise Free Synagogue   *Reform*
30 West 68th Street 10023   877-4050

No, the membership here is not free, but the spirit is. Stephen Wise was founded in 1907 to provide a forum for social justice issues, and the "free" in this case referred to the rabbi's right to say from the pulpit what conscience dictated, something that wasn't often the case in those days. Stephen Wise Synagogue still has a commitment to that tradition, and it is carried out in many of its social service programs: the synagogue has its own part-time social worker who helps in individual counseling and referral, and such programs as senior citizen's support groups, shelter for the homeless and the synagogue's day care center (one-and-a-half to four). They are also hoping to establish a parenting center. These services, as well as a men's club, sisterhood, young marrieds group, seniors group, *havurot* (fellowship), and several youth groups ranging from elementary school to high school, are all open to nonmembers. Stephen Wise also has a full religious school program and worship services here are held Friday evening and Saturday morning; on the first Friday of every month there is a family service. On Sunday mornings there are mini-courses for adults, on topics such as the book of Joshua, or Mideast prospects for peace, and sometimes there are guest lecturers. Very popular is the synagogue's B'nai Mitzvah program for adults, encompassing the study of language, culture, lifestyle and aspects of the Jewish life cycle—open even to those who don't want to participate in the group B'nai Mitzvah at the end. The Stephen Wise gift shop is open Friday after services and on Sunday mornings.

Synagogue of the Jewish Theological Seminary
Conservative   3080 Broadway 10027   678-8000

The Seminary Synagogue has two concurrent worship services daily (as well as on Shabbat and holidays), which draw the faculty and students of the Seminary as well as Jewish residents of Morningside Heights. The chapel *minyan* has separate seating for men and women, and does not allow women to participate equally in the service. Upstairs, a newer *minyan* has been formed, with mixed seating and a completely egalitarian style. The Seminary uses the synagogue from time to time for lectures and other programs as well.

West End Synagogue   *Reconstructionist*
270 West 89th Street 10024   769-3100

This new synagogue opened in the Lindenbaum Center on the Upper West Side just a year ago, and already it's a flourishing community busy developing many new programs as its membership grows. Services are held every Saturday morning, and on the first and third Friday night each month. In addition they hold monthly Shabbat dinners on Fridays at 6:00 P.M. on a pay-as-you-go basis. They also occasionally have bag lunches following Saturday morning services. An enrichment program for ages five to eight runs during Shabbat morning services, with singing, dancing and dramatic techniques; there is separate child care for those not participating. The synagogue has a religious school that meets in students' homes (ages eight to eleven) and an afternoon pre-Hebrew program for children five to six.

West Side Institutional Synagogue *Orthodox*
120–138 West 76th Street 10023 877-7652

Founded in Harlem in 1917 and then established on the West Side in 1937, the West Side Institutional Synagogue was one of the centers of the Labor movement, but the synagogue today retains none of that character. It holds daily and Shabbat services, and offers a variety of programs including a men's club, sisterhood, singles, young marrieds and seniors groups.

Yeshiva Chofetz Chaim *Orthodox*
310 West 103rd Street 10025

Chofetz Chaim is not far from Columbia University. Its membership is small and it is eager to attract new, young members, since the facility itself is quite spacious. There is no programming here, but there are services on Shabbat.

Young Israel of the West Side *Orthodox*
210 West 91st Street 10024 787-7513

The uptown Young Israel synagogue is housed in what used to be the Reform Temple Israel of the City of New York, now on the Upper East Side. A true Young Israel *shul*, it is characterized by daily and Shabbat services with lots of participation and spirit. The sanctuary is huge, with a multi-story dome. Next door is the Schreiber Community Center, where cultural, educational and social events are held. The synagogue also has a gym, used by the 92nd Street Y West Side branch.

SHTEEBLACH

Ahavath Chesed
303 West 89th Street 724-8065

American Congregation of Jews from Austria
118 West 95th Street 663-1920

Beth Israel Center
646 West End Avenue 874-6135

B'nai Israel Chaim
353 West 84th Street 874-0644

B'nai Yitzhuk
441 West End Avenue

Chasidei Ger
  215 West 90th Street (1D)   799-0075

Congregation Morya
  2228 Broadway   724-6909

Hechal Moshe
  303 West 91st Street   362-1091

Ohav Sholom
  270 West 84th Street   877-5850

Torath Chaim
  489 West End Avenue   874-3823

WASHINGTON HEIGHTS AND INWOOD

Many people have forgotten about this enclave in upper Manhattan separated from the Upper West Side by Harlem. It once was a flourishing Jewish community, its avenues lined with comfortable apartment houses and a large number of synagogues. Its apartment houses are still well kept, the apartments spacious, the parks still beautiful, but many of the Jews have left, and what remains for the most part is a large population of elderly Jews whose roots are still strongly tied to the German Orthodox synagogues that dominate the area. This is not as open or fluid a community as in other parts of Manhattan, but its attractiveness (Ft. Tryon Park is a popular place to stroll on Shabbat), as well as the quality and value of the housing, has led more and more young professionals to settle here. They remain unaffiliated, however, because the very traditional Jewish synagogues with their elderly leadership have been unable to offer services that appeal to a younger population. Washington Heights is also where a number of Russian immigrants have settled, and some of the synagogues are attempting to reach them (although again, it is hard for these *shuls* to cope with immigrants who may not have a strong religious background). The Washington Heights YM–YWHA does commendable outreach to this group, and we have listed their programs in our sections on learning and culture. As we drove around the area with one of its residents, he pointed out not only the famous Orthodox *shuls*, but also the many unmarked doorways that house other Orthodox communities—too small to warrant a large building, and perhaps too private to want one. Those who know where to find a *minyan* here don't need any signs. The synagogues we list are those with enough programs to be able to answer our questions.

Beth Am–The People's Temple *Reform*
178 Bennett Avenue 10040   923-5979/942-0869

This small congregation meets in the Cornerstone Center, which houses a Lutheran church and a Seventh Day Adventist church as well, something considered quite radical for the neighborhood. There is a sisterhood, and its seniors participate in citywide groups run by the Reform movement. There are only Friday evening services at Beth Am, but they have a regular adult education program. There are also once a month *havurah*-style Shabbat morning services at people's homes.

Congregation Beth Hillel of Washington Heights *Orthodox*
571 West 182nd Street 10033   568-3933

This is a large synagogue with two daily services, as well as a complete schedule of Shabbat services. Although it has a large congregation and building, because it is an older congregation there are no school programs, youth groups or young singles groups. The synagogue has a sisterhood and a "couples club" for all ages. There is some adult education programming but no other activities.

Congregation K'hal Adath Jeshurun *Orthodox*
85 Bennett Ave. 10033   923-3582

This is the power synagogue of Washington Heights, the crown of the German Breuer movement, and it dominates the neighborhood, including the butchers, groceries and commercial establishments. It occupies several large buildings which include its day school, the Yeshiva Rabbi Raphael Hirsch, which includes a post–high school program, and it runs a weekday nursery school that is part of Yeshiva. There are daily (two in the evening) and Shabbat services, and a number of other programs including a sisterhood and organized events for young marrieds. There are separate youth groups for boys and girls, and an adult education program for men only. The congregation does some outreach to the Russian immigrants in the neighborhood, with hopes of drawing them into the Orthodox community.

Congregation Nodah bi Yehuda *Orthodox*
392 Ft. Washington Avenue 10033   795-1552

This may be the only active synagogue left with a building south of the George Washington Bridge where the neighborhood quickly dissolves into Harlem, but even so, it lists a congregation of only forty, and the doors are shut when there is no *minyan*. There are services weekday mornings and Shabbat, but very little else going on outside of monthly luncheons and sisterhood, although the synagogue has some adult education and claims to have a small religious school operating two days a week.

Congregation Ohav Sholaum *Orthodox*
4624 Broadway 10040 567-0900

In an austere building next door to an excavated site that used to be the Jewish Memorial Hospital, Ohav Sholaum is considered to be the third-largest congregation in the area. Although not adhering to the Breuer movement, the synagogue is definitely German-Jewish and very Orthodox. This is an older congregation (in fact, on our questionnaire they wrote "no school, no children") and offers services for that membership, including an active men's club, sisterhood, and Golden Age Club. There are occasional Sunday morning breakfast-study sessions throughout the year, but no regular education programs. Since they feel that there are very few singles or young marrieds in the neighborhood, they offer no programs for these groups.

Congregation Shaare Hatikvah Ahavath Torah v'Tikvoh Chadoshoh *Orthodox*
711 West 179th Street 10033 927-2720

Another of Washington Height's heavily German-Jewish congregations, this one has a modern building facing the approach to the bridge. Just past its fiftieth birthday, this congregation has a fairly large membership and holds daily services as well as Shabbat services. Again, since its membership is in the over–fifty-five range, the services are geared to them. There is a men's club, sisterhood, and adult education programming, and JASA (Jewish Association for the Aged) has an office in the building. There are no programs for children or young people.

Ft. Tryon Jewish Center *Conservative*
524 Ft. Washington Avenue 10033 795-1391

Ft. Tryon Jewish Center is a close-knit synagogue with no Hebrew or religious school. It has a daily morning *minyan* and Shabbat services, but no full-time rabbi and very few programs besides a sisterhood and senior citizens group.

Hebrew Tabernacle Congregation *Unaffiliated*
551 Ft. Washington Avenue 10033 568-8304

Hebrew Tabernacle is one of Washington Heights' major synagogues, and houses the largest German-Jewish group outside the Orthodox movement. It is a progressive synagogue, with services Friday evening and Saturday morning that combine liberal Reform elements with the use of a

Conservative prayerbook. Although the majority of its members is over fifty-five, Hebrew Tabernacle is the only synagogue in the area that has a substantial afternoon religious school two afternoons a week, and children from outside the congregation attend school here (in fact the Y provides bus service to make sure the children get home safely after dark, which the Y hopes will keep the school active). The synagogue is a beautiful building with a dome and an art deco interior, and in addition to a large sanctuary and chapel, there are a library, gift shop and a gallery that has revolving art exhibits by known Jewish artists. There is an active men's club and sisterhood, a young married group, and the sisterhood runs luncheon and card playing for seniors on Wednesdays. There is also a high school youth group. There is a regular adult ed program and the synagogue is active in fund-raising to provide food and shelter for seniors.

Inwood Hebrew Congregation *Conservative*
111 Vermilyea Avenue 10034   569-4010

This is another older congregation in a lovely Federal-style red brick building in a neighborhood without Jewish character. There is a daily morning and evening *minyan,* as well as Shabbat morning worship services, but few other activities. There has been no Hebrew school for the past eight years, and most of the social activities revolve around the sisterhood and its programs.

Inwood Jewish Center *Orthodox*
12 Elwood Street 10040   569-4311

This small congregation has been held together in recent years by its elderly president, who we were told runs almost everything by himself. There are services most mornings, when they can get a *minyan,* and there are services every Shabbat. The rabbi serves the community part-time, and services during the High Holidays are more crowded because many of the area's Russian immigrants are invited to attend. There are no clubs or programs and there is no school.

Mt. Sinai Jewish Center *Orthodox*
135 Bennett Avenue 10040   928-9870

We were told that this is probably the most progressive Orthodox synagogue in the neighborhood, and because of that it draws a younger crowd, including students from Yeshiva. Its modern building still has seating that separates men from women, but it has a younger rabbi than most synagogues in Washington Heights and it sees itself as a growing, dynamic *shul.* Mt. Sinai has active singles and young married groups in addition to a sisterhood and adult education programs during the week. There is also a youth group affiliated with N.C.S.Y. There is a daily morning *minyan* and Shabbat services every weekend. In addition to a library and gift shop open during the day, the synagogue has a gym that is open evenings.

Washington Heights Congregation   *Orthodox*
815 West 179th Street 10033   923-4407

The rabbi here teaches at Yeshiva University, and this synagogue is considered more liberal than some others in the neighborhood, though not as progressive as Mt. Sinai. The building sits on a corner, and its white brick exterior looks like a model of a medieval castle, complete with crenelations. There are daily and Shabbat services. In spite of its rabbi's affiliation, this is still an older congregation and there are no groups here for young people, singles, or young marrieds. There is a sisterhood and a men's *Kiddush* club. There are separate men's and women's adult education programs.

SHTEEBLACH

Congregation Beth Hamedrash of Inwood
1781 Riverside Drive 10034

Congregation Machzikei Torah
851 West 181st Street 10033   927-6740

Congregation Shmuel Josef Vchayah
587B Ft. Washington Avenue 10033   927-9012

HAVUROT AND MINYANIM

The term *havurot* is used these days to refer to what are usually small Jewish groups that come together for worship or study or celebration or mutual need. Derived from the Hebrew word meaning friend *(haver)*, *havurot* are often as different from one another as they are from the rest of synagogue life, making generalizations about them difficult. But we'll try anyway, because these groups have provided a much-needed place for many Jews searching for community, which is perhaps the unifying point about *havurot*. Most of these groups were born after the turmoil of the sixties, and were given life by Jews who felt a yearning to experience Judaism but felt excluded or alienated from regular synagogues. Reflecting a strong commitment to participatory Judaism, and revolting against the predominant role of the American clergy, most of these groups do not have rabbinic leadership, though rabbis are often members of them.

In a reaction against what has been called the "edifice complex" of American Jewish life, *havurot* by definition do not own buildings, choosing instead to borrow space from existing facilities or meet in members' homes. Although many *havurot* are called independent—unrelated to institutions or denominations—more and more we find these groups as subsets of existing synagogues, created to make possible a sense of intimacy within the larger congregations. As we've said, the activities of individual *havurot* vary from group to group—some function essentially as prayer communities, while others spend time studying, eating or celebrating holidays together. *Havurot* are constantly changing in every way—who comes, what happens, where it happens and why it happens, so while we've listed the ones we know about, both those within synagogues and those that are independent, there will certainly be more around by the time you read this, and some of these we mention may look very different.

The best resource for information about the *havurah* movement in general, and Manhattan *havurot* specifically, is the National Havurah Committee, 270 West 89th Street, 10024 (496-0055). This group is best known for its summer institutes, held in various locations across the country, where individuals of all ages come together for the intensive study of Jewish texts and subjects. While there, they also pray, eat and socialize in a kind of adult summer camp atmosphere. When the NHC is not planning institutes, they're busy helping *havurot* to form, publishing a journal and newsletter, and connecting people with groups. Another umbrella organization, specifically for Orthodox women's davening groups, is the Women's Tefilla Network (928-2001), which provides information about the location of groups and how to form one. The issue of women's davening groups is a hot one in Orthodox circles these days, and this network provides support for new groups and helps them deal with the challenges they confront.

Ansche Chesed, 251 West 100th Street, 10025 (865-0600) is one location that has either provided space or given birth to several Manhattan *havurot*. This synagogue had been declining before many of New York's Upper West Side Jews became active and helped to revive it as a model of religious pluralism. All of the *havurot* and *minyanim* that live at Ansche Chesed function both as separate groups for regular worship or study, and as part of the larger community for other activities.

Minyan M'at: This group meets on Shabbat mornings and holidays at ten o'clock on the second floor of the building. All members of the group are urged to participate in leading the liturgical and study aspects of the service, which is egalitarian. Worship itself is fairly traditional, though individual members have diverse views concerning prayer and study. *Minyan M'at* also holds discussions throughout the year on topics of Jewish interest.

The West Side Minyan: One of the first *havurot* in Manhattan, the West Side *minyan* is a davening group. Each Shabbat and holiday they come together for egalitarian worship led by members of the group. People in this *minyan* come from diverse backgrounds, with less experienced members participating in informal classes to improve their skills.

The Chapel Minyan: The oldest of the Ansche Chesed groups, this *minyan* developed out of original Ansche Chesed members, as well as others in the neighborhood, so the age range here is broader than in some of the other *minyanim.* This group meets in the synagogue chapel, a medium-sized room on the main floor. Lay people conduct all worship, and newcomers are enthusiastically welcome.

Minyan Hamakif: On the lower level at Ansche Chesed you'll find another egalitarian *minyan,* which follows a traditional format. There's a full Torah reading, haftarah, and Musaf service here, as well as a d'var Torah, all handled by members of the group. Once a month people get together for Shabbat dinners, and there are periodic Saturday late-afternoon meals together as well. *Minyan Hamakif* holds monthly Friday night services at the Jewish Home and Hospital for the Aged.

Other *havurot* and *minyanim* throughout Manhattan include:

CONNECT at the 92nd Street Y: CONNECT is the outreach program at this Y, attempting to provide unaffiliated Manhattan Jews a family education program, which also happens to include singles and older adults. The goal here is to help those who come (forty or so adults and about as many children), learn and experience the Jewish heritage. In addition to other programs described throughout the book, CONNECT holds a weekly

Shabbat dinner program on the first Friday evening of each month. There is candle lighting, blessings over challah and wine, and an introduction to Shabbat traditions. Dinner is followed by short discussions or programs. For more information, or to reserve a space, call the Y at 427-6000, ext. 162, or stop by at 1395 Lexington Avenue.

Educational Alliance West: This West Village branch of the Educational Alliance has what they call an "Intergenerational Havurah," which meets once a month, usually on the first Friday of the month. There's a potluck dinner, candle lighting, lots of singing, but no formal service. It is open to anyone in the community (the age range here is from babies through grandparents), but it's a good idea to call first and let them know you're coming. There is also a study *havurah* that meets every other Sunday. For more information, call 420-1150, or stop by 51 East 10th Street, where they meet.

Greenwich Village Havurah: This group meets once a month in people's homes for Shabbat morning services, discussion and lunch. Members, about half of whom are connected with New York University, take turns handling the liturgy and the d'var Torah. They describe themselves as Conservative-Reconstructionist, using the Conservative prayerbook and a Reconstructionist approach, including discussion and lots of participation. Once a year the group goes away for the weekend, to study, celebrate Shabbat and socialize. For more information, call 475-7831.

The New York Havurah: Once extremely active on the Upper West Side, this group meets now mostly for High Holidays, when they hold a public service at Ansche Chesed. Otherwise, they get together for life-cycle events of members, festivals and other Jewish holidays. The group identifies itself ideologically as Conservative-Reconstructionist.

Washington Heights Havurah: This area of town has had some trouble creating informal prayer and study groups, for reasons not entirely clear to us, because there certainly is an increasing number of young Jews from the Upper West Side moving uptown in search of more space and less rent. In spite of the predominantly Orthodox character of the neighborhood, this group—made up of a mix of "modern" Orthodox, Conservative and Reform Jews—operates as a "traditional egalitarian" *havurah* where women participate actively. The group meets once a month in members' homes on Shabbat afternoon, beginning with a potluck parve or dairy lunch, followed by prayer and then a d'var Torah or discussion. The group sees itself as a social as well as prayer fellowship; the discussion may sometimes focus on Torah or at other times on current family issues, such as single parenting. For more information or to be put on their mailing list, call 942-8808.

Women's Davening Group of Washington Heights: This group, some of whose members also belong to the Washington Heights Havurah, functions as an Orthodox women's *minyan*. It meets once a month (usually the Shabbat right before Rosh Hodesh) in members' homes, and they also have some special holiday celebrations. There are about fifteen or twenty women who participate, and they welcome newcomers. For more information, call 928-4177 or 795-8867.

Women's Minyan at Lincoln Square: Formed by Orthodox women at this Orthodox *shul,* with the rabbi's endorsement, this group meets some Shabbat mornings across the street at the Esplanade Hotel. For more information, call 874-6105.

The following synagogues told us that they have *havurot* within their congregations:

> **Congregation Kehilath Jeshurun**
> 125 East 85th Street   427-1000
>
> **Congregation Ohav Sholaum**
> 4624 Broadway   567-0900
>
> **Conservative Synagogue of Fifth Avenue**
> 11 East 11th Street   929-6954
>
> **Hebrew Tabernacle Congregation**
> 551 Ft. Washington Avenue 10033   568-8304
>
> **Sutton Place Synagogue**
> 225 East 51st Street   593-3300
>
> **Young Israel of Manhattan**
> 225–229 East Broadway   732-0966

FRATERNAL AND WOMEN'S ORGANIZATIONS

Many, if not most, of the groups listed in this section are involved in cultural, social service, religious or educational activities on a local and national level. Some, because of their particular programming, are mentioned elsewhere in the book. One important function of each of these organizations, however, is fellowship or sisterhood. People come together through these groups as Jewish men, Jewish women, Jews from particular countries or with particular interests, to shmooz, take trips together, enjoy a program, help each other out and receive personal benefits from being part of a group. Please note that what we've called Fraternal Organizations, listed first, are not necessarily or even mainly men's groups. Women's Organizations, however, generally direct their programming to women.

FRATERNAL ORGANIZATIONS

Association of Yugoslav Jews in the U.S.A., Inc.
247 West 99th Street 10025 865-2211

This is a group of 378,000 Jews from Yugoslavia, who participate in fraternal, Israel-oriented and social service activities.

American Veterans of Israel
15 East 26th Street 10010 532-4949

This group of 500 members was founded in 1949 by those who fought in the War of Independence and later came to the United States and Canada.

B'nai B'rith District No. 1
823 United Nations Plaza 10017 490-2525

B'nai B'rith lodges throughout the city and the nation hold regular meetings to provide local community services and to discuss issues of Jewish concern. Through Project Hope, lodges undertake large-scale food distribution to the needy before the holidays.

B'nai Zion 136 East 39th Street 10016 725-1211

The oldest Zionist fraternal organization in the United States, B'nai Zion and its affiliate Brith Abraham provide benefits to its members, and cultural programs through its local chapters. It also raises money for Israel and runs outreach programs here.

Charitable Fund American Far Eastern Society, Inc.
250 West 57th Street 10019 586-7934

Former Far Eastern Jewish residents participate in this organization, which provides social programming and financial aid to its 240 members.

Federation of Jewish Men's Clubs
475 Riverside Drive 10027 749-8100

This Conservative organization has 300 local men's groups throughout the United States. Activities include a Hebrew literacy campaign, Laymen's Institute for adult study, and other programs to enrich Jewish life on the synagogue level.

Free Sons of Israel 932 Broadway 10010 260-4222

With about fifty local groups throughout the country, this organization participates in social service projects, raises money for Jewish causes, and provides benefits for its members.

Jewish Cultural Clubs 1133 Broadway 10010 675-8854

Comprised mainly of retired older adults, this Yiddish and English-speaking group offers social, cultural and social action programs for its members, and raises money for Jewish education. It also provides some benefits for members.

Jewish War Veterans of the U.S.A.
51 Chambers Street 10007 349-6640

Founded in 1896 by a group of Jewish Civil War veterans (it was then called the Hebrew Union Veterans), to combat insinuations that Jews had not participated in that war, this national organization still works to publicize the fact that throughout this nation's history—beginning with colonial times in New Amsterdam—Jews have served in the armed forces in numbers beyond their proportion to the general population. JWV is committed to fighting bigotry of all kinds, and to assisting oppressed Jews worldwide. Another of its concerns is the security of the state of Israel. In addition to providing hospital, rehabilitation and veterans' service programs for its membership, which it does through its local posts, JWV also supports and raises money for the Israeli Military Rest and Rehabilitation Home in Beersheba, Israel.

National Federation of Temple Brotherhoods
838 Fifth Avenue 10021 570-0707

Almost every Reform synagogue has a men's group, which meets on a weekly or monthly basis for programs of a cultural, social or religious nature. The National Federation of Temple Brotherhoods is the umbrella organization for some 500 local groups, and helps them with programming. It also sponsors the Jewish Chautauqua Society, which endows courses of Jewish studies at universities.

New World Club   2121 Broadway 10023   873-7400

This is a group of 2000 German-speaking Jews who participate in cultural and social activities. The club publishes the German-language Jewish newspaper *Afbau*.

The Workmen's Circle
45 East 33rd Street 10016   889-6800

Among the many activities of this Yiddish organization are fraternal and cultural activities. Founded as *Der Arbiter Ring* in 1900 as a Socialist, secularist organization, the Workmen's Circle supports Yiddish schools and theater, and labor and citizen's groups. It provides travel services, camps, services for the aged, Jewish schools and benefits for its members.

WOMEN'S ORGANIZATIONS

Amit Women   817 Broadway 10003   477-4720

This Orthodox Zionist women's organization (known formerly as American Mizrachi Women) has 425 chapters across the country. Women partcipate in educational and cultural programs, and help support Amit's twenty major educational facilities in Israel.

B'nai B'rith Women, Empire Region
823 United Nations Plaza   599-2123

The women's division of B'nai B'rith meets in regular chapters for education, social service, cultural, and social activities in support of B'nai B'rith.

Emunah Women of America
370 Seventh Avenue 10001 564-9045

An extremely religious Zionist women's organization, Emunah has eighty local groups that participate in various programs and raise money for many Israeli institutions.

Hadassah, The Women's Zionist Organization of America
50 West 58th Street 10019   355-7900

With 1700 groups across the country, Hadassah is one of the largest Jewish women's organizations in the world. Its many programs for youth are described in our chapter on "Children." Its groups engage in cultural, social, educational and Zionist activities, as well as fund-raising for Hadassah's programs in Israel, which include the Hadassah Hebrew University Medical Center, Hadassah Israel Education Service and Youth Aliya (services for resettlement of refugees to Israel from places like the Soviet Union and Middle Eastern Countries).

Na'amat USA 200 Madison Avenue 725-8010

Formerly known as Pioneer Women, this group with 500 chapters is part of the World Labor Zionist Movement. In addition to Jewish and Zionist programs, chapters help to support Na'amat in Israel, which maintains several educational and social service facilities.

National Council of Jewish Women, Inc.
15 East 26th Street 10010   532-1740

The National Council has 200 sections in 39 states, with local groups within each section. Over 100,000 women participate in its programs, which include volunteer work for social service agencies, cultural and Jewish activities, political action for women's rights, aid to other women, children and the aged, and programs in Israel. The New York Chapter sponsors the Jewish Women's Resource Center, founded in 1977 to help deal with Jewish issues raised by the women's movement. (Its programs are described throughout this book.)

National Federation of Temple Sisterhoods
838 Fifth Avenue 10021   249-0100

With close to 700 local synagogue chapters, this Reform women's organization provides educational, cultural and religious programming help to its affiliates. They also are involved in youth activities, scholarship aid, service to the elderly and countless other activities on behalf of the Reform movement.

Women's League for Conservative Judaism
48 East 74th Street 10021   628-1600

This is the Conservative movement's women's division, which sponsors 800 local Conservative synagogue sisterhoods. In addition to religious, cultural, educational and social programming, the local clubs raise money for Conservative institutions in the United States and Israel.

Women's League for Israel, Inc.
515 Park Avenue 10022   838-1997

This group is a member of the American Zionist Federation, and has about 5000 members in 39 local chapters across the country. The groups participate in programs, and raise money for a wide range of Israeli institutions.

Women's American ORT
315 Park Avenue South 10010   505-7700

As the women's branch of ORT (Organization for Rehabilitation through Training), this group—with 145,000 women in chapters throughout the United States—participates in programs and raises money for ORT's many vocational training programs.

Chapter 9
HOW WE OBSERVE: RESOURCES FOR JEWISH HOLIDAY CELEBRATION

"The Jewish people," writes Michael Strassfeld in *The Jewish Holidays: A Guide and Commentary,* "has developed a map for traveling in time . . . called the festival cycle." Jewish holidays like Rosh Hashana, Hanukkah, Passover and others serve as markers for us, times to connect to the tradition as well as one another and our families. In New York, where community is so illusive and people often live without extended families, the holidays can be particularly challenging times, but you'd be surprised what's out there and available for you.

In this chapter we give you some of the resources in New York that can help make your holiday celebrations more meaningful and accessible. In addition to holiday worship services and celebrations, many synagogues in Manhattan also have pre-holiday study groups and workshops, and most welcome participation by nonmembers. Community centers and Ys also have activities around holidays, especially Hanukkah, Purim and Passover, so you should check their calendars for these events. Since many of these programs change from year to year, your best bet is to consult *The Jewish Week* or other local Jewish publications a few weeks before a specific holiday; they are likely to list current programs.

Rosh Hashana and Yom Kippur

The High Holidays are regarded by most Jews as the most important set of holidays on the Jewish calendar. Even very assimilated Jews often seek some kind of Jewish contact during this ten day period, only to find their neighborhood synagogues unable to accommodate them. Synagogues vary in their policies; some have seats only for members, while others sell tickets on a first-come first-served basis. Others are filled to capacity, but have an unspoken policy of not turning anyone away. Check Chapter 8 for a complete listing of synagogues in Manhattan, and call ahead to find out what kind of seating is available. The following synagogues and community centers open their doors during the High Holidays, at least to the extent of their facilities:

The Brotherhood Synagogue   *Conservative*
28 Gramercy Park South 10010   674-5750

Congregation Beth Simchat Torah   *Unaffiliated*
57 Bethune Street 10014   929-9498

Lincoln Square Synagogue   *Orthodox*
200 Amsterdam Avenue 10023   874-6105

The 92nd Street YM–YWHA
1395 Lexington Avenue 10128   427-6000

Some synagogues have created special services for the High Holidays that are geared specifically toward singles. Although these services are not generally free, the cost is usually low.

Maimonides Temple   *Unaffiliated*
P.O. Box 20374 10017   722-6984

Sutton Place Synagogue   *Conservative*
225 East 51st Street 10022   593-3300

Temple Israel of the City of New York   *Reform*
112 East 75th Street 10021   249-5000

Sukkot

Sukkot, which occurs right after the High Holidays, is called in English the Festival of Booths, because it commemorates the time in Jewish history when the Israelites camped out in the desert in temporary structures. It is a mitzvah—a commandment—to sit, even eat in a sukkah, a hut-like dwelling whose principle feature is that it looks like it's about to collapse. This poses great challenges to New Yorkers, who are mostly apartment dwellers, but we've seen sukkot constructed on the roofs of buildings, on terraces, as well as in some courtyards. For the less experienced there are even sukkah-building kits sold at Jewish bookstores. If you wish to fulfill the mitzvah but have no opportunity to create your own sukkah, there are several more or less public sukkot in Manhattan in which you can have a meal or spend some time. Almost every synagogue builds a sukkah, and will be happy to have you use it, provided you call first and let them know. In addition, there is a very large and quite beautiful sukkah erected each year in the courtyard of the Jewish Theological Seminary, located at the northeast corner of 122nd Street and Broadway. Call 678-8000 first for information. In past years, the 92nd Street YM–YWHA has offered a walking tour of great New York sukkot, including those in other boroughs; call 427-6000.

Part of the celebration of Sukkot includes shaking the lulav (a long palm branch surrounded by willow and myrtle) and the etrog (a citron). Although all public sukkot will have these available, many people buy their own set, which can range in price from fifteen to fifty dollars, depending on where you make the purchase and the quality of the lulav and etrog. Most of the bookstores we list will be happy to order a set for you; if you'd like the opportunity to choose a set for yourself, go down to Canal Street near Essex Street right after Yom Kippur. There you'll find ten or fifteen tables set up on the sidewalk, each with a different merchant hawking his wares. You can compare quality and prices, and have the fun of making the best deal you can.

Hanukkah

Several events in Manhattan announce the coming of the Festival of Lights. The world's largest menorah (thirty-two feet tall) is set up by the Lubavitch Youth Organization in Grand Army Plaza, at Fifth Avenue and 59th Street. The same group places menorot at all New York City bridge and tunnel crossings. The Educational Alliance lights a menorah in Washington Square Park each year, and invites people to bring their own menorot to light as well. Congregation Ansche Chesed, located at West End Avenue and 100th Street

(865-0600) sponsors a Hanukkah Arts Festival each year, usually on the Sunday immediately preceding Hanukkah. There is live entertainment, lots of good food, and all kinds of Judaica gift items to buy for the holiday. The Women's Organization of Yeshiva University sponsors an annual pre-Hanukkah Holiday Boutique to benefit the University. All kinds of things are sold, most of quite high quality. Art, Judaica, jewelry, gift certificates to Tiffany's, as well as special Hanukkah food baskets prepared by Barbara Plasse can all be purchased here. For exact date, time and location, call 960-5400.

The bookstores and gift shops we list in Chapter 7 sell a variety of menorot, from inexpensive brass to ornate or beautifully handcrafted silver and ceramic. In addition, many of the artists we list create beautiful menorot in a variety of media and some will even custom design items.

Tu b' Shevat
The New Year of Trees occurs during January or February, and is acknowledged in the United States largely through the planting of trees in Israel. This is usually done through the Jewish National Fund, an agency whose work is described in our chapter on Israel. If you would like to plant a tree in Israel, either in honor or in memory of someone, or for some occasion, call JNF at 737-7441. When the transaction is completed, you or the person you are honoring will receive a certificate. Many other Jewish organizations—Hadassah for example—have volunteer JNF representatives who can arrange tree planting for you as well.

Purim
The most raucous holiday in the Jewish Year, Purim celebrates the salvation of the Jewish people from the evil Haman through the efforts of Esther and Mordecai. Verisimilitude aside, New Yorkers mark this day in lively fashion with the reading of the Megilla—the scroll of Esther—in synagogues and *havurot* all over the city. The noise and merriment essential to the day are abetted through the use of greggers and costumes. Although most communities supply greggers, they can be purchased at any of the bookstores and gift shops listed in Chapter 7. Collectors of Judaica may be interested in own-

ing Megillot; some magnificent ones can be purchased at The Hecker Corporation (593-2424), In The Spirit (861-5222), The Jewish Museum Gift Shop (860-1895), and Moriah Art Crafts (751-7090). Judaica auctions at Sotheby-Park Bernet and antique dealers around town may also offer antique Megillot.

The Jewish Museum and the Yeshiva University Museum often run family programs before Purim, designed to display their collections that relate specifically to the holiday and to provide hands-on workshops, where parents and children make greggers, costumes, or other Purim-related artifacts. Purim festivals, usually before the holiday, have been held in the past in several locations in Manhattan, sponsored by the Hebrew Arts School, 129 West 67th Street (362-8060), Ansche Chesed, 251 West 100th Street (865-0600), and the American Jewish Heritage Committee, 535 Fifth Avenue (772-6190). There has also been a Purim carnival for learning-disabled children, sponsored by B'nai B'rith Hillel–Jewish Association for College Youth, held at the Town and Village Synagogue, 334 East 14th Street (677-8090).

It is customary to send gifts, usually of food, to friends and family on Purim. Hamantaschen, the cookies baked in the shape of the villain Haman's hat, can be found at almost all the bakeries we list, and are the traditional food eaten on Purim. You can assemble them in a basket with fruits and/or wine and send them to friends. We know at least one resource that will do it all for you: Barbara Plasse, formerly of the Gingham Garden, specializes in preparing beautiful baskets with fruit, baked goods, and imported kosher gourmet items like chocolate and jams (860-8368). Be sure to call early.

Purim is also a holiday during which we help those in need, even beyond our normal contributions, because we wish all to share in the happiness of the holiday. The following Jewish organizations in New York, described more fully in Chapter 11, provide help to the needy in town, and are grateful for any and all contributions.

Dorot   251 West 100th Street 10025   864-7410
Project Ezra   197 East Broadway 10002   982-4124

Gemiluth Chessed of Greater New York, Inc.
P.O. Box 178 10033   923-8701

**Metropolitan New York Coordinating Council on Jewish
Poverty** 9 Murray Street 10007   267-9500

**Homeless Project of Jewish Board of Family and Children's
Services** 235 Park Avenue South 10003   460-0900

United Jewish Council of the East Side
235 East Broadway 10002   233-6037

Please note that Dorot, Ezra, and the United Jewish Council
send packages of food to the needy before each major holiday.

Passover

According to studies done by the American Jewish Committee, more Jews celebrate Passover than any other holiday on
the Jewish calendar, and while Passover itself lasts eight days
(or seven for Reform Jews), preparation for the festival can
take weeks!

Since everything eaten during Passover must be made
without leaven, special products begin appearing on supermarket shelves weeks before the holiday. Virtually every major
supermarket in Manhattan carries a full line of kosher-for-
Passover products. In addition, Miller's opens a store a few
weeks before the holiday that carries only Passover products.
Since the location varies from year to year, your best bet is to
call (496-8855 or 475-3337) and check where the store will be
opening. Although matzah is sold everywhere, you can go
right to the source by visiting the Streit Matzo Company at 150
Rivington Street (475-7000) on the Lower East Side.

Many bakeries close for Passover, though several sell
"Passover Baked Goods" before the holiday. This often means
that no flour is used in the baking; if you observe the laws of
Passover, or are bringing cake to someone who does, you will
need to know if special utensils were used and if the kitchen
was made kosher for Passover. To be on the safe side, ask if the
bakery has been rabbinically supervised as being kosher for
Passover.

The story of Passover is told in the Haggadah, which is
read during the seder. All the bookstores listed in this book

carry a variety of Haggadot. There are also Haggadot published by individual movements; you can find these at bookstores or by calling:

Central Conference of American Rabbis *Reform,* 684-4990
Federation of Reconstructionist Congregations and Havurot *Reconstructionist,* 496-2960
Rabbinical Assembly *Conservative,* 678-8060

The Jewish Braille Institute provides free Haggadot in braille, large type, or audiocassettes. They have Orthodox, Conservative and Reform editions as well as a children's Hagaddah. Call 889-2525 for information.

Seder plates come in various styles, and can be made of clay, silver or other materials. Many of the bookstores and gift shops we list carry several kinds of seder plates, and we've seen some particularly lovely ones at The Hecker Corporation, In the Spirit Gallery, The Jewish Museum Gift Shop, J. Levine, and West Side Judaica. Many of the artists we list in Chapter 8 also create seder plates.

If you're looking for a seder outside the home, you may find one in a neighborhood synagogue or community center, or at a restaurant. Many synagogue seders are open to nonmembers; many advertise in *The Jewish Week* and other Jewish periodicals. Restaurants in Manhattan that have held communal seders in past years include Lou G. Siegel, 209 West 38th Street (921-4433), Moshe Peking, 40 West 37th Street (594-6500) and Tavern on the Green, Central Park West & 67th Street (873-4111). Lou Siegel and Moshe Peking are also among the few restaurants that remain open throughout the intermediate days of Passover. For more information about seders open to the public, call the Jewish Information and Referral Service (753-2288).

There are also a number of Passover celebrations designed for special groups. Sutton Place Synagogue (225 East 51 Street, 593-3300) has two such seders: one for singles and one designed for single parents and their children. The New York Society for the Deaf holds a seder each year sponsored by the Hebrew Association for the Deaf. Call 673-6500 for more information.

For seniors, The Jewish Association for the Aged (JASA)

holds communal seders at senior centers, synagogues, community centers and Ys throughout the city. For more information call 724-3200. UJA–Federation camps offer Passover programs for older adults at their camp facilities in Connecticut, upstate New York, and Pennsylvania. For more information, call 753-2288. For elderly Jews on the Upper West Side who need assistance walking to a seder, Dorot (864-7410) provides an escort service.

There are even options for students away from home who wish to share a seder but do not want to try a local synagogue. Hebrew Union College–Jewish Institute of Religion holds a seder for college students at 1 West 4th Street (674-5300). B'nai B'rith Hillel–JACY holds a city-wide model seder for students before Passover. Call 696-1590 for date, time, and location.

If you wish to send a food gift to the hosts of your seder, you can call Barbara Plasse (860-8368). She'll send out an attractive basket of chocolates, grape juice, and other gourmet items all labeled kosher for Passover.

Several organizations and groups reach out to those in need at Passover. They are usually happy to have volunteers helping out, as well as contributions to enable them to continue providing help. Project Ezra (982-4124), Dorot (864-7410), and the United Jewish Council (233-6037) send out holiday packages of food to the needy before Passover. The Joint Passover Association, a subvention of UJA–Federation, provides stipends for needy Jews to help them celebrate Passover. There are application sites throughout the city, staffed by trained volunteers under the auspices of JBFCS (460-0900). Other outreach programs are run by the Jewish Community Council of Washington Heights (568-5450), Ansche Chesed (865-0600) and the Educational Alliance (475-2600).

Yom Hashoa: Holocaust Memorial Day

The government of Israel established the 27th day of Nisan as the day on which we commemorate the Holocaust. Annual observances in Manhattan include one sponsored by the Warsaw Ghetto Uprising Memorial, held at Madison Square Garden on the Sunday nearest April 19th.

Many other groups, described in our list of Holocaust organizations, hold annual events. To learn about various programs, call the American Federation of Jewish Fighters, Camp Inmates, and Nazi Victims (697-5670).

The sidewalk on the west side of First Avenue between 42nd and 49th Streets has been named "Raoul Wallenberg Walk," after the famous non-Jewish hero of the war who some think is still alive. There are often commemorations held here as well.

Solidarity Sunday

In recent years, one Sunday in May has been set aside to honor Jews in the Soviet Union and to demonstrate the will of all Jews to help those who seek freedom from religious persecution. Sponsored by the Coalition to Free Soviet Jewry (354-1316), a parade starts on the Upper East Side, heads down Fifth Avenue, and ends up at United Nations Plaza.

Yom Ha-atzmaut: Israel Independence Day

In Manhattan, this joyous holiday is marked by a rain-or-shine massive parade on Fifth Avenue, between 57th and 86th Streets, sponsored by the American Zionist Youth Foundation. For more information call 751-6070. There has also been a street fair at Yeshiva University's main center on Amsterdam Avenue, between 184th and 186th Streets.

Chapter 10
WHERE WE EAT

There's an old joke that says that aboard all El Al Israeli airplanes, in addition to the signs that say "No Smoking" and "Please Fasten Your Seat Belt," there is one that says "Have a Piece of Fruit." The image of the Jewish mother pushing food ("ess, ess, mein kindt") is perhaps unfair, but food does play an important role in Jewish life. The mere mention of certain holidays conjures up visions of roast chicken, tzimmes, noodle pudding, matzo brie or potato latkes. New York's dense Jewish population has influenced the food of all its peoples, and it's not unusual to see an Italian noshing a knish or a non-Jew sitting down to Sunday brunch at Ratner's. It would be impossible to list every bakery and food shop that carries some Jewish-style food (bagels are now an all-American bread, but it still hurts to see people order them with bologna and mayonnaise on top), so our listings in this section concentrate on those places serving kosher food. We couldn't, of course, resist including in our restaurant section a few of the most well-known "Jewish-style," though not kosher, establishments.

According to current Jewish practice in most places, *kashrut* is determined not only by the type of food, how it is slaughtered, or how it is prepared. The final stamp of approval must be given by a recognized authority—a *mashgiach*. Recognized by whom, you ask? Therein lies the problem. Some very Orthodox Jews eat only glatt kosher food, which doesn't mean the food is "more" kosher, but that the animal from which the food comes was smooth-lunged (hence "glatt"). Many Jews do not require glatt kosher food, but some will eat only foods their rabbi permits; others will eat anything with a recognized *hashgacha* (supervision mark) like Ⓤ or K. Still others will eat dairy anywhere. We make no claims concerning the *kashrut* of any restaurants, delis, butchers, bakeries, groceries or caterers listed here. We do tell you what is rabbinically supervised (and by whom); if you have questions about a particular eating place or its supervision, check with your rabbi or the New York Board of Rabbis (879-8415). There are a few places on the Lower East Side that are so trusted by everyone that they require no supervision, and we've so indicated. Finally, some establishments have a sign that reads Cholov Yisroel. This designation tells you that all dairy products have been derived from kosher animals. Since federal law requires this anyway, Cholov Yisroel is not generally required by Orthodox rabbis, and we omit mention of it.

Because we tend to do our cooking and eating by neighborhood, our listings in this section will be arranged by location, like our synagogue listings. First hours are A.M., second P.M., unless otherwise specified.

SUPERVISED BUTCHERS

Many supermarkets and delis carry some kosher meats such as chickens and hot dogs, and some even keep them in a separate section. These are usually the kinds of things that can be frozen and packaged under supervision, and you will not find kosher steak or other cuts of beef in a regular supermarket. For that you will want to try one of our kosher supervised butchers. Since they cannot keep meat for more than a few days, if you want an unusual cut you should call a day or two ahead so they can stock it for you. None of these butchers has a self-service counter. None will accept credit cards, but once they know you many will arrange for a house charge, and most will deliver reasonably-sized orders. Most will *kasher* meat for you, and some even prepare things so that you can just pop them in the oven when you get home.

DOWNTOWN AND LOWER EAST SIDE

Goldberg Butcher Store
500 Grand Street 10002   475-6915
> Supervision: Union of Orthodox Rabbis
> Hours: Sun–Thurs 7–7, Fri. 7–3   Delivery: no minimum

Murray's House of Prime Kosher Beef
507 Grand Street 10002   254-0180
> Supervision: Rabbi Pesach Akerman, Am. Fed. of Retail
> Kosher Butchers
> Hours: Mon–Tues 7–7, Wed–Thurs 7–7:30, Fri 7–2:30
> Delivery: free. No minimum in area,
> $40 minimum uptown

Morris Stahl Kosher Meats & Poultry
62 Avenue A 10009   228-2668
> Supervision: Rabbi Pesach Akerman, Am. Fed. of Retail
> Kosher Butchers
> Hours: Mon–Thurs 6–6, Fri 6–2 hours before sundown
> Delivery: none

UPPER EAST SIDE

Irving Berger Kosher Meats & Poultry
202 East 87th Street 10128   289-7234
> Supervision: Rabbi Pesach Ackerman, Am. Fed. of Retail
> Kosher Butchers, glatt
> Hours: Mon–Thurs 6:30–5, Fri until 1:30
> Delivery: East Side only, $50 minimum

Park East Kosher Butcher
1163 Madison Avenue 10028   787-3545
> Supervision: Midtown Board of Kashrut
> Hours: Mon–Wed 7:30–5:30, Thurs until 7:30, Fri until 3
> Delivery: no minimum

I. Salzman
1384 Second Avenue 10021   650-1996
> Supervision: Rabbi Pesach Ackerman, Am. Fed. of Retail
> Kosher Butchers
> Hours: Mon–Tues 6–6, Wed–Thurs until 8, Fri. until sundown
> Delivery: no charge

UPPER WEST SIDE

Paul Feldstein
2370 Broadway 10024   873-3560
> Supervision: Midtown Board of Kashruth
> Hours: Mon–Thurs 7–6, Fri until 3
> Delivery: $15–25 minimum

Fischer Brothers & Leslie
230 West 72nd Street 10023   787-1715
> Supervision: Midtown Board of Kashruth
> Hours: Mon–Thurs 7–7, Fri until 3 (a little later in summer)
> Delivery: for reasonable order

Jonas Stern & Sons
229 West 100th Street 10025   662-7081
> Supervision: Midtown Board of Kashruth
> Hours: Mon–Tues 8–5, Wed–Thurs 8–6, Fri 8–noon
> Delivery: yes

WASHINGTON HEIGHTS AND INWOOD

Bloch & Falk Meat
4100 Broadway 10032   927-5010
> Supervision: Rabbi Weinbach, Rego Park
> Hours: Sun–Thurs 7:30–6, Fri until 4
> Delivery: depends where

Gruenspecht Meat Products
3830 Broadway 10032   568-5656
> Supervision: Union of Orthodox Rabbis
> Hours: Mon–Thurs 6:30–4, Fri until noon
> Delivery: $40–50 minimum

Gutmann & Mayer
4229 Broadway 10033   923-1989
> Supervision: Rabbi Abraham Gross
> Hours: Mon 7–5, Tues–Thurs 7–6, Fri until 1
> Delivery: $35 minimum in area

Sidney's Kosher Meats
4230 Broadway 10033   927-8188
> Supervision: Rabbi Pesach Ackerman, Am. Fed. of Retail
> Kosher Butchers
> Hours: Mon–Thurs 8–6:30, Fri until 3
> Delivery: $50 minimum

BAKERIES

If you're on a search for the perfect challah, you'll have plenty of opportunities in Manhattan, for in addition to our bakeries there are many specialty food shops that also carry challah on Fridays. While we can't list every bakery that sells challah, our list includes those that clearly identify themselves as Jewish. We're too worried about weight to have sampled *every* baked good available in New York, so we have limited ourselves to including what items the bakeries generally carry. When appropriate, we indicate supervision. Bakeries do not take credit cards. Our own searches for challah over the years have led to some wonderful eggy varieties to which we happen to be partial, but we have lots of friends who prefer bread that is sweet and cakey. You'll have to do the sampling and be the judge!

LOWER EAST SIDE

Gertel's
53 Hester Street 10002 982-3250

Hours: Sun–Thurs 7–6, Fri until 2
In addition to both dairy and parve challah, Gertel's has a big selection of baked goods including traditional Jewish pastries like mohn cakes and honey cakes. It is supervised by the Orthodox Union and the Boro Park Board of Rabbis.

East Broadway Kosher Bakery–Israelbeigel Bakery
181 East Broadway 10002 228-1110

Hours: Sun–Thurs 7–7, Fri until sundown
This small bakery carries challah, kichel, honey cake, and other breads in addition to wine and Shabbat candles.

Kossar's Bialys 367 Grand Street 10002 473-4810

Hours: Open 7 days, 24 hours
Kossar's, which is also known as Kossar's Bialystoker Kuchen Bakery, has stacks of fresh bagels and bialys and looks like a factory. In fact, their bagels are so good they are trucked all over the city to retail outlets.

Moishe's Bakery
211 East Broadway 10002 982-0960

Hours: Sun–Thurs 7–9, Fri until sundown
Moishe's shop has strictly kosher breads and will take large orders by phone.

Moishe's Homemade Kosher Bakery
181 East Houston 10002 475-9624

Hours: Sun–Thurs 7–6, Fri until sundown
The lines here are long for the Russian health bread and cornbread, for which Moishe's is famous, and the challah, bagels, bialys and cakes.

Moishe's Second Avenue Homemade Kosher Bake Shop
115 Second Avenue 10003 505-8555

Hours: Sun 7–8, Mon–Thurs 7:30–8:30, Fri until sundown
There are challahs here as well as strudel and delicious-looking hamantaschen. The shop says it has Satmar supervision.

Ratner's
138 Delancey Street 10002 677-5588

Hours: Sun–Fri 6–11, Sat. 6–2
Everyone comes to Ratner's for the mushroom barley soup and blintzes, but the front of the restaurant has a large bakery counter where you can purchase challah, brownies, strudel, mohn pastries, cookies and cakes.

Zaro's Bread Basket
South Street Seaport 608-6962

Hours: open 7 days, 7:30–10
The Zaro's at the seaport (there are several in Manhattan) sells only baked goods, and these include cakes, rolls, breads, and the big muffins for which Zaro's has become well known—fourteen kinds, including chocolate chip, banana walnut, zucchini, and granola in addition to more traditional flavors. The shop is supervised by Rabbi Norman Twersky.

MIDTOWN

Broadway's Jerusalem 2
1375 Broadway 10018 398-1475

Hours: Mon–Thurs 7:30–midnight, Fri until sundown
This restaurant has a large bakery section in front, with everything from bagels to cakes. Supervision is by the Rabbinical Board of Flatbush.

Kosher Delight
1365 Broadway 10036 563-3366

Hours: Mon–Thurs 8–10, Fri until 4
This midtown restaurant also has an assortment of baked goods, including breakfast items and cakes. It is supervised by the Rabbinical Board of Flatbush.

Underground Kosher Gourmet
1196 Sixth Avenue 10036   391-8729

Hours: Mon–Thurs 7–5:30, Fri until 12:30
This take-out shop is run by the people who own the Edible
Pursuits restaurant. They have a large assortment of baked
goods including muffins and brownies, chocolate, cheese and
fruit danish, apple strudels, Russian coffee cake, and of course
challah on Fridays.

Zaro's Bread Basket
466 Lexington Avenue 10017   972-1560

Hours: Mon–Sat 6–8

625 Eighth Avenue (Port Authority)   279-7663

Mon–Fri 6:30–10, Sat–Sun 7–8:30

Grand Central Station   599-1515

Hours: Mon–Sat 6–8
Zaro's bakery section is filled with cakes, rolls, many different
kinds of breads, including pumpernickel and challah, and their
many kinds of big muffins including zucchini, granola, chocolate
chip, and banana walnut in addition to bran and corn. All items
at the bakery counter are kosher and some things are also parve
(you have to ask). Zaro's also has nonkosher deli sections that
carry baked goods (there are ham-filled croissants, for example),
so be sure you have chosen from the supervised section if this is
important to you. There are signs everywhere, indicating which
is which, but it can get tricky since not all staff are
knowledgeable. Supervision is provided by Rabbi Norman
Twersky.

Zooky's
180 Third Avenue   10003   982-4690

Hours: Mon–Fri 8–8:45, Sat–Sun until 7
Zooky's Deli sells hot bagels and bialys, challah, rye and
pumpernickel, as well as Mrs. Grimble's cheesecake.

UPPER EAST SIDE

H & H Bagels
1551 Second Avenue 10028   799-9680

Hours: Open 7 days, 24 hours
This Upper West Side establishment was so much in demand
that it opened an East Side branch to save everyone carfare on
the crosstown bus. The bagels are certified by the Kosher
Supervision Service. For mail-order delivery, see the H & H
listing on the Upper West Side.

Orwasher Bakery

308 East 78th Street 10021 288-6569

Hours: Mon–Sat 7–7

It may not be a big storefront on a main street, but everyone knows where Orwasher's is, and it is famous for its potato bread and pumpernickel as well as its challah.

UPPER WEST SIDE

Grossinger's Home Bakery

337 Columbus Avenue 10023 362-8672

Hours: Mon–Sat 8–8, Sun until 6

Grossinger's is a traditional Hungarian bakery that sells parve challah, hamantaschen, almond horns and, of course, Hungarian cheesecake.

H & H Bagels

2239 Broadway 10024 799-9680

Hours: open 7 days, 24 hours

The lines never shorten here and the bagels just keep coming and coming, the best in New York. The bagels are certified by the Kosher Supervision Service. And good news for all expatriates and homesick New Yorkers: H & H now ships fresh bagels to any state in the country by Express Mail. Orders are taken Monday through Friday 9 to 5 (New York time, of course) and can be charged to American Express cards. The special numbers to call are 1-800-882-2435 from anywhere in New York State including Manhattan, and 1-800-692-2435 from outside the state. There is a minimum order of three dozen bagels plus a postage charge, and you must provide an exact zip code. Call before 10:00 A.M. for next day delivery.

Lichtman's Bakery

532 Amsterdam Avenue 10024 873-2373

Hours: Mon–Sat 8–6, Sun until 5

Lichtman's is an Upper West Side tradition among Jews and non-Jews alike. The aroma from the corner of 86th Street and Amsterdam has been known to reach parts of Long Island! It is well-known for its Hungarian and French pastries, and also sells parve challah.

Meal Mart

2189 Broadway 10023 787-4720

Hours: Sun 10–7, Mon–Wed 10:30–7:30, Thurs 10–8, Fri 8–2

This take-out deli imports its baked goods, which include bread, rolls, cakes and water challah, from Williamsburg and Boro Park. Some of their cakes are from Gruenebaum.

Miller's Kosher Cheese

2192 Broadway 10023 496-8855

Hours: Sun 8:30–7, Mon–Wed until 8, Thurs until 9, Fri until 2
Although it is not a bakery, Miller's carries a large range of
baked goods, from bagels, rolls, challahs and breads (including
pumpernickel raisin) to fancy cookies and cakes. Specialties are
lemon rolls, raspberry rolls and Green's chocolate loaf.

Royale Pastry Shop

237 West 72nd Street 10023 874-5642

Hours: open 7 days, 6–9:45
A fixture on 72nd Street west of Broadway, Royale, which has
a few tables for those who can't wait to eat until they get
home, has Polish baba rhum, delicious Russian kuliche, hot
bagels and, of course, challah.

WASHINGTON HEIGHTS

Bagel City

720 West 181st Street 10033 927-3424

Hours: Sun–Mon 6–6, Tues–Thurs 6–8, Fri until 1 hour
 before sundown
This take-out bagel shop is supervised by the Kosher
Supervision Service of Hackensack.

Gideon's

810 West 187th Street 10033 927-9262

Hours: Sun 6:30–7, Mon–Thurs 7–8, Fri 6 to sundown
The window is full of mocha torte, layer cakes, and European-
style baked goods, and there is plenty of bread and rolls. It is
supervised by K'hal Adath Jeshurun of Washington Heights.

Grandma's Cookie Jar

2543 Amsterdam Avenue 10033 568-4855

Hours: Sun 8–5, Mon–Thurs 8–7, Fri until 1
David, watch out! To judge from the lines stretching from the
doorway down Amsterdam Avenue toward the dorms,
Grandma's has hit Yeshiva University with all the force of the
cookie franchises downtown. In addition to the many varieties
of cookies, there are muffins, ice cream and hot drinks to go.
Grandma's is supervised by Rabbi Ashen and a sign in the
window says "approved by S.O.Y." Can Yeshiva University
students already have their own supervision service?

Gruenebaum Bakery

725 West 181st Street 10033 781-8813

Hours: Sun–Thurs 6:30–8, Fri until sundown
This bakery serving the Breuer community has German-style
water challah, heart cakes on Valentine's Day, and all kinds of

good baked goods for Pesach. Supervision is by K'hal Adath Jeshurun of Washington Heights.

Stern's Bakery

257 Dyckman Street   569-3630

> Hours: Sun 8–4:30, Mon–Thurs 8–4, Fri until 3
> This tiny bakery with tin ceilings must be the last outpost of Washington Heights (in fact it's at the western end of Dyckman Street almost under the Henry Hudson Parkway). It has cakes and turnovers, bread and rolls. It is supervised by K'hal Adath Jeshurun of Washington Heights.

RESTAURANTS AND DELIS

Restaurants in New York come in all varieties, and it is some-times difficult to decide if some restaurants are really restaurants or just glorified delis with a few tables. We have used both names in our listings and have included virtually any place with tables where you can sit down and eat. Whether you want a quick knish and a cup of coffee, or an elegant birthday dinner, we hope our descriptions will give you an indication of what place to choose. Those restaurants that are rabbinically supervised are so indi-cated, and listed together with dairy restaurants and other estab-lishments that are either trusted within observant circles despite the lack of supervision, or seem to us to serve only permitted foods. At the end of the section, we've also listed some of the well-known "Jewish-style" delis, which make no claim to being kosher, and in fact may serve nonkosher meats as well. Hours change frequently, particularly among restaurants that close be-fore sundown on Friday and reopen for dinner on Saturday evening, so it is always best to call ahead. Again, first hour given is always A.M., second hour P.M., unless otherwise specified. Many of our listings also do catering and deliver.

DOWNTOWN AND LOWER EAST SIDE

Bernstein-on-Essex

135 Essex Street 10002   473-3900

> Supervision: Harav Jacov Yitzchok Spiegel, glatt
> Hours: Mon–Thurs 8–1 A.M., Fri until 2:30, Sat 8 P.M.–1 A.M., Sun 9:30–10:30
> Credit: Most major cards
> Bernstein-on-Essex now has a deal with the First Roumanian-

American Congregation on Rivington Street to use their premises for its catering business, and the Roumanian pastrami is why most people eat here. Bernstein has two large dining rooms as well as a take-out counter, and it serves in classical deli style, with jacketed waiters and formica tables. Portions on its all-meat menu are enormous, and this is a popular stop on a shopping trip to the Lower East Side. Bernstein's also advertises a glatt kosher Chinese party for twenty-five, with free delivery in Manhattan.

B & H Dairy
127 Second Avenue 10003   777-1930
Hours: Mon–Sat 6–11, Sun until 10
Credit: No credit cards
This luncheonette has good food, especially the kasha varnishkes. Menu items include vegetarian chopped liver, vegetable cutlets, omelets and traditional dairy dishes.

Broadway Kosher Delicatessen
321 Broadway 10013   964-2116
Hours: Mon–Fri 8–6
Credit: No credit cards
This typical deli has a convenient location across from Federal Plaza, and it offers company charge accounts and free delivery in the neighborhood. The lunch menu includes popular meat dishes, combination sandwiches, deli platters and salads, all washed down with Dr. Brown's and polished off with strudel. There is also a breakfast menu. Broadway Kosher caters office parties and does platters for all occasions.

Burger Spot
25 Essex Street 10002   473-5255
Supervision: Rabbi Avraham Fishelis, Grand Street
Hours: Mon–Thurs 9–5:15, Fri until 2:15, Sun 9–5:45
Credit: No credit cards
If you're a brisk walker you'll miss this spot that looks like a newsstand in between all the pickle stands and religious article stores on Essex Street. In fact, you can make a quick stop here and stand up and have a hamburger, hot dog, knish or parve soup.

Canal Street Kosher Dairy Restaurant
43 Canal Street 10002   226-6493
Hours: Sun–Thurs 8–5
Credit: No credit cards
There are about five formica tables in this small restaurant

that specializes in homemade knishes, pirogen, noodles and cabbage, blueberries and cream, and malteds. A sign in the window announces that they speak Russian here.

The Dairy Planet
182 Broadway 10013   227-8252

Supervision: Rabbi Bernard Levy
Hours: Mon–Thurs 11–9, Fri until 2:30
Credit: American Express, Mastercard, Visa
As you walk downstairs to the large dining room of The Dairy Planet you will pass a waterfall and small pond. This is definitely a more formal atmosphere than in most dairy restaurants, with red-velvet seats, black and chrome walls, and table settings that include white tablecloths. The full menu here includes daily soup choices, sandwiches, salads, omelets, and dairy dishes ranging from potato pancakes and matzah brei to broiled salmon steak, vegetable cutlet, broccoli and cheese souffle, and eggplant parmigiana. There are also cream dishes (in season) as entrees. The formal atmosphere and size (it accommodates 200) make it popular for private parties (they don't yet do weddings), and Saturday evenings the restaurant becomes The Comedy Planet, "New York's Only Kosher Comedy Club," with reserved seating and a cover charge (dinner is available). For reservations for the club, call 964-3177 or the restaurant.

Gertel's Bake Shop
53 Hester Street 10002   982-3250

Supervision: Orthodox Union
Hours: Sun–Thurs 7–6, Fri until 2
Credit: No credit cards
Tucked away on Hester Street around the corner from the heavy traffic on Essex, Gertel's still draws many people with its big pastry selection. This is a small shop with a counter and formica tables; in addition to coffee and cake, there is a small menu offering simple dairy dishes like scrambled eggs, pot cheese and sandwiches.

Grand Dairy Restaurant
341 Grand Street 10002   673-1904

Hours: Sun–Thurs 6–4, Fri until 3
Credit: No credit cards
This luncheonette has great blueberry blintzes and other traditional dairy dishes. The formica tables are jammed together to provide maximum patronage and the turnover is very quick.

Great American Health Bar

Supervision: Rabbi Chaim Dov-Ber Gulevsky

55 John Street 10038   227-6100

Hours: Mon–Thurs 7–5:30, Fri until sundown

11 Park Place 10007   962-4444

Hours: Mon–Thurs 7:30–6

Credit: No credit cards

There are several of these franchised restaurants in
Manhattan, and while not all of them are supervised, those
that are serve dairy menus and have an attractive decor for a
quick lunch spot. There are some unusual items, including
freshly squeezed fruit juices and carrot, spinach, parsley and
celery juice (in any combination you like) and what the
restaurant calls tonics, combinations of yogurt, milk, yeast and
fruit. Their lunch menu includes many health salads,
sandwiches on health breads, and hot specials like pita pizza,
linguine with mushroom sauce, and apple-cheddar quiche. For
dessert there are cakes, cookies and frozen yogurt with a
variety of toppings. There is also a breakfast menu with
muffins, health breads (including whole wheat bagel) and eggs.
You can sit at the counter but there is also table service, and
the restaurants have an attractive atmosphere. They will
deliver in the area.

Henry's Delicatessen & Restaurant

195 East Houston 10002   473-9781

Supervision: Rabbi G. Taylor

Hours: Open 7 days, 9–9

Credit: No credit cards

Henry's has recently been redecorated in early Burger King,
but it is clean and spacious if noisy (the video games don't
help). There are many formica tables as well as the deli
counter, and Henry's has the usual assortment of hot dogs,
knishes, cole slaw, potato salad and other meat deli items.
They do a large take-out and catering business, and make hot
hors d'oeuvres for parties as well as various platters of
sandwiches and salads, and they offer free delivery.

J–II Kosher Pizza

112 Fulton Street 10038   732-6523

Supervision: Va'ad Harabonim of Flatbush.

Hours: Mon–Thurs 7:30–6:30, Fri until 2 hours before
sundown

Credit: No credit cards

Israeli specialties here include falafel, tahina, baba ganoush
and hummus, as platters and sandwiches, individually or as
combinations. There are also American dishes like tuna salad

and egg salad, sandwiches and knishes. The Italian foods feature pizza, baked ziti and eggplant parmigiana. J–II also has a breakfast menu. The large, simply-decorated restaurant has cafeteria-style seating. J–II will cater office parties in the area.

Just-a-Bite
106 Greenwich Street 10013   425-5470

Supervision: Va'ad Harabonim of Bensonhurst
Hours: Mon–Thurs 8–6, Fri until 3:15
Credit: No credit cards
This long and narrow deli in the shadow of the World Trade Center has a long counter with stools where you can select from a meat or *parve* menu, including burgers, sandwiches, platters and side orders of knishes, kugels, and salads. There is also a breakfast menu. Delivery is free with a minimum order, and they cater office parties.

Pizza Plaza
92 Chambers Street   732-8150

Supervision: Orthodox Union
Hours: Mon–Thurs 11–6, Fri until 2:30
Credit: No credit cards
This new dairy restaurant in a busy downtown area is pleasant, even if the music volume is a little high. Everything from the graph-print wallpaper, formica tables, bentwood chairs and modern lighting to the counter in the back of the restaurant is fresh looking. The menu is a mix of Italian and Middle Eastern specialties—pizza, baked ziti, falafel, hummus—and just to add more variety there are traditional favorites as well: kugels, knishes and cheese blintzes among others. There is also a breakfast menu and free delivery in the area.

Ratner's
138 Delancey Street   10002   677-5588

Hours: Sun–Fri 6–11, Sat 6–2 A.M.
Credit: No credit cards
The prices keep going up, but everyone keeps going to Ratner's. They are famous for their blintzes, vegetable cutlets and of course their mushroom barley soup. The lines here are very long on Sunday, and you may have to wait quite a while for a table even though their dining room is large. The front of the restaurant has a large bakery counter. Ratner's does party catering.

Rishon II

2 Lafayette Street 732-4780

Supervision: Rabbi Bernard Levy
Hours: Sun noon–5, Mon–Thurs 7:30–7, Fri until 2 hours
 before sundown, Sat after sundown until midnight
Credit: No credit cards
Just below Foley Square and the courthouses, Rishon II is
another kosher fast-food place that serves a combination of
pizza, calzones and Italian fast foods and falafel, hummus and
baba ganoush on platters or as sandwiches. There are also
knishes, kugels and fish and chips. The breakfast menu includes
bagels, blintzes and danish. There are two stand-up tables in the
front room, along with the counter and the pizza ovens, and a
small dining room through an archway.

Sabra

505 Grand Street 10002 260-6330

Supervision: Rabbi Avraham Fishelis
Hours: Sun–Thurs 10–10, Fri until 3:30
Credit: No credit cards
The newspaper clipping in the window says that the Lower East
Side is lucky to have Asazmi, the former chef at Cafe Tel Aviv, El
Avram, and David's Harp, right here on Grand Street. The
menu in this pleasant-looking informal restaurant (plastic
tablecloths) is Middle Eastern. Specialties include shish-kebab,
baba ganoush and Middle Eastern meatballs. You may also order
knishes and gefilte fish.

Sam's Famous Knishes

25 Canal Street 10002 598-4178

Supervision: K'hal Adath Jeshurun of Washington Heights
Hours: Sun–Thurs 7–7, Fri until 3
Credit: No credit cards
There is a long counter here, with sections marked for each
specialty (a little like the motor vehicle bureau): pizza, falafel,
knishes, blintzes and Italian items like ziti and eggplant
parmigiana. You stand on line to wait for your order and then
sit down at one of several tables that are usually pretty busy.

Someplace Special Deli & Restaurant

401 Grand Street 10002 674-0980

Supervision: Orthodox Union, glatt
Hours: Sun–Thurs 10:30–9, Fri until 1:30
Credit: American Express, Mastercard, Visa
This deli, which has a traditional menu of hot dogs, cold cuts,
kasha varnishkes and many side dishes, has a counter and about
eight formica tables with waiter service. In addition there is a
nicer-looking party room, open when there are enough people

to warrant it and available for rental on Saturdays after
sundown, even when the restaurant is closed.

Steinberg's Dairy Restaurant
21 Essex Street 10002 254-7787

Hours: Sun–Thurs 6–6, Fri until 3
Credit: No credit cards
This tiny dairy restaurant has a large counter and just five
tables, with a typical dairy menu that includes knishes, falafel,
lasagna and vegetable dishes.

Yonah Schimmel
137 East Houston 10002 477-2858

Hours: Open 7 days, 8–6
Credit: No credit cards
This is *the* original knish maker, and still the best known, and
you will often see cars (and even taxis) double-parked outside
waiting for their owners to emerge with savory hot potato,
cabbage, kasha, fruit and cheese knishes, as well as cheese
bagels. There is also homemade yogurt and borscht. There are
tin ceilings, the original fixtures, and several tables (some of
them often covered with trays of knishes that there is no other
room for anywhere else) where you can sit down to have a hot
knish and coffee. Yonah Schimmel also does catering, hors
d'oeuvres trays of knishes, meat balls, kreplach and other
goodies sold per 100 pieces.

GREENWICH VILLAGE, SOHO, CHELSEA, GRAMERCY PARK

Marrakesh West
149 Bleecker Street 10012 777-8911

Supervision: Rabbi Josephy
Hours: Mon–Thurs 5:30–11, Sat 8 P.M.–1 A.M., Sun 2–11
Credit: All major cards
In the heart of the Village you will find one of Manhattan's
few restaurants serving Moroccan specialties, and the
atmosphere one flight up is a little exotic too—it's the way you
might imagine a harem to look. Moroccan specialties here
include couscous, bisteeya (chicken and nuts baked in phyllo
dough), tagines (stews that often combine meat with fruit) and
m'shwya, a roast lamb dish.

Shalom Japan
22 Wooster Street 10012 925-0930

Supervision: Rabbi Moishe Lehon
Hours: Mon–Thurs noon–10:30

Credit: All major cards
In the southern reaches of Soho, just north of Canal Street, on a block that has more warehouses than art galleries, you will see a colorful red banner whose insignia will at first startle you. It is a Jewish star vertically bisected with Japanese characters. You have arrived at Shalom Japan, the only restaurant in New York featuring kosher Japanese food. The windows are decorated with large kimonos and Japanese art objects, and inside the dining room is informal but comfortable and has tablecloths. All the traditional Japanese favorites are here: beef and chicken teriyaki, sukiyaki, even sushi and sashimi.

MIDTOWN

Boychik's Pizza Parlor
19 West 45th Street 10036 719-5999

Supervision: Orthodox Union
Hours: Sun–Thurs 11–8, Fri until 3:30
Credit: No credit cards
A few years ago, Mimi Sheraton called this "the most convincing kosher pizza we have tasted," and the review still hangs on the walls of this pleasant-looking place. It is large, the walls baby blue, and the tables attractive for this kind of quick-lunch restaurant. The main thing here is the pizza and the other Italian dishes like eggplant parmigiana and baked ziti, but there are also Israeli specialties like hummus, tahina and falafel, as well as vegetarian liver, quiches and salads. They offer delivery service for a minimum order.

Broadway's Jerusalem 2
1375 Broadway 10018 398-1475

Supervision: Va'ad Harabonim of Flatbush
Hours: Mon–Thurs 7:30–midnight, Sat late evening
Credit: No credit cards
This very large and attractive place in the middle of the garment district combines a take-out counter in the front with tables, and offers hot soups, pizza and falafel. They have a large bakery section and seem to do a big business early in the morning as well as at other times of the day. Upstairs there is a nightclub (Upstairs at Jerusalem 2, 819-1891) that opens at 8:00 P.M. and runs until quite late, where you can have dinner and listen to Israeli and Hassidic music.

Diamond Kosher Dairy Luncheonette
4 West 47th Street 10036 719-2694

Hours: Business hours of the neighborhood
Credit: No credit cards
Located on the mezzanine of the National Jewelers Exchange,

the chief virtue of this luncheonette seems to be the view of all the jewels being bought and sold below. The clientele here are mostly people who work right on the block and the hours of the restaurant are those of the Exchange itself.

Edible Pursuits
325 Fifth Avenue 10016   686-5330

Supervision: OK Labs
Hours: Sun–Thurs for lunch and dinner until 9:15,
Fri for lunch
Credit: American Express, Visa, Mastercard
An oasis in the Midtown area full of kosher fast-food restaurants, this new restaurant is really beautiful, with a gentle pink and gray decor, tablecloths and formal service at its thirty-two tables. There is a dairy menu with specials every day that include dishes like lasagna, baked bluefish, tofu chicken, salmon steak, and various salads.

Gefen's Dairy Restaurant
297 Seventh Avenue 10001   929-6476

Hours: Mon–Thurs 6:45–8, Fri 6:45–3, Sun 11–7
Credit: No credit cards
This informal restaurant offers typical dairy dishes in a convenient midtown location.

Girlchik's Restaurant
155 West 47th Street 10036   391-2933

Supervision: K'hal Adath Jeshurun of Washington Heights
Hours: Mon–Thurs until 8, early Friday closing
Credit: No credit cards
A few blocks away from its brother Boychick's, this pizza restaurant is also attractive, with pink walls and several tables. There are pastas with sauces, antipasto, eggplant parmigiana, and Italian tuna salad in addition to the pizza. The prices are reasonable and the restaurant delivers.

Great American Health Bar
Supervision: Chaim Dov-Ber Gulevsky at all locations below
except 44th Street
Credit: No credit cards

35 West 57th Street 10017   355-5177

Hours: Mon–Fri 7:30–7, Sat 7:30–4

30 West 48th Street 10036   921-1750

Hours: Mon–Thurs 7–6, Fri 7–sundown

2 Park Avenue   685-7117

Hours: Mon–Thurs 7–7, Fri 7–sundown

15 East 40th Street   532-3232
Hours: Mon–Thurs 7–7, Fri 7–sundown

154 East 43th Street   682-5656
Hours: Mon–Thurs 11–9, Fri 11–sundown

10 East 44th Street   661-3430
Hours: Mon–Fri 7–7, Sat 8–5
The menus here are about the same as at the other branches of this franchise, including fruit and vegetable juice drinks, salads made with vegetables and sprouts, and frozen yogurt and tofutti desserts. These are attractive and fresh-looking restaurants, and quite popular in these days of concern with what we eat. The restaurant on 40th Street has counter service and a rear dining room that seats 100. The 57th Street restaurant has an upstairs dining room that makes it attractive for a casual business lunch.

Greener Pastures
117 East 60th Street   10022   832-3212
Supervision: Rabbi Chaim Dov-Ber Gulevsky
Hours: Mon–Thurs noon–9:30, Fri & Sun noon–8:30,
 Sat noon–10
Credit: No credit cards
Across the street from Bloomingdale's and around the corner from the UJA–Federation of Jewish Philanthropies building, this is a very popular restaurant for many who work in this part of Midtown. The restaurant is very attractive; several rooms have a clean, woodsy look with lots of plants. The food here is dairy and "health-food style," with salads and sandwiches. Although the restaurant is open on Shabbat, they employ non-Jews to run it and diners can make reservations and pay in advance so that they can come without violating Shabbat observance.

Kirschenbaum's Deli Restaurant
18 East 33rd Street   10016   683-0748
Hours: Mon–Thurs 6:30–4, Fri until 3
Credit: No credit cards
There is a small dairy section in the front with pastry, bagels and beverages (as well as packaged snack foods with the Orthodox Union label), and in the back are cases with deli meats and parve salads (egg salad, salmon salad, chopped herring, potato salad and macaroni salad). In between is a counter that seats about fifteen. After receiving your order for sandwich or platter, you can sit with paper plate and plasticware (a sign near the coffee reminds you to tell them which you are eating, meat or dairy). Although the deli is not supervised, all meats are glatt kosher and Kirschenbaum's customers know that he observes all dietary laws. The deli offers delivery in the area and will also do catering.

Kosher Delight

1365 Broadway 10036   563-3366

Supervision: Rabbinical Board of Flatbush, glatt
Hours: Mon–Thurs 7:30–10, Fri until 4, Sat 9:30 P.M.–2 A.M.,
Sun 11–10
Credit: No credit cards
This pleasant-looking kosher equivalent of McDonald's (the sign
says "where fast food is good food") is large, and offers
breakfast specials, delivery and catering for office parties. The
menu includes burgers, hot dogs, and deli sandwiches, as well as
boxed fried chicken. There are also cakes and pastries.

Kosher Hut

866 Sixth Avenue 10001   686-8319

Supervision: Rabbi Bernard Levy of Boro Park
Hours: Mon–Thurs 8–8, Fri 8–sundown, Sun 10:30–6:30
Credit: No credit cards
This luncheonette with a take-out counter and seating for about
forty-eight serves dairy only. The menu, which you can read in
English or Yiddish, has pizza, several pasta dishes, falafel and
salads. Kosher Hut also serves Klein's Cholov Yisroel ice cream.

Levy's Pizza and Vegetarian Cafe

330 Seventh Avenue   594-4613

Supervision: Rabbi Avraham Fisheles
Hours: Mon–Fri 7–6:30
Credit: No credit cards
This cafeteria-style restaurant, with its simple decor, is attractive
and has good pizza, with a variety of dairy toppings. In addition
there is falafel, other pita sandwiches, cold platters, and some
inexpensive hot plates such as eggplant parmigiana and spinach
pie.

Lois Lane's

9th Avenue & 42nd Street 10036   695-5055

Supervision: Rabbi Chaim Dov-Ber Gulevsky
Hours: Mon–Fri 9–8, Sat 10–7
Credit: American Express, Mastercard, Visa
You might really be able to fly if you order the "Superman, a
meal in a drink." Other power beverages are wheatgrass juice,
papaya juice, and fresh vegetable juices. Or you can try a
meatless burger with brown rice. These are just a few of the
macrobiotic selections at this combination health-food store and
restaurant. The restaurant has a large take-out business, but if
you decide to stay the seating area is quite pleasant, with butcher
block tables, track lighting, and lots of greenery. Even the
background music here is healthy.

Macabeem Restaurant

147 West 47th Street 10036   575-0226

Supervision: Orthodox Union, supervisor on premises
Hours: Mon–Thurs 11–11, Fri until 2, Sat sundown–2 A.M.
Credit: American Express, Mastercard, Visa
This is a plain but not unattractive meat-only deli in the
diamond district. There is both cafeteria-style service and a
dining room with tablecloths and waiters. Macabeem has both
Middle Eastern Jewish specialties such as stuffed grape leaves
and hummus, and American dishes such as tuna salad and
goulash. Wine is sold by both the bottle and the glass, and there
are tofutti desserts.

Moshe Peking

40 West 37th Street 10018   594-6500

Supervision: Orthodox Union, glatt
Hours: Sun–Thurs noon–9:45, Sat 7:30 P.M.–12:30 A.M.
Credit: All major cards
A Chinese restaurant where the waiters wear yarmulkes! The
menu features a large repertoire of Chinese food that can be
prepared according to *kashrut,* including Peking duck. The
restaurant has an attractive and formal atmosphere and is on the
expensive side.

New Gross Dairy Restaurant

1372 Broadway 10018   921-1969

Supervision: Orthodox Union
Hours: Mon–Thurs 7–10, Fri until 3, Sat after sundown–1 A.M.,
  Sun 11–10
Credit: American Express, Carte Blanche, Diners Club
This new restaurant (on the site of an old one) seats 150, is very
attractive, with tablecloths, baskets of rolls on the tables, and
waiters in jackets. The menu is vegetarian and there are fish
platters, soups, omelets, and entrees that include pirogen,
eggplant steak, vegetarian chow mein, and vegetable cutlets.
The desserts include some delicious-looking pastries.

Shalom Kosher Pizza

1000 Sixth Avenue 10018   730-0008

Supervision: Orthodox Union
Hours: Mon–Thurs 7:30–midnight, Fri closes early
Credit: No credit cards
This small restaurant does a busy breakfast take-out business of
danish and rolls, but also serves at a counter and an adjacent
room. Israeli newspapers are available along with the pizza,
falafel and hot dishes like spinach vegetarian loaf. The decor is a
cheerful Mediterranean motif with white stuccoed walls and
colorful murals. Free delivery is offered.

Lou G. Siegel

209 West 38th Street 10018 921-4433

> Supervision: Orthodox Union, glatt
> Hours: Sun–Thurs 11:30–10, Fri until 3
> Credit: All major cards
> This glatt kosher restaurant in the middle of the garment district is the best-known and most old-fashioned formal restaurant in the area. The inside is attractive if a little dark by today's standards, with dark paneling and mirrored columns, and the menu is fairly traditional with items like brisket, chicken and roast beef, although they have added some new dishes like duck (which they still prepare like traditional Jewish food).

Verve Naturelle

157 West 57th Street 10019 265-2255

> Supervision: Orthodox Union
> Hours: Mon–Thurs 11:30–9:30, Fri until 2:30, Sat sundown–midnight, Sun noon–9
> Credit: No credit cards
> Another Midtown find, this new dairy vegetarian restaurant has beautiful decor and advertises candlelight dinners. Everything here is very fresh and the menu is "California vegetarian cuisine," with lots of fish and pasta salads. There are sandwiches and salads at lunch also.

West 35th Street Dairy

218 West 35th Street 10001 947-2167

> Hours: Mon–Thurs 7–6, Fri until 3
> Credit: No credit cards
> This is a small pizza and falafel take-out with a few tables. They offer free delivery.

Yahalom

49 West 47th Street 10036 575-1699

> Supervision: on premises
> Hours: Mon–Thurs until 8, Fri closes early
> Credit: Most major cards
> In the heart of the diamond district, this glatt kosher cafeteria and dining room is one flight up, has bare floors, and is not attractive. Its menu is Middle Eastern Jewish and American, and there are chicken dishes, kebabs, veal stew and different sandwiches.

UPPER EAST SIDE

Cafe Masada

1239 First Avenue 10021 988-0950

Supervision: on premises
Hours: Sun–Thurs 8–11, Fri until 3, Sat from 1 hour after
sundown until 1 A.M.
Credit: All major cards
This small new restaurant is informal and attractive. There are
grilled entrees, such as shish kebab and schnitzel, and salads
with an Israeli or Moroccan flair, like hummus and tahina.
One of their specialties is Moroccan cholent, made with
chicken, lamb, chick peas and vegetables, cooked by a
Moroccan chef. Masada will do small orders to go.

Deli King II Kosher Deli

1162 First Avenue 10021 355-5577

Hours: Open 7 days, 9–9
Credit: All major cards
This deli has several tables, comfortable looking chairs, and
quiet music playing. The menu is typical New York deli, with
pages of hot and cold selections, as well as sodas and beer.
There is meat only, with fish platters and salads, and hot
dishes like roast chicken, flanken and stuffed cabbage. They
also serve cold cuts, deli sandwiches, and parve blintzes. Deli
King delivers, does a big business in platters that serve from
eight to forty, and will cater for up to 400 people.

UPPER WEST SIDE

Benjamin of Tudela

307 Amsterdam Avenue 10023 496-9492

Supervision: Orthodox Union, glatt
Hours: Mon–Thurs noon–3, 5:30–10, Sun 5–9:30, Sat dinner
from 2 hours after sundown
Credit: American Express
This is one of the most attractive—and most expensive—
kosher restaurants in Manhattan, and the setting is sleek
enough to attract the most sophisticated diner, with soft
carpeting and lighting, and elegantly set tables. The menu is
also elegant, and offers lunch choices like fancy salad, cold
chicken vinaigrette and omelets, and dinner entrees like
smoked brook trout and duckling. There are special desserts
every day. Reservations are recommended.

Famous Dairy

222 West 72nd Street 10023   595-8487

Supervision: K'hal Adath Jeshurun of Washington Heights
Hours: Sun–Thurs 7–11, Fri until 2:30
Credit: American Express, Visa, Mastercard
This is where you will find a complete dairy menu that includes typical dishes like blintzes and potato pancakes as well as vegetable chopped liver and sour milk. Their "special combination" will hold you for days. They offer a special Sunday brunch in addition to their regular menu, and will do take-out platters and outside catering.

Fine & Shapiro

138 West 72nd Street 10023   877-2874

Hours: Open 7 days, 11–11
Credit: American Express
What can you say about one of the Upper West Side's institutions? They have beautiful-looking turkeys in the window and a big deli counter inside with all the expected meats and salads, as well as good soups. They do a big business in party catering.

Levana

141 West 69th Street 10023   877-8457

Supervision: OK Labs
Hours: Sun 3 P.M.–11, Mon–Thurs noon–11, Sat from 2 hours after sundown to 2 A.M.
Credit: American Express, Visa, Mastercard
Levana has recently moved to this brownstone and is working to create an upscale atmosphere, with tablecloths and a slightly dressier decor than at their former location. The specialty here is fish, and all their selections are bought fresh each day. They also have salads, pastas and quiches, and they are well known for their baked goods. They have take-out service and will make party platters.

WASHINGTON HEIGHTS

Continental Kosher Deli & Restaurant

732 West 181th Street 10033   568-0571

Supervision: K'hal Adath Jeshurun of Washington Heights
Hours: Mon–Wed 10–8, Thurs until 8:30
Credit: No credit cards
This small home-style restaurant has a deli counter and five formica tables. It has a meat menu, with staples like pot roast and roast chicken, and the waiters are Yeshiva University students who really try hard.

Kosher Inn 2

2500 Amsterdam Avenue 10033   927-5858

Supervision: Rabbinical Council of Bergen County
Hours: Sun–Thurs 10–9, Fri until 3
Credit: No credit cards
This is the Y.U. pizza joint, and you will always see students
scurrying back to class with a slice in hand. There are a few
formica tables and the required video game. You can also have
falafel, knishes, egg roll, eggplant parmigiana, and hummus in
addition to the pizza, and they carry some dessert items.

Kum 'n Ess Homestyle Food

2549 Amsterdam Avenue 10033

Step inside this luncheonette and you've entered another
world: only the video games tell you it's not 1953. The crowd
here is from Y.U.'s high school for boys and it's so crowded
you can't find the counter. But who comes here to eat
anyway?

McDovid's

2520 Amsterdam Avenue 10033   928-4497

Supervision: K'hal Adath Jeshurun of Washington Heights
Hours: Sun–Thurs 11–2, 4–9:30, Sat after
 Shabbat to 11
Credit: No credit cards
Is the "Mc" a giveaway? Although you can get a corned beef
sandwich, the popular items here are the hot dogs and
chicken by the bucket with side orders of french fries. It is
self-service and there are formica tables.

My Place

2553 Amsterdam Avenue 10033   568-4600

Supervision: K'hal Adath Jeshurun of Washington Heights
Hours: Sun–Thurs 11–11, Fri until 1:30, Sat after
 Shabbat to 11
Credit: No credit cards
The latest addition to Y.U. row is nicer-looking than most of
the others, with a fresh interior and butcher block tables. It's
still a hamburger–hot dog menu, but there are no video
games and the crowd inside seems tamer. Maybe it just hasn't
caught on yet.

JEWISH-STYLE RESTAURANTS

DOWNTOWN AND LOWER EAST SIDE

Kaplan's Old New York
90 Broad Street   747-0722

Hours: Mon–Thurs 5–9, Fri–Sun 5–4
Credit: All major cards
This is the original Kaplan's, no longer associated with the
uptown restaurants of the same name. Located in the most
historic part of the Wall Street area, Kaplan's features wood
paneling, deep red banquettes, and pictures of old New York.
The traditional deli menu includes both meat and dairy
specialties; separate slicing machines are used for each.

Katz's
205 East Houston Street 10002   254-2246

Hours: Sun–Thurs 7–11:30, Fri–Sat until 1:30 A.M.
Credit: No credit cards
A neighborhood landmark is Katz's, which used to be a lot
more famous than it is now ("send a salami to your boy in the
army") but otherwise hasn't changed much. On Sundays it's
still tough to get around the cars double-parked in front, and
the lines for the hot dogs and other deli sandwiches are long.

Sammy's Famous Roumanian Restaurant
157 Chrystie Street 10002   673-5526

Hours: Mon–Fri 5 P.M.–10, Sat & Sun 5 P.M. until last
customer leaves
Credit: American Express, Diners Club
Eating at Sammy's is like taking a nostalgic trip to your
grandmother's kitchen—that is, if your grandmother was in
the habit of putting pitchers of schmaltz on the table, right
next to the ever-present bottles of seltzer and syrup.
Roumanian specialties here include mamaliga, kasha
varnishkes, gribenes, Roumanian steaks (the kind that hang
over the rim of your plate), and every kind of potato you can
imagine. The waiters love to serve you off the menu"'I'll bring
you the best"—but if you're counting pennies watch out: all
those special extras will show up on the bill.

Second Avenue Deli
156 Second Avenue 10003   677-0606

Hours: Open 7 days, 6:30–11:30
Credit: No credit cards
The Second Avenue Deli is as old as the stars it now has
immortalized on the sidewalk out front, and it was long the

center of Yiddish Broadway. Most of the theaters are gone now, but the Second Avenue Deli still thrives and the Molly Picon room is filled with memorabilia of Jewish theater. The restaurant is large, comfortable and pleasant, and its large menu includes all the traditional New York favorites: hot and cold deli sandwiches, flanken, stuffed derma, eggs, beef and fish dishes. They are famous for their chopped liver, of which they often hand out samples when the wait for a table is long.

GREENWICH VILLAGE, SOHO, CHELSEA, GRAMERCY PARK

Pastrami Factory
333 East 23rd Street 10010 689-8090
> Hours: Open 7 days, 11–9:30
> Credit: American Express, Carte Blanche, Diners Club
> This very pleasant and comfortable delicatessen has a full menu of favorites including pastrami, corned beef and Hebrew National meat sandwiches, soups, entrees like goulash and southern fried chicken, omelets, salads, falafel and Reuben sandwiches. The Pastrami Factory offers free delivery and a complete catering menu including sandwich and meat platters, hors d'oeuvres (by the piece or pound), main dishes and desserts.

Zooky's
180 Third Avenue 10003 982-4690
> Hours: Mon–Fri 8–8:45, Sat–Sun until 7
> Credit: Carte Blanche, Diners Club
> Zooky's Jewish-style food includes popular appetizers and deli foods. There is a take-out service and tables in the back where you can enjoy a variety of deli sandwiches including brisket, chopped liver, salami, bagels and lox, sturgeon and salads. Zooky's has a selection of breads and also carries Miss Grimble's cheesecake.

MIDTOWN

Carnegie Delicatessen
854 Seventh Avenue 10019 757-2245
> Hours: Open 7 days, 6:30–4 A.M.
> Credit: No credit cards
> Always very crowded, especially after the theater, the Carnegie is an institution, with sandwiches so big they hardly fit in your mouth. There is a big deli counter on one side, formica tables on the other and in the back, and the waiters are outrageously familiar. The Carnegie Deli is famous for its pastrami and corned beef, and for its rich cheesecake.

Kaplan's Deli
71 West 47th Street 10036 391-2333
> Hours: Mon–Fri 7–7, Sat 8–4
> Credit: American Express, Diners Club
> Another big New York deli, this one right in the middle of
> the diamond district. The menu includes appetizers, salads,
> bagels and lox, pastrami and deli sandwiches. Although both
> meat and dairy are served, there are separate slicing machines
> behind the counter near the front of the restaurant. The
> decor is old-world deli style, with wood banquettes and walls,
> and lots of stained-glass lamps. Kaplan's does party platters.

Lattanzi
361 West 46th Street 10036 315-0980
> Hours: Jewish menu after 8 P.M.
> Credit: American Express
> Although this is not strictly a Jewish restaurant, and makes no
> claims to being kosher, its devotion to "traditional Roman
> Jewish cooking" is so interesting that we are including it. If
> you want to try these Roman Jewish specialties, you must
> come after 8:00 P.M. and ask for the menu that includes
> "artichokes à la Judea" and other specialties that developed in
> the ghetto surrounding the fabulous synagogue in Rome. The
> owner grew up in that neighborhood and had such fond
> memories of these dishes that he decided to recreate them in
> New York. He flies to Rome several times a year to make sure
> that he is doing them right.

The New York Delicatessen
104 West 57th Street 10019 541-8320
> Hours: Open 7 days, 24 hours a day
> Credit: All major cards
> Located in the old Horn & Hardart on 57th Street (which has
> seen many tenants come and go in the past few years), this 500-
> seat deli has maintained many of the art deco fixtures and decor,
> while adding some of its own to create a Jewish restaurant with a
> different look. The large menu though remains New York deli,
> with corned beef, pastrami, chopped liver, blintzes, overstuffed
> sandwiches and platters. Its location seems to create a glut on the
> market—the area is already crammed with similar delis—but it is
> open around the clock and we're always glad to have another
> place to go at 4 A.M. There are private party rooms and they will
> do party platters.

Pastrami Factory
7 West 47th Street 10036 819-0202

Hours: Mon–Thurs 6–6, Sat 10–4
Credit: No credit cards
This large, noisy, quick-in-and-out deli has all the atmosphere of a honky-tonk boardwalk. The menu is mixed meat and dairy, but they seem to keep the pizza separated from the typical deli meats such as hot dogs and salamis. Pastrami Factory offers free delivery and seems to do a large outgoing business to offices in the area. They also do catering.

Stage Delicatessen
834 Seventh Avenue 10019 245-7850

Hours: Open 7 days, 8:30–2 A.M.
Credit: No credit cards
New York's most famous delicatessen has served the famous with unbelievably big pastrami, corned beef, and other deli sandwiches. Try one of their combination sandwiches. They also have very good, very rich desserts.

Wolf's Sixth Avenue Delicatessen
101 West 57th Street 10019 586-1110

Hours: Open 7 days, 6–2 A.M.
Credit: No credit cards
If only New York deli prices were what they once were—which, according to the replica of the original Wolf's displayed in the 57th Street window, was five cents for coffee with a free donut thrown in! This delicatessen has a prime location on the corner of Sixth Avenue and is jammed during lunch hour, particularly on matinee days. It has a big deli menu with sandwiches, omelets and salads.

UPPER EAST SIDE

Cornucopia Kosher Deli & Appetizers
1651 Second Avenue 10021 879-0733

Hours: Open 7 days, 10–10
Credit: No credit cards
This is a traditional-looking deli, with a large appetizer counter up front, hot dishes continuing toward the rear, and some tables along the side and in the back. The menu includes appetizer specialties, sandwiches, deli platters and salads. They do catering for up to 600 people, and will make platters for parties. On Sundays, Cornucopia will deliver a bagels-and-lox breakfast together with the Sunday *Times*.

Mama Leah's Restaurant and Blintzeria
1400 First Avenue 10021   570-2010
>   Hours: Open 7 days, 11–11
>   Credit: American Express, with $25 minimum
>   This very attractive restaurant fits right into its Upper East
>   Side location: clean walls, track lighting, small tables with
>   white tablecloths under glass tops. Don't let the decor fool you
>   though, Mama Leah's—which advertises "nonkosher Jewish-
>   American cuisine"—has everything your grandmother ever
>   made: lukschen, potato latkes, pirogen, chicken soup,
>   homemade chopped chicken liver, daily specials, and of
>   course, blintzes with a variety of fillings and toppings. There
>   are also salad platters, sandwiches, and a big dessert selection.
>   Brunch is served on Saturday and Sunday, and there is take-
>   out service and delivery in the neighborhood for a small
>   charge with a minimum order. Mama Leah's also does
>   catering.

UPPER WEST SIDE

Barney Greengrass
541 Amsterdam Avenue 10024   724-4707
>   Hours: Tues–Sat 8:30–5:45, Sun until 5
>   Credit: No credit cards
>   In the battle for who had the best smoked fish on the Upper
>   West Side, Barney Greengrass was definitely a top contender.
>   In addition to the fish and deli salads, there are cheese,
>   imported coffees and teas, and a pumpernickel raisin bread
>   that's addictive.

GROCERS AND TAKE-OUT PLACES

These are primarily take-out shops, although some may have
space to sit down for a quick bite. Remember that not all Jewish
delis are rabbinically supervised although many will indicate that
they use kosher products or separate meat and dairy. If they
have supervision, we've indicated that; others see themselves as
kosher-style and still others simply specialize in Jewish-style
food. Most places listed will make up platters, do some catering,
and offer delivery.

Bennett Grocery
4 Bennett Avenue 10033   923-7140
>   Hours: Mon–Thurs 7–6:30, Fri until 2, Sun 8–2
>   This grocery store carries a full line of kosher products
>   including items imported from Israel (smoked Israeli carp is

one). It also stocks "Start Fresh," a line of kosher diet dinners. Supervision is by K'hal Adath Jeshurun of Washington Heights. As the sign in the window says, they even have "school supplies with a Yiddishe taam."

Ben's Cheese
181 East Houston 10002 254-8290

Hours: Sun 7:30–6, Mon–Thurs 8:15–6, Fri until 2
Ben's carries both kosher and nonkosher cheeses, although the nonkosher cheese is sold in unopened packages. The homemade baked farmer and cream cheeses are supervised by the Orthodox Union. Credit cards are not accepted.

Leibel Bistritzky
27½ Essex Street 10002 254-0335

Hours: Sun–Thurs 9:30–6:30 (sometimes later), Fri until sundown
This shop carries kosher cheeses and sells cheese from the wheel. We've been told that at four o'clock every day, Mr. Bistritzky locks up the store, moves the women to one side, and davens mincha services. This is one of those places that, though carrying no supervision sign, clearly is recognized as strictly kosher.

Dairy Appetizing
510 Grand Street 10002 473-6161

Hours: Sun–Thurs 7–7, Fri until 4:30
This grocery store carries a full line of kosher products, including Miller's cheese, and offers free delivery. No credit cards are accepted.

Deli Glatt Sandwich Shop
150 Fulton Street 10038 349-3622

Supervision: Va'ad Harabonim of Flatbush, glatt
Hours: Mon–Thurs 7:30–6, Fri until 3
Credit: No credit cards
The traditional deli menu includes meat sandwiches, franks and hamburgers, parve sandwiches, kugels, eggplant cutlet and Middle Eastern specialties. There are also breakfast specials. Deli Glatt caters office parties in the area with platters and salads, and offers free delivery in the neighborhood with a minimum order.

G & M Kosher Caterers
41 Essex Street 10002 254-5370

Hours: Sun–Wed 9–6, Thurs 9–7:30, Fri 8–2
This tiny shop has homemade foods prepared on the premises to take out. Dishes are traditional meat favorites, and although the store is not formally supervised, everything is strictly

kosher, and everyone trusts that fact. No credit cards are accepted.

Guss Hollander Pickle Products
35 Essex Street 10002   254-4477

Hours: Sun–Thurs 9–5, Fri until sundown
To some people, a trip to the Lower East Side isn't complete without a stop here. On Sundays, there are lines waiting to get close to the fragrant barrels.

Jerusalem Falafel
1275 Lexington Avenue 10028   534-8541

Hours: Sun–Thurs 7–11, Fri until 3:30, Sat from sundown until 11
With Yonah Schimmel now on the Upper East Side (see below), can it be long before others follow? A few doors down—and sharing the same address—you can have Israeli Middle East specialties to go, including hummus, falafel, tabouleh, health salad, and cheese or spinach borkas as well as pizpuffs. You can have cream cheese or salads on pita or bagel, and french fries and homemade soups. For breakfast you can get a plain omelet or scrambled eggs on pita. Jerusalem Falafel offers free delivery for a minimum order and will do catering. The shop is supervised by the Midtown Board of Kashruth.

Kedem Winery
107 Norfolk Street 10002   673-2780

Hours: Mon–Thurs 9–5:30, Fri until 2:30, Sun 10–5
Just like Heinz, Kedem has forty-seven kinds. There are wines from Austria, Italy and Israel. The store is supervised by the Orthodox Union and Rabbi Weinberger of the Mt. Kisco Yeshiva. Credit cards are not accepted.

Meal Mart
2189 Broadway   787-4720

Hours: Mon–Wed 10:30–7, Thurs 10–8, Fri 8–2, Sun 10–7

4403 Broadway   568-7401

Hours: Sun–Wed 10–6, Thurs until 7:30, Fri until 2 hours before sundown
In addition to its big catering business based in Brooklyn, Meal Mart has two stores in Manhattan that sell prepared foods. You can get brisket and p'cha, casseroles and salads. Platters can be ordered for any occasion. There is also a full line of baked goods, many of them from Boro Park, Williamsburg, and Gruenebaum's bakery, including water challah. Meal Mart carries a large variety of kosher products and prepared foods, and also stocks "Start Fresh," a line of

kosher diet dinners. Supervision is provided by the Midtown Board of Kashruth. All meat is glatt. No credit cards are accepted.

Miller's Kosher Cheese

13 Essex Street 10002 475-3337

Hours: Mon–Thurs 9–5:30, Fri until 1:30, Sun until 6

2192 Broadway 10023 496-8855

Hours: Sun 8:30–7, Mon–Wed until 8, Thurs until 9, Fri until 2

Miller, which opened for business in New York City in 1898, carries a variety of kosher cheeses including brie and camembert (for what they perceive as the "kosher hip market"), yogurt cheeses, and low-salt and low-fat cheese. There is homemade farmer cheese, baked farmer cheese with vegetables and a variety of fruit flavors, and fresh pot cheese. Miller's also has a selection of baked goods, including bagels, challah and cakes. They do catering and their Lower East Side store will also host a wine and cheese-tasting party for charity groups.

Murray's Sturgeon Shop

2429 Broadway 10024 724-2650

Hours: Sun & Tues–Fri 8–7, Sat until 8

A tiny shop but heaven couldn't have such nice sturgeon, whitefish, sable and lox. Everything for brunch including specialty cheeses, and the window is full of beautiful dried fruit. No credit cards are accepted.

Russ & Daughters

179 East Houston 10002 475-4880

Hours: Tues–Thurs 9–6:45, Fri–Sun 8–6:45

On one side of this appetizing store you will see all kinds of smoked fish, salads, deli items and breads, and on the other cases of dried fruits and nuts. There are many other gourmet items like imported mushrooms and oils. No credit cards are accepted.

Schapiro's Wine Co.

126 Rivington Street 10002 674-4404

Hours: Sun–Thurs 10–5, Fri until 3

The retail store sells fruit and concord wines as well as chablis, burgundy, rosé and kosher imported wine from France and Italy. Schapiro's operates free tours every Sunday 11–4 (every hour on the hour), to see the winery, have a tasting, and hear how the history of the winery (which was established in 1899) relates to the history of the Lower East Side. It is supervised by the Orthodox Union.

Streit Matzo Company
150 Rivington 10002   475-7000

> Hours: Sun–Thurs 8:30–5

Underground Kosher Gourmet
1196 Sixth Avenue 10036   391-8729

> Hours: Mon–Thurs 7–5:30, Fri until 12:30
> Owned by the same people who own Edible Pursuits, this shop offers sandwiches and deli items. They also sell packaged milk and cheese products, but will not prepare take-out food with them. They carry a big selection of baked goods and sell challah on Fridays. No credit cards are accepted.

Yonah Schimmel
1275 Lexington Avenue 10028   722-4049

> Hours: Mon–Thurs 6:30–8, Sat 7–7, Sun 9–6
> Now you can have the same heartburn without making a trip downtown. The most famous knishes in New York are currently available on the Upper East Side, right near 86th Street—potato, cabbage, kasha and cheese knishes. Something's different though: the help are young uptown types and the small shop with a stand-up snack bar also sells croissants, muffins and espresso.

Zabar's
2245 Broadway 10024   787-2000

> Hours: Mon–Thurs 8–7:30, Fri until 10,
> Sat until midnight, Sun 9–7:30
> You may wonder why we include a store that does as much business in fancy Italian sausages and prosciutto as it does in smoked fish and herring salad. Zabar's is undoubtedly the king of all gourmet shops in Manhattan (not to mention the entire metropolitan area) and such a large proportion of its customers are Jewish that to many secular Jews it has always represented *the* place to buy deli food. Their appetizers counter carries several varieties of herring and smoked salmon, sable and other kinds of fish, as well as an assortment of creamed cheeses and salads. All this and now they've added a knish bar in the back. They also sell bagels and challah. They accept American Express, Mastercard and Visa.

CATERERS

Whether it's a wedding or a bris, you will be concerned about having the right caterer. Many of the restaurants and delis we have listed will make up platters for a small affair, but if you are interested in an entire meal, or hot dishes, you will want to call a full-service caterer. If you are getting married in a synagogue, or planning a Bar or Bat Mitzvah, the synagogue will probably provide you with a list of recommended or required (to comply with the synagogue's *kashrut* policy) caterers. If your affair is at home, here is a list of Manhattan kosher caterers. Be sure to ask them about their requirements for a kitchen—many will bring their own ovens and cooking utensils and others will be unwilling to do any preparation in a nonkosher kitchen. Remember that there are many other kosher caterers in the New York area, and many will be happy to come into Manhattan.

K & C Caterers, Inc. (Karmazin Caterers) 362-0412

Supervision: Midtown Board of Rabbis
Michelle Karmazin is the director of food services at Ramaz High School, and the catering business she runs with her husband does a big business in both meat and dairy (they have done catering in many hotels). Menus are tailored to customers' needs—most of their dairy menus are nouvelle cuisine—and they are used to handling full meals for about 450, although they will cater for up to 800. They have also catered cocktail parties for 1200. They provide full service, including waiters, dishes and linens, and will recommend florists, photographers and bands.

Kay Caterers

200 Amsterdam Avenue 10023   362-5555

Supervision: K'hal Adath Jeshurun of Washington Heights, glatt
Kay Caterers, which is the exclusive caterer for Lincoln Square Synagogue, will do off-premises catering as well, and they have done catering in all the leading clubs and hotels in Manhattan. They offer a large menu of both meat and dairy, and usually cater for between 100 and 400 at Lincoln Square. They will handle up to 1800 off premises. Their service includes dishes and linens, and they will recommend florists and bands.

Manna Catering

189 Franklin Street 10013   966-3449

Supervision: available
Joni Greenspan and Dan Lenchner, who specialize in nouvelle kosher cuisine, design menus for all kinds of events, based on clients' needs, and they have done catering for up to 500. Menus are primarily dairy but they will also do meat, and they provide the food, service and dishes. Manna follows the Conservative movement's standards for *kashrut,* but will also call in a supervision service at a customer's request. They can also provide the flowers and will give referrals for other arrangements including location, photographer and music.

Mr. Omelette
505-5520

Supervision: Va'ad Harabonim of Long Island
Although its address is on Long Island, Mr. Omelette has a
New York phone number because it does so much business in
Manhattan. The dairy menu features a variety of omelets,
salmon mousse, pasta salad, vegetable strudel, falafel, blintzes
and smoked fish platters, as well as many breads and desserts.
There are several Mr. Omelette party menus from which to
choose or you may embellish on any of them. Mr. Omelette
provides china and linen as well as waiters and waitresses, will
put together preprinted items like *keepot* and matches, and will
recommend florists, photographers and bands. They prepare
the food on their own premises but will travel anywhere, and
have catered meals in synagogues, lofts and even on yachts.

Newman & Leventhal
45 West 81st Street 10024 362-9400

Supervision: Rabbi Isaac Morgenstern, glatt
Newman & Leventhal serves both dairy and meat, and will
devise individual menus to suit their clients' tastes. They also
provide waiters, dishes and linens, and will recommend florists
and bands. They do most of their catering at Park East
Synagogue (where dinner for about 250 is most comfortable)
but they will serve as many people as can be accommodated in
a facility. They will cater in major hotels that are prepared for
a kosher caterer, but they prefer not to go to private homes.

Papilsky
305 West End Avenue 10023 724-3761

Supervision: Orthodox Union, glatt
Papilsky has been catering major affairs at hotels and
synagogues for years. They have no minimum number of
people and have catered for as many as 2400. They prepare
both meat and dairy menus, provide waiters, dishes and
linens, and will recommend florists and bands. They will go
almost anywhere.

Somerstein Caterers
936-7110

Supervision: available
Stuart Somerstein gets to be in this book because, although his
restaurant is in Queens (and not kosher), he's got the best
view of Manhattan we've ever seen! Actually, you can arrange
a kosher party at his facility in Long Island City, but
Somerstein also does the kosher catering for the Water Club
and will come to other Manhattan locations as well. He serves
both meat and dairy, and supervision is provided by Rav
Gulofsky.

Chapter 11
HOW WE HELP EACH OTHER

"All Israel is responsible one for the other." Such a motto has been the starting point for a network of Jewish social service agencies, projects and programs that have gone far beyond anything anyone could have imagined in the latter part of the nineteenth century, when this network was born. Then it was German Jews, well established on these shores, helping newer, Eastern European Jews get settled. Today, the "new" Jews might be from Russia or Iran or maybe Israel. They might not even be Jews at all, but immigrants from Cuba, Puerto Rico or Haiti. And it isn't only immigrants that the Jewish community reaches, but all people with need, be it illness, loneliness or poverty, family stress, legal trouble or job difficulties.

Some of the programs we describe are run by or funded through large agencies, while others are run by synagogues or ad hoc committees. In all cases the programs are subject to change, depending on the needs of the community and the availability of funds. For more information about social service agencies run by the Jewish community, a good resource is the **Jewish Information and Referral Service (753-2288).** This is a department of UJA–Federation of Jewish Philanthropies of Greater New York, and is staffed by trained volunteers who are eager to answer your questions (they answered plenty of ours!).

While we're talking about UJA–Federation, we should point out that approximately 130 agencies receive funding from them, either as beneficiary agencies (whose prime or only source of funds is the Jewish community) or as subventions. We've tried to indicate which programs and projects are supported by UJA–Federation.

THE ILL

Jewish hospitals began primarily as a response to the anti-Semitic exclusion of Jewish physicians from many existing hospitals. While today that is of course no longer the case, the UJA–Federation still provides support to these Manhattan hospitals.

Beth Israel Medical Center
10 Nathan D. Perlman Place 10003   420-2000

> This is a full-service hospital which, in addition to its other programs and facilities, has a Tay-Sachs clinic. Everyone, even non-Jews, eats kosher food here; the hospital follows dietary laws.

Hospital for Joint Diseases–Orthopedic Institute
301 East 17th Street 10003   598-6000

Mount Sinai Hospital   Fifth Avenue and 100th Street 10029   650-6500

> Mount Sinai is a full-service hospital which services the Jewish community particularly through its Tay-Sachs Center and its comprehensive clinic for Goucher's disease, another, rarer, genetic disease afflicting Eastern European Jews in disproportionate numbers. Kosher food is available on request. Another hospital program targeted to servicing Jews suffering from a rare genetic disease is at New York University Hospital. The Dysautonomia Clinic (340-7225) provides diagnostic and treatment services for those afflicted with this disease. For more information about this program, as well as other agencies that deal with Jewish genetic diseases, see Chapter 1, and later in this chapter under Children in Need.

It is a mitzvah, a Jewish obligation, to visit the sick. Though in the United States this service is normally performed by the clergy, Jewish tradition relegates no special responsibility to rabbis in this regard; every Jew should visit those who are ill, even if they are strangers. *Bikur cholim* (Illness Visitation) groups exist in many Manhattan synagogues; they make visitations on request and on a regular basis at hospitals and homes in their communities. Groups that visit elderly Jews who are sick are listed in our section on the Elderly in Need.

The Task Force on *Bikur Cholim* is a joint venture of the Commission on Synagogue Relations of UJA–Federation and the New York Board of Rabbis. Rabbinic visitations are coordinated in virtually all of Manhattan's hospitals, both public and private, as you can see by the list that follows. Should you or someone you know desire a visit by a rabbi in one of the hospitals listed below, ask at the hospital, or call the New York Board of Rabbis (879-8415).

Bellevue Hospital
Beth Israel Medical Center
Cabrini Medical Center
Coler Memorial Hospital
Columbia–Presbyterian Hospital
Doctors Hospital
Goldwater Memorial Hospital
Gouvernor Hospital
Gracie Square Hospital
Hospital for Joint Diseases–Orthopedic Institute
Hospital for Special Surgery
Lenox Hill Hospital
Manhattan Eye and Ear Hospital
Manhattan State Hospital
Medical Arts Center
Memorial Sloan Kettering
Mount Sinai Hospital
New York Hospital
New York Infirmary–Beekman Downtown
New York Psychiatric Institute
New York University Hospital
Roosevelt Hospital
St. Clare's Hospital–Health Center
St. Luke's Hospital
Veteran's Administration Hospital

OTHER PROGRAMS

Congregation Beth Simchat Torah
57 Bethune Street 10014 929-9498

The gay and lesbian synagogue has a group who make visitations to AIDS victims, and offers a referral service involving several area rabbis who visit and counsel AIDS patients.

ARC, AIDS Resource Center
235 West 18th Street 10011 206-1414

This is a nonsectarian group that provides a list of rabbis who do spiritual counseling for AIDS patients.

E.A.R.S. Educational Alliance
197 East Broadway 10002 475-6200

This is an emergency alarm system, which the homebound ill individual can activate in an emergency. A responder is then sent to help.

Community Homemaker Service
235 Park Avenue South 10003 460-0900

A division of the Jewish Board of Family and Children's Services, they provide homemakers for those who are ill or unable to function. The service is free when the situation warrants it. All homemakers have received training in "kosher awareness."

Satmar Bus (718) 387-0546

This Brooklyn Hassidic sect operates a free bus between Brooklyn and Manhattan's East Side hospitals for people who wish to make visits.

THE PHYSICALLY OR DEVELOPMENTALLY DISABLED

Adults with physical or developmental disabilities are aided by the organizations listed below.

PHYSICALLY DISABLED ADULTS

Altro Health and Rehabilitation Service
40 East 30th Street 10016 684-0600

This UJA–Federation supported agency provides various medical, psychological, social and vocational help to disabled adults. The Day Care Program services those who are not yet prepared for work or training.

Federation Employment and Guidance Service
510 Sixth Avenue 10011 741-7424

At the Diagnostic Vocational Evaluation Center, physically (as well as emotionally and developmentally) disabled adults are assessed in order to determine vocational skills and aptitudes for potential training or workshops.

The Jewish Braille Institute of America, Inc.
110 East 30th Street 10016 889-2525

The Jewish Braille Institute maintains a lending library containing books in braille, large-print volumes, and sound recordings and tapes, many in Hebrew and Yiddish as well as English. The elderly blind and visually handicapped are provided special services. Many prayerbooks have been published in braille and are available here along with braille periodicals. Counseling is provided for college and graduate school admission, as well as to those interested in pursuing careers in the Jewish community as rabbis, cantors and other professionals. This agency, with the Brotherhood Synagogue and Central Synagogue, also cosponsors three cultural programs a year for the elderly blind.

The Jewish Guild for the Blind
15 West 65th Street 10023 595-2000

The Jewish Guild for the Blind offers vocational training and job placement, special education and school programs, Adult Day Care, a library, residential services for elderly and developmentally-disabled visually-impaired people, and a wide range of social, mental health and community outreach programs. Services in Manhattan include *Rehabilitation Services,* where visually-impaired and blind persons can acquire the necessary skills to lead more productive lives. Vocational assessment, counseling, special physical education, teaching communications skills and placement services are all part of the work done in this part of the Guild. *Mental Health Service* provides outpatient diagnosis and evaluation, crisis intervention, psychiatric social work, testing and behavior modification for the visually-impaired or blind person who requires additional help. The Guild's *Day Treatment Program* offers a wide range of services to the psychiatrically-impaired, multidisabled individual, including physical education, art therapies and psychotherapy. The elderly blind and visually impaired often have special needs, and are serviced through *Group Work Services.* Hand skills, adult education and discussion groups, special programs and a summer program are all designed especially for the elderly blind and visually-impaired. Joselow House (46 West 74th Street) is the Guild's community residence in Manhattan for visually-impaired and blind adults with developmental disabilities. For special programs for children, see our section on Children in Need.

Mentor International Travel for the Handicapped
1 East 57th Street 10022   753-8393

This Israeli-staffed agency specializes in helping physically-disabled Israel-bound travelers choose hotels, tours and activities that will make travel easier for them.

National Council of Jewish Women
15 East 26th Street 10010   532-1740

NCJW's Jackson–Stricks Scholarship Fund helps goal-oriented handicapped people to earn a degree or develop marketable skills to improve the quality of their lives.

New York Society for the Deaf
344 East 14th Street 10003   673-6500 (673-6974 TTY)

Located on the 4th floor of the Emanu-El Midtown Y, the New York Society for the Deaf is an agency of UJA–Federation. Service is provided here to the profoundly deaf through sign language programs, information and referral, job placement and counseling. The society's housing project, Tanya Towers, 612 East 13th Street, has 137 units for deaf, elderly and handicapped adults. In conjunction with the Hebrew Association of the Deaf, a fraternal organization open to deaf Jews, the Society sponsors a number of religious and cultural events. Monthly Shabbat services are held right in the agency. Services are signed and there are cue cards that make it easier to follow the prayers and watch the rabbi at the same time. There are creative ways of celebrating Jewish holidays to make them meaningful for the deaf, such as a special time during the High Holidays when everyone has an opportunity to touch the shofar to feel the vibrations, or popping balloons representing Haman instead of shaking greggers. The society has a part-time rabbi who is also available to do weddings and funerals for deaf Jews.

Vocational Rehabilitation Workshops (FEGS)
62 West 14th Street 10011   741-7581

Physically disabled adults can participate in sheltered workshops here. Vocational training is provided as well.

DEVELOPMENTALLY DISABLED ADULTS

The Brotherhood Synagogue
23 Gramercy Park South   674-5750

This Conservative synagogue runs Sunday school classes and lunch each week for retarded adults.

Federation Employment and Guidance Service
510 Sixth Avenue 10011   741-7709

The center for vocational training in the Jewish community for the young and the old, the developmentally disabled, the immigrant and the homeless, FEGS has several programs specifically geared to the retarded or developmentally disabled adult who can benefit from vocational counseling. Although its residential facilities are all in the Bronx (for more information on them, call 741-7956), there are day programs in Manhattan. The *Developmental Day Treatment Program* assesses and treats individuals who are mentally retarded or developmentally disabled, in order to help them become ready for training programs or jobs. The focus here is on personal and self-care skills, socialization and activities of daily living. The *Diagnostic Vocational Evaluation* provides assessment to determine vocational possibilities for mentally-retarded adults. Through this program, recommendations are made concerning programs, workshops, and vocational training. Through the *Skills Training Program,* clients learn how to repair and rebuild automobiles, air-conditioning units, refrigeration and heating units, jewelry and typewriters. FEGS also provides clerical training at the Manhattan Business School, 114 Fifth Avenue (741-6245). At the Manhattan Center of Vocational Rehabilitation Workshops, 62 West 14th Street (741-7581), FEGS operates a sheltered workshop that services developmentally-disabled adults. The *Day Programs* (741-7139) are full-time day treatment centers for long-term psychiatric patients.

The Jewish Heritage Program   Board of Jewish
Education at the Educational Alliance
197 East Broadway   10002   255-6472

The goal of this BJE program, funded through a UJA–Federation grant, is to provide a supportive atmosphere for retarded adolescents and adults to learn about Jewish tradition and to develop a positive Jewish identity.

Adult Vacation Program
Cummings Campgrounds Brewster, N.Y.
Educational Alliance
197 East Broadway   10002   475-6061

The Adult Vacation Program provides a two-week vacation for retarded adults who are currently employed or in workshops. There is a full range of activities, with counselor supervision in the cabins. Dietary laws are observed.

THE POOR

Perhaps one of the most important acts that a Jew performs in her or his lifetime is to care for the needy. In Jewish tradition, such acts are not what we call charity in English, but rather *tzedaka*—"righteous behavior." For the Jew, providing help for those in need is not a voluntary act, but rather a moral obligation, an integral part of life. Below is a list of Jewish agencies and programs that serve poor people in Manhattan.

Metropolitan New York Coordinating Council on Jewish Poverty 9 Murray Street 267-9500

This umbrella group is the Jewish community's primary agency for identifying and responding to the needs of urban Jewish neighborhoods. Through the network of local Jewish Community Councils (which it funds), MNYCCJP develops city-wide and community programs for Jewish poor. It tries where possible to stabilize Jewish neighborhoods, provides linkages between the Jewish poor and government agencies, and does research for the Jewish community on issues relating to the needs of the Jewish poor. Specific programs that the Coordinating Council is involved with include emergency shelters for the homeless, emergency food, entitlement advocacy, housing improvement, health-related services, and protective services for adults.

AID TO THE HOMELESS

A few years ago, Mayor Ed Koch publically chastised (as only he can do) the Jewish community for failing to respond to the needs of homeless men and women in New York City. Although some agencies and institutions had been responding for a long time, others took notice, and today there are several synagogues, agencies and other community resources that provide shelter for the homeless and those in need of temporary low-cost housing.

Federation Joint Services of the Lower East Side
197 East Broadway 10002 475-6200

This agency reaches out to the poor with counseling, crisis intervention, information and referral, vocational guidance and placement.

Great Northern–Regent Children's Center
JBFCS 2720 Broadway 10025 662-1591

The Jewish Board of Family and Children's Services uses this Upper West Side facility to provide temporary shelter and relocation for those who are the victims of disasters such as fire.

Homeless Project of the Jewish Board of Family and Children's Services
235 Park Avenue South 10003   460-0900

This umbrella agency for families and children in need provides temporary shelter, food, job retraining and counseling for the homeless.

Project Contact   Educational Alliance
197 East Broadway 10002   533-3570

This extension service of the Lower East Side Y provides aid to homeless teenagers, runaways, school drop-outs and drug abusers.

Respite House   Serovich Senior Center
331 East 12th Street 10002   505-0722

Respite House is a community service provided by the Educational Alliance. It is a temporary shelter for senior adults in crisis as a result of crime in their home, fire, eviction, domestic violence or building abandonment.

United Jewish Council of the East Side
235 East Broadway 10002   233-6037

Among the many services of this agency is to help families who must relocate.

The following synagogues currently provide temporary shelter to the homeless. More may already exist; for further information, call the Partnership for the Homeless, an interfaith organization, 208 West 13th Street, 807-6653, which has a list of churches and synagogues that have opened their doors to the homeless.

The Brotherhood Synagogue
28 Gramercy Park South 10010   674-5750

Congregation Ansche Chesed
251 West 100th Street 10025   865-0600

Congregation B'nai Jeshurun
257 West 88th Street 10024   787-7600

Congregation Rodeph Sholom
7 West 83rd Street 10024   362-8800

Congregation Shearith Israel
8 West 70th Street 10023   873-0300

Stephen Wise Free Synagogue
30 West 68th Street 10023   877-4050

FINANCIAL HELP

Agudath Israel of America
5 Beekman Street 10038 791-1800

This large Orthodox agency makes interest-free loans to those in need through its Benevolent Fund.

The Blue Card, Inc. 2121 Broadway 10023 873-7400

This group provides financial aid to victims of the Holocaust and their children when no other help is available. They help sort out entitlement programs.

Federation Joint Services Educational Alliance
197 East Broadway 10002 475-6200

The Hebrew Free Loan Society has an extension service here which gives interest-free loans up to $750, with the endorsement of responsible people. The elderly poor can borrow up to $100 without a cosigner.

Gemiluth Chessed of Greater New York, Inc.
P.O. Box 178 10033 923-8701

This small, independent organization provides financial aid for people in need of medical assistance or who have other emergencies. Annual dues that support the work of the group are $10.

Hebrew Free Burial Association
1170 Broadway 10001 686-2433

Free Orthodox burials are provided by this association.

Hebrew Free Loan Society
205 East 42nd Street 10017 687-0188

For almost a century, this Jewish agency has been providing interest-free loans throughout Greater New York. There is a minimum of red tape here and a maximum of respect for the person in need. The society gives the borrower ten months to repay the loan, which is normally granted within a few days of the request (sooner, if necessary). Through a subvention from the Federation of Jewish Philanthropies, the society also provides free loans to yeshivot and day schools. Under this program, the society also provides interest-free loans to be used toward down-payment costs on the purchase of homes or apartments in selected neighborhoods.

Joint Passover Association of the City of New York
235 Park Avenue South 10003 460-0900

Through a grant from UJA–Federation, the Joint Passover Association provides cash stipends for needy Jews to help them celebrate Passover. There are application sites around the city, staffed by trained volunteers under the auspices of the Jewish Board of Family and Children's Services.

Self Help Community Center
300 Park Avenue South 10003   533-7100

Holocaust survivors have special needs, and Self Help Community Services tries to meet them through a variety of programs, including financial aid. Money is distributed through local service agencies for survivors, and help with various government financial aid programs is provided.

LEGAL AID

Agudath Israel of America
5 Beekman Street 10038   964-1620

Orthodox Jews in need of advocacy with governmental and legislative groups get help here.

Cardozo Bet Tzedek Legal Services
Yeshiva University, Benjamin Cardozo School of Law
55 Fifth Avenue 10012   790-0200

Law school students at Cardozo help people in need of legal assistance, through this program funded by UJA–Federation and operated through Yeshiva University.

Colpa   450 Seventh Avenue 10001   563-0100

The National Jewish Commission on Law and Public Affairs is a volunteer group comprised of attorneys who handle issues concerning religious discrimination. These lawyers advocate for many who are powerless, such as those in prisons, hospitals and nursing homes.

Court Liaison and Referral Service
Jewish Board of Family and Children's Services
235 Park Avenue South 10003   460-0900

JBFCS has a trained volunteer at New York Family Court, 60 Lafayette Street, who aids in all aspects of court-related problems with children and families.

Family Location and Legal Services
Jewish Board of Family and Children's Services
235 Park Avenue South 10003   460-0900

JBFCS offers legal assistance involving family and civil matters to those who are unable to afford private counsel.

United Jewish Council of the East Side
235 East Broadway 10002   233-6037

Once a week an attorney comes to this center in order to help people who can't afford legal services.

FOOD AND CLOTHING

B'nai B'rith District No. 1
823 United Nations Plaza 10017 490-2525

Through their lodges, the regional chapter of B'nai B'rith does large-scale food distribution to the needy before the holidays.

Metropolitan New York Coordination Council on Jewish Poverty 9 Murray Street 10007 267-9500

This group serves as the clearinghouse for distribution of surplus food. It also provides emergency food for those in need.

National Council of Jewish Women
15 East 26th Street 10010 532-1740

Both through the facilities of the Katharine Engel Center, and through the New York chapter, the Council participates in soup kitchens to assist the growing numbers of hungry people in New York.

United Jewish Council of the East Side, Inc.
235 East Broadway 10002 233-6037

At Passover and Hanukkah, the council distributes food to the needy. It also distributes surplus food when it comes in. Drives are conducted to collect clothing for those in need.
Headstones for proper burial are provided for those who can't afford to buy them.

JOB TRAINING

Diagnostic Vocations Evaluation
Federation Employment and Guidance Service
510 Sixth Avenue 10009 741-7709

FEGS offers assessments for poor people who need help with vocational planning. Through this program, recommendations are made for workshops, vocational training or other appropriate programs. The agency also provides vocational training to economically disadvantaged individuals, mostly in the repair of automobiles, jewelry, air conditioning and typewriters.

CHILDREN IN NEED

Children with special needs are a particular concern of the Jewish community, through its religious, educational and social service agencies. The physically and mentally-impaired child, the abandoned or learning-disabled child, the poor or abused child, each one needs more than any one parent or family can often provide. And with the new-found sense of pride among disabled adults and their advocates, there are increasingly more programs and services for the disabled child as well. Before we delineate some of those services, we should point out that there are two main agencies, both within the UJA–Federation of Jewish Philanthropies orbit, that are good general resources for parents with disabled children. The Jewish Board of Family and Children's Services, 120 West 57th Street (582-9100), helps disturbed, disabled, disadvantaged and abused children through its more than sixty different mental health and social services programs, on both a residential and outpatient basis. The Jewish Child Care Association, 575 Lexington Avenue (371-1313), maintains residential treatment centers, community-based placement services, and day and preventive mental health services. As with all UJA–Federation constituent agencies, these serve not only the Jewish community, but the community at large. Several other organizations—religious, educational and social service—provide help to children in need. For a complete listing of educational programs for Jewish children with special needs, call Rabbi Martin Schloss, Director of Special Education Center of the Board of Jewish Education, 426 West 58th Street (245-8200). Although our list below is according to specific category of help, if you or someone you know has a disabled child, read through the whole chapter. There is some overlap in the various agencies, as there is in the categories of disability.

PHYSICALLY-DISABLED CHILDREN

Dysautonomia Treatment and Evaluation Center
New York University Medical Center
530 First Avenue 10016   340-7225

> Dysautonomia (Riley-Day Syndrome) is a rare hereditary disease afflicting Ashkenazic Jews. It is a malfunction of the autonomic nervous system, which affects processes such as heart rate, digestive system and reflexes. Although there is no genetic screening or prenatal test yet available, the Dysautonomia Foundation, 370 Lexington Avenue (889-5222), maintains and supports a treatment and evaluation center at

New York University Medical Center. The center maintains a 24-hour answering service (340-7225), and sees patients and their families.

Educational Alliance   197 East Broadway   475-6200

There is a Head Start program for physically disabled three and four-year olds. It meets five days a week, 8:15–11:15 A.M. or 12:45–3:45 P.M.

Jewish Braille Institute of America, Inc.

110 East 30th Street 10016   889-2525

This agency, dedicated to providing a way for blind and partially-sighted individuals to participate fully in Jewish life, offers a number of children's services. It provides a complete Jewish education for blind and partially-sighted children in neighborhood synagogues, side by side with sighted children. Bar and Bat Mitzvah preparation is aided by the use of special materials in braille or large type. The agency has children's prayerbooks in braille as well as all textbooks necessary for a Jewish education. Finally, the agency consults with rabbis and Jewish educators to mainstream visually-impaired children with those who are sighted.

The Jewish Guild for the Blind

15 West 65th Street 10023   595-2000

This is a nonsectarian agency that, among other activities, operates under a contract with the New York City Board of Education to provide education for the visually impaired, blind, and deaf-blind children ages five to twenty-one, who are also developmentally, psychiatrically, orthopedically or otherwise disabled.

Mitzvah Corps   New York Federation of Reform Congregations   838 Fifth Avenue 10021   249-0100

Mitzvah Corps runs a unique Jewish summer camp for hearing Jewish youth and deaf Jewish youth, where each group learns from the other. It's designed for children fourteen to seventeen.

92nd Street YM–YWHA

1395 Lexington Avenue 10028   427-6000

The 92nd Street Y has a Sunday Recreational Program for Children who are orthopedically disabled. These kids, ages six to sixteen, participate in a variety of organized activities, including adapted sports, games, cooking, and arts and crafts.

Camp Oakhurst Oakhurst, N.J.
New York Service for the Handicapped
853 Broadway 10003 533-4020

> This summer camp for the physically disabled has activities
> adapted to meet the needs of these one hundred or so boys
> and girls from six to seventeen. There are three two-week
> sessions, with a double-session option.

Our Way National Conference of Synagogue Youth
45 West 36th Street 10018 563-4000

> Our Way is an outreach group for deaf Jewish youth,
> sponsored by the Union of Orthodox Jewish Congregations.

LEARNING-DISABLED CHILDREN

Board of Jewish Education of Greater New York
426 West 58th Street 10019 245-8200

> If your learning-disabled child is currently attending a Yeshiva
> or day school (or has recently graduated) and is between the
> ages of sixteen and twenty-five, the BJE can help provide
> vocational training and evaluation.

Jewish Braille Institute
110 East 30th Street 10016 889-2525

> Children with major reading problems are assisted by this
> agency, which provides Judaic textbooks and recreational
> material on sound cassettes for study and enjoyment.

Jewish Board of Family and Children's Services
120 West 57th Street 10019 582-9100

> JBFCS provides, through its Educational Therapy Services,
> help for learning-disabled children and adults who are already
> in treatment at the agency for other problems.

Mogen Avraham Learning Disabilities Program
Swan Lake, N.Y. 114 Fifth Avenue 10003 691-5548

> Mogen Avraham, which is a camp for Orthodox boys, has a
> separate learning-disabilities program within an otherwise
> integrated camp setting.

92nd Street YM—YWHA
1395 Lexington Avenue 10028 427-6000

> The Y runs an after-school program for children six to
> thirteen who are minimally learning disabled. Classes include
> scouting, sports, modern dance and a TV/Drama Workshop.
> There is also a teen program for children thirteen to
> eighteen, with volunteer activities and a Sunday Social Club.

Camp Tova   92nd Street YM—YWHA
1395 Lexington Avenue 10028   427-6000

Camp Tova is a day camp for children and teens with minimal learning disabilities. Most of the week they spend at the Henry Kaufman Campgrounds, in Pearl River, N.Y. (to which they are bused), while Fridays are spent at the Y and around the city.

Two Together   Jewish Child Care Association
345 Madison Avenue 10017   490-9160, ext. 137

Two Together is a remedial-reading program that provides one-to-one tutoring for children with reading problems. Under the guidance of a specialist, volunteers work with school-age children referred by schools, courts, hospitals and social agencies.

The following Manhattan day schools provide special classes or programs for learning-disabled children. For more information about each school, see Chapter 1.

Manhattan Day School
310 West 75th Street 10023   595-6800

Ramaz
125 East 85th Street 10028   427-1000

Tonya Soloveitchik–Yeshiva University High School for Girls
425 Fifth Avenue 10016   340-7800

Marsha Stern Talmudical Academy–Yeshiva University High School for Boys
2540 Amsterdam Avenue 10033   960-5337

Yeshiva Rabbi Samson Raphael Hirsch
85–91 Bennett Avenue 10033   568-6200

Rodeph Sholom Day School
10 West 84th Street 10024   362-8769

DEVELOPMENTALLY-DISABLED CHILDREN

Jewish Board of Family and Children's Services
Mental Health Consultation
120 West 57th Street 10019   582-9100

JBFCS provides on-site consultation services to nursery and day schools with developmentally-disabled and emotionally-disturbed children.

Educational Alliance
197 East Broadway 10002   475-6200

The Educational Alliance runs several summer programs in Brewster, N.Y. Sparc is designed to aid in the socialization of retarded kids, ages eight to sixteen, and runs for one or two months. Loeb provides a full summer prevocational experience for young adults, ages fifteen to twenty-five. Back to Nature, also for young adults, emphasizes outdoor activities and farm-animal care, and, finally, A.I.M. provides a full summer program for autistic teenagers. All programs are kosher and serve the greater New York Jewish community. There is also a winter program on Sundays and after school, which focuses on self-care and social development.

Jewish Child Care Association
345 Madison Avenue 10017   490-9160

JCCA places severely-retarded children, ages sixteen to twenty-one, in community-based residences and group homes. All the facilities are outside Manhattan, but you can call the JCCA headquarters for more information.

The Jewish Heritage Program   Board of Jewish Education at the Educational Alliance
197 East Broadway 10002   255-6472

This program is designed to give retarded adolescents and adults a supportive atmosphere in which to develop a positive self-worth and Jewish identity. Weekly classes are held on Sundays at the Educational Alliance.

92nd Street YM–YWHA
1395 Lexington Avenue 10028   427-6000

The Y has a program of Jewish education, leading to Bar and Bat Mitzvah, for retarded children.

The Tikvah Program
Camp Ramah   3080 Broadway 10027   749-0754

Held each summer at Camp Ramah in Palmer, Mass., this program provides summer camping for children who are neurologically impaired, mentally retarded or emotionally handicapped. The eight-week program is for children between the ages of twelve and seventeen, and there is a two-week trip to Israel during the Hanukkah vacation.

Yachad   National Conference of Synagogue Youth
45 West 36th Street 10018   563-4000

This national Orthodox youth agency holds weekend retreats, holiday celebrations, and publishes a newsletter for developmentally-disabled teenagers. Yachad also has a special summer trip to Israel, where Yachad kids join other NCSYers on a tour and study program.

CHILDREN WITH EMOTIONAL OR
BEHAVIORAL PROBLEMS

Jewish Board of Family and Children's Services
120 West 57th Street   10019   582-6300

JBFCS provides services for emotionally-disturbed children (as well as families and individuals in need) throughout the Greater New York region. In Manhattan, there are several programs, some at the above address and others located around the borough. Below is a list of Manhattan programs.

Child Development Center
120 West 57th Street   10019   582-9100

The Child Development Center offers outpatient and therapeutic nursery services for children with behavioral, emotional and developmental problems or organic conditions, from infancy through six years of age. There is a clinic that does diagnostic assessment, and a nursery program for children ages three to six. The CDC also consults in nursery schools and day care centers throughout Manhattan.

Court Services
235 Park Avenue South   10003   460-0900

JBFCS runs a Court Clinic which provides diagnostic evaluations and treatment for children and their families referred by the Family Court. There's also an office of JBFCS at the Manhattan Family Court, 60 Lafayette Street, Room 1A (582-5564), that serves as a court liaison and referral service. The Tri-Agency Family Court Services, located at the Manhattan Family Court and also at 66 Allen Street (966-2705), runs a preventative program providing casework, group work, mental health, educational, vocational and recreational services to high-risk, court-referred children and families.

Madeline Borg Counseling Services
120 West 57th Street   10019   582-9100

Children who are doing poorly in school or exhibiting behavior problems, either at home or in school, are among the many people that Madeline Borg Counseling Services seeks to help. Although it is a treatment resource for families in stress, MBCS sees children separately as well. Manhattan regional offices are located at 33 West 60th Street (586-2900), 1651 Third Avenue (860-3500), and 84 Sherman Avenue (304-1900).

Stuyvesant Residence Club
74 St. Marks Place   10003   477-1565

This is a residential facility for emotionally-disturbed older adolescent boys, ages sixteen to twenty-one. Like other

JBFCS programs, it services a diverse population of kids, many of whom have been referred from other programs.

West Side School of New York City
328 West 48th Street 10036 307-6641
This is a day treatment program for delinquent boys fourteen to seventeen, who have been referred by the courts.

Jewish Big Brothers and Big Sisters–Fatherless Boys Program
120 West 57th Street 10019 582-9100
This program, one of the oldest in the agency, aims to establish a meaningful relationship between a child with only one parent, and an adult of the same sex. There are support programs for the big brothers and sisters, and a special Fatherless Boys Program for Jewish children who are paired with Jewish adults.

Jewish Child Care Association

345 Madison Avenue 10017 490-9160
The JCCA maintains several residential treatment centers (some of which are out of the city; call for more information about these) for emotionally-disabled youth. The agency also has some community-based services as well as day and preventive mental health services.

Youth Residence Center
217 East 87th Street 10028
This is a threshold facility, designed for young men and women sixteen to twenty, many of whom have serious emotional problems and a history of mental illness, and who are now almost ready to live on their own. They attend high school or work, and receive therapy as well.,

Friendly Home for Girls
320 West End Avenue, 14A 10023
465 West End Avenue, 2A 10024
Through its community-based placement services, JCCA maintains two small group-homes in Manhattan for young women (homes for boys are located in Queens) who cannot live at home, but are in need of the structure of a residential treatment center. Trained child-care workers manage the residences and create a homelike environment. Children attend regular or special schools or work at regular or sheltered jobs in the community.

Foster Homes
345 Madison Avenue 10017 490-9160, ext. 222
JCCA places children in foster homes when they cannot live at home, do not need the structure of an institutional setting, and are able to accept care in a family atmosphere. The agency screens foster parents and offers a variety of support systems to the child and foster family.

The Manhattan Child Guidance Center
575 Lexington Avenue 10022   371-1313
JCCA maintains an outpatient clinic for children currently
under the care of the agency.

Project Contact   Educational Alliance
197 East Broadway 10002   475-6200
A wide array of services for adolescents in trouble is
provided through this division of the Educational Alliance,
funded by the National Institute on Drug Abuse. The Crisis
Center, 315 East 10th Street, seeks out runaway youth at
bus terminals and other places where homeless teenagers
might be. At the Center, emergency aid is provided,
including food, shelter and counseling. The Short-Term
Crash Pad gives teenage runaways and homeless a place to
live for up to two weeks, until a referral can be made.
There is also a twenty-four hour hotline maintained
(533-3570). Counseling, vocational help and educational
services are handled at the Day Treatment Facility, 380
Lafayette Street. The Group Home, 315 Second Avenue,
offers long-term residential facilities in a therapeutic
atmosphere for teenage runaways and homeless. A drug-
free therapeutic rehabilitation residence is maintained at
Pride Site, 371 East 10th Street.

THE ELDERLY IN NEED

Just as the general population of the country is growing older, so
too is the Jewish population. Jews are living longer, trying to
remain independent for longer periods of time, and requiring
more services from the community they worked so hard to
maintain. The New York UJA–Federation of Jewish Philanthropies estimates that they service the needs of 75,000 Jewish older adults yearly, and they don't reach everybody. We've
listed services designed for older adults basically in two places in
this book. In Chapter 5, we've listed educational, cultural and
social programs specifically geared to the healthy older adult.
The programs described here have been created specifically to
help older adults in need, whether that need be physical, legal,
financial, religious or psychological.

Umbrella groups that serve older adults in a variety of over-
lapping programs and facilities include the **Jewish Association
for Services for the Aged,** the largest voluntary agency for the

aged in the city, and a beneficiary agency of UJA–Federation. Its main office is at 40 West 68th Street (724-3200), but it has programs, facilities and offices throughout Manhattan and the other boroughs. In addition to cultural and social programs listed elsewhere, JASA serves as a central address for referral and information on services for older adults, provides home care and maintains residential facilities, and operates nursing homes, all of which are described in detail below. Another agency serving older adults in need and recently supported by UJA–Federation is **Self Help,** 300 Park Avenue South (533-7100). Self Help was founded by refugees from the Holocaust, and has unique services designed for elderly Jewish survivors. Self Help also provides home care, programs addressing the needs of adults whose children live far away, and community services, again described in detail below. Several UJA–Federation agencies and subventions, such as JASA, JBFCS, FEGS, Beth Israel Hospital, the Hebrew Free Loan Society and the Educational Alliance have all joined forces under the auspices of an organization called **Federation Joint Services,** 197 East Broadway (475-6200, ext. 203), to provide a full range of social services for the elderly on the Lower East Side. Finally, the **Central Bureau for the Jewish Aged,** part of UJA–Federation and located in its central office in Manhattan, 130 East 59th Street (308-7316), is a membership organization of Jewish-sponsored nursing homes and recreation centers for the aged, which serves as a coordinating agency to study the needs of the metropolitan Jewish elderly.

Although we've divided the services by category—financial, housing, homecare, nursing home services—there is a certain amount of overlap, not only in what a given agency does, but in any given individual's needs. So if you or someone you know is an older adult in need of help, read through the whole chapter.

ELDERLY POOR

Dorot 251 West 100th Street 10025 864-7410
> This group, housed at Congregation Ansche Chesed, serves the frail elderly and homeless of Manhattan's Upper West Side. Like Project Ezra, Dorot (which means "generations") works with college students and other volunteers, who visit the

elderly on a weekly basis. Dorot also delivers special holiday food packages during Passover and Rosh Hashanah. Through its Homelessness Prevention Project, 316 West 95th Street (666-2000), Dorot provides a safe Jewish communal atmosphere for the homeless elderly. Assistance is provided in obtaining government entitlements, housing relocation and supportive counseling. Dorot is a subvention agency of the UJA–Federation.

Project Ezra   197 East Broadway 10002   982-4124

This unique multifaceted agency serves the elderly of the Lower East Side, most of whom are poor. Receiving no direct financial help from the organized Jewish community, this remarkable group of people works with volunteers to provide a myriad of services, always with the goal of helping the elderly poor stay in their own homes whenever possible. Project Ezra distributes food for the holidays to those in need and also shops and delivers food for the homebound. In a joint program with Self Help, Ezra has a home-care worker to help the needy who are awaiting government assistance. A van provides transportation for the elderly to attend programs sponsored by Ezra, such as luncheons and *havurot* fellowship groups. Through a synagogue clean-up program, poor and dying synagogues are cleaned and maintained by volunteers. Finally, Project Ezra supports a breakfast and *Kiddush* program at Congregation Anshei Berzan, where Rabbi Joseph Singer maintains special accounts with the local butcher and grocer to help feed the hungry. In addition to contributing to these accounts, Project Ezra has renovated the *shul's* kitchen so that food can be provided for those who drop in.

Respite House   331 East 12th Street 10003   505-0722

Under the auspices of the Educational Alliance, Respite House provides an eighteen-bed temporary shelter for older adults in crisis as a result of crime in their home, fire, eviction, domestic violence or building abandonment. Clients are helped with relocation, entitlements and counseling.

United Jewish Council of the East Side
235 East Broadway 10002   233-6037

Another community-based group that serves Jewish elderly and poor on the Lower East Side, the United Jewish Council sponsors cultural events as well. Outreach programs include food distribution for the holidays, legal assistance for those who can't afford lawyers, social workers to assist with government entitlements, a representative from Social Security to meet with the elderly who can't get to the Social Security office, and information and referral.

HOUSING

Rising rents and decreased availability of rental housing have created a serious problem for older adults in Manhattan. For the Jewish older adult who wishes to live independently, but with some support—financial, emotional or fraternal—the opportunities are slim indeed. Most if not all facilities have long waiting lists and few spaces. We've listed facilities in Manhattan; several comparable apartment buildings, some maintained by the UJA–Federation, are located in other boroughs.

Evelyn and Louis A. Green Residence at Cooper Square
200 East 5th Street 10003   724-3200

> This is JASA's newest housing facility for the well elderly. Built in 1985, it has 150 one-bedroom units, twenty-four hour security, a library, arts and crafts shop, lounge, multipurpose rooms, outdoor sitting area, classes and social events and services. There is at least a two-year waiting list.

David Podell Residence
179 Henry Street 10002   475-6200

> The Educational Alliance operates this fifty-unit residence for the elderly, who participate in all activities of the Alliance. Although no meals are provided, some residents go to the Alliance for kosher food.

Stern Residence   156 West 106th Street 10025   870-4836

> This residence, attached to The Jewish Home and Hospital for the Aged, has eight apartments for the elderly who wish some services, such as a daily hot meal and homemaker help. Residents can also make use of facilities at Central House, the JASA Nursing Home down the block which has a library and communal activities.

Tanya Towers   612 East 13th Street 10009   673-7719

> This is a 137-unit facility under the auspices of the New York Society for the Deaf, designed for the deaf, elderly and handicapped.

United Jewish Council Bialystoker Synagogue
Grand Street and Bialystoker Place 10002   677-4451

> The United Jewish Council operates housing for the well elderly, both Jewish and non-Jewish, and this building has 128 units.

EMPLOYMENT AND VOCATIONAL TRAINING

Senior Aides Program Federation Employment and Guidance Service 2 West 17th Street 10011 741-6309

This Federally-funded program at FEGS sends older adults (55+) who meet federal income guidelines to worksites at nonprofit organizations, where they work for twenty hours per week and receive at least minimum wage. They also receive training, preemployment counseling and placement assistance.

CARE FOR THE HOMEBOUND

Dorot 251 West 100 Street, 5th floor 10025 864-7410

This Upper West Side organization, in addition to its emergency crisis assistance and help for the homeless, has brightened the lives of the area's homebound with visits by volunteers and with food packages on Jewish holidays. It also brings the homebound out to special intergenerational programs and helps them to make graveside visits.

EASY-RIDE West Side Jewish Community Council 210 West 91st Street 10024 496-0401

This is a para-transit service that aids people without other access to transportation to get medical and other kinds of help.

Educational Alliance
197 East Broadway 10002 475-6200

Several programs at the Educational Alliance serve the homebound elderly. Alliance Home Care provides housekeeping services to the frail elderly, including light cleaning and shopping. E.A.R.S.–Lifeline, an emergency alarm system, is also operated by the Educational Alliance. The Alliance's Telephone Reassurance Program is made up of volunteers supervised by a trained professional. The Senior Companions Program is made up of low-income seniors who visit the sick and disabled on a regular basis and also do some light shopping as well as escorting the frail to clinics or on local errands. The volunteers also visit patients in two neighborhood nursing homes. They are paid and receive free kosher lunch and carfare.

Project Ezra 197 East Broadway 10002 982-4124

In a joint program with Self Help Community Services (see below), Project Ezra provides a home-care worker for the elderly who need short-term help while awaiting government-assisted home care. These workers, who often stay with their clients around the clock, are offered a weekly support group for their stressful jobs, as well as technical nursing training and information about *kashrut,* Sabbath observances, and traditional Jewish life. In addition to this home care, Project Ezra also operates a transportation program that brings the frail elderly to programs at the Y or to healthcare facilities in a van equipped with a wheelchair lift.

Federation Joint Services

197 East Broadway 10002 475-6200

Federation Joint Services, a combined service with JASA, JBFCS, FEGS, Beth Israel Medical Center and the Hebrew Loan Society, provides counseling and home visits to the elderly.

FEGS Home Attendant Services, Inc.

c/o Kennedy Community Center
34 West 134th Street 10037 694-0800

This subsidiary of the Federation Employment and Guidance Service provides attendant services to enable the frail elderly to live independently at home. The service is responsible for recruiting and screening the attendants and for taking care of their employment needs, as well as providing on-the-job training. It only serves clients who have been referred by the General Social Services and who are Medicaid eligible.

Project HOPE YM–YWHA of Washington Heights and Inwood 54 Nagle Avenue 10040 569-2004

This Y-sponsored Homebound Outreach Program for the Elderly provides support for homebound seniors who are able with this help to stay in their own apartments. Services include shopping, light housekeeping, laundry, escort for errands or doctor visits, and counseling and information. Services are provided to all residents over sixty living between 168th Street and 218th Street. Additional housekeeping is available as well as personal care services by a trained staff member. Another component of Project HOPE is Teens Serving Seniors (569-7647) which employs community teenagers to help with some of the services to the frail elderly, such as shopping, laundry and visitation. Telephone reassurance and visiting are part of the program, and the volunteer staff may be senior citizens or teens involved in the project.

JASA 40 West 68th Street 10023 724-3200

In its efforts to allow the elderly to remain in their own homes, JASA offers several assistance programs, including homemakers and meals-on-wheels. It offers help obtaining Medicaid and food stamps, and gives personal counseling and legal advice. You must be over sixty years old to be eligible for these services.

Metropolitan New York Coordinating Council on Jewish Poverty 15 Park Row 10038 267-9500

This agency provides home care for the over sixty-five elderly and the physically frail, within a maximum income level well below the poverty line. There are two offices for this service, one on the Lower East Side and one in Washington Heights (569-5450).

Project Sages YM–YWHA of Washington Heights and Inwood 54 Nagle Avenue 10040 569-6200

The Washington Heights Y and Yeshiva University have joined forces in a new program to provide intergenerational visiting. College and rabbinical students visit the homebound elderly, most of whom are clients of Project HOPE. The program runs only during the academic year.

Self Help Community Services 300 Park Avenue South 10003 473-6230

Self Help has been providing home care to clients and hospitals and is now opening up its services to the public. A registered nurse visits all clients to give a consultation and evaluation of needs, after which a worker is assigned. There are housekeepers, homemakers, home health aids, and live-in companions available for short-term, long-term and acute care. Home care is tailored to individual needs.

NURSING HOMES

Bialystoker Home and Infirmary for the Aged 228 East Broadway 10002 475-7755

This nursing home has fifty skilled-nursing units and fifteen health-related facilities. Patients must be over sixty-five. There is a synagogue with a daily and Shabbat *minyan*. *Kashrut* is observed.

Fort Tryon Nursing Home 801 West 190th Street 10040 923-2530

This is a private nursing home that is loosely connected with the Breuer community in Washington Heights. It is an Orthodox facility, with kosher food and a daily *minyan*. There are 205 patients, many of whom are Jewish.

Jewish Home and Hospital for the Aged JASA Central House 120 West 106th Street 10025 870-5000

This long-term health center is comprised of several buildings that house more than 500 patients and provide diagnostic laboratories and rehabilitation facilities. Residents receive complete hospital care and medical attention including psychiatry and physical and occupational therapy. This complex also contains the Stern Residence which does not have nursing care but provides hot meals, homemaker services and geriatric outreach. Residents must be sixty and over. The food is not kosher.

Home of the Sages of Israel
25 Willett Street 10002   673-8500

This is an Orthodox nursing home that states it is for scholarly men over sixty-two. It is a health-related facility that also has study groups. *Kashrut* is observed.

THOSE UNDER STRESS

It might be some specific counseling you need for a child in a cult, a relative with an alcohol problem, a marriage in trouble. Maybe your problem is of a more general nature, and you'd like someone to talk to, or to refer you to a place where you can get more help. The agencies or programs described below, in alphabetical order, try to help those in need of counseling or psychological assistance. Some are broadly defined, while others address a specific problem you may be experiencing.

Alzheimer Support Group   Brotherhood Synagogue
23 Gramercy Park 10010   674-5750

This synagogue, which reaches out to the community in many ways, has a support group for those who are caring for victims of Alzheimer's disease or are friends of families where a person is afflicted with the illness.

Beth Israel Hospital
10 Nathan Perlman Place 10003 420-2900

Mount Sinai Hospital
Fifth Avenue and 100th Street   650-6500

Both of these UJA–Federation-supported Manhattan hospitals maintain substance-abuse clinics.

Dysautonomia Foundation
370 Lexington Avenue 10017 889-5222

This genetically-transmitted neurological disorder (also known as Riley-Day syndrome) is an illness that afflicts those of Ashkenazic ancestry. There have in the past been attempts to set up support groups for victims and their families, but because of the high level of secrecy and denial about the disease (some of whose symptoms, such as drooling and speech and motor difficulties, can be embarrassing to those affected or their families) these have not been successful. The Foundation is very interested in helping people deal with the stressful effects of this disease, and it can be called for information.

Group Project for Holocaust Survivors and Their Children 345 East 80th Street 10021 737-8524

This organization reaches out to survivors and their children who may need psychotherapeutic services on an individual, family or group basis. The Project also holds seminars for mental health professionals who work with survivors to help articulate and treat specific problems that arise among victims of Nazi persecution.

JACS Foundation, Inc. 197 East Broadway 473-4747

Funded through a subvention of UJA–Federation, JACS is one of the first organizations under Jewish auspices to acknowledge and reach out to individuals and families suffering from alcoholism and substance abuse. It is a volunteer, grass roots group that provides supplementary Jewish cultural programming to these individuals, who are often in treatment programs. JACS is not a direct service therapeutic agency; rather it tries to offer those who are looking for spiritual and cultural guidance a Jewish context in which to do that. The group works in conjunction with the New York Board of Rabbis.

Jewish Board of Family and Children's Services
120 West 57th Street 10019 582-9100

JBFCS provides a wide range of programs to help individuals and families facing crises or in need of counseling. Below is a list of these programs, which are located at the above address unless otherwise indicated.

Cult Hotline and Clinic
1651 Third Avenue 349-2177

The clinic provides counseling for families and their children involved with cult and missionary groups.

Divorce and Mediation Service

If you're in the process of a divorce and would like to avoid the court ordeal, the Divorce Mediation Service will mediate separation agreements, property division, spousal maintenance, and child support and visitation.

Family Location and Legal Service
235 Park Avenue South   460-0900
In addition to providing legal assistance, this service will help in locating missing family members.

Jewish Conciliation Board of America
235 Park Avenue South 10003   460-0900
Evaluation and conciliation of disputes within the Jewish community, including interpersonal, familial and business conflicts, are handled through this department of JBFCS.

Madeleine Borg Community Services
120 West 57th Street   582-9100
This department of JBFCS has branches throughout Manhattan and the other boroughs, offering a wide range of mental health and social services to adults and families, as well as children. Offices are located at 1651 Third Avenue (860-3500), 84 Sherman Avenue (304-1900), and 120 West 57th Street (582-9100). For more information, call the central office of Madeleine Borg, listed above.

Remarried Consultation Service
For those who are remarried or contemplating second marriages, this service provides counseling, therapy and support services for step-families.

Services to the Widowed
For those coping with loss, this service provides counseling, information and referral services.

Sex Therapy and Counseling Program
The program provides treatment for all types of sexual dysfunction, as well as providing sex-education programs for both adults and adolescents.

Jewish Braille Institute
110 East 30th Street 10016   889-2525
Among many other activities, this organization provides counseling for the children, parents and friends of blind or visually-impaired individuals.

Jewish Child Care Association
345 Madison Avenue 10017   490-9160

There is an outpatient Psychiatric Clinic for families whose
children are being treated by JCCA. The Preventative Services
Program (cosponsored with the Jewish Board of Family and
Children's Services), 2521 Broadway (864-5600), is designed to
prevent family dissolution and avoid or shorten foster
placement by providing support services to families in need.

Project Contact   Educational Alliance
197 East Broadway 10002   533-3570

This federally-funded project helps adolescents with drug
problems, including shelter for runaways, counseling and
getting back to school. For more information, see Children in
Need.

National Council of Jewish Women   New York Section
9 East 69th Street   535-5900

The Council provides support for family members testifying
in domestic violence cases. The Jewish Women's Resource
Center here also holds pregnancy-loss peer counseling.

National Tay-Sachs and Allied Diseases Association, Inc.   516-569-4300

This Long Island-based association sponsors parent peer-
group networks throughout the country for those whose
children are afflicted with Tay-Sachs or other Jewish genetic
diseases.

New York Board of Rabbis
10 East 73rd Street 10021   879-8415

The New York Board of Rabbis is the umbrella organization
for rabbis of all denominations. Its outreach programs include
help to individuals and families who have recently suffered a
loss in the family. Help is of a pastoral nature, provided on a
short-term basis by trained rabbinic counselors. One of the
Board's special outreach projects is Project RAV (Rabbinic
Answering Voice), which provides information, counseling and
referral to individuals who would like to speak to a rabbi. Call
the Board of Rabbis for the number.

92nd Street YM–YWHA
1395 Lexington Avenue 10028   427-6000

Personal development classes at this Y include courses in
Divorce, Families of Gay People, Dialogue between Holocaust
Survivors and Their Children, and Widowhood (cosponsored
by the Jewish Board of Family and Children's Services).

Pareveh: The Alliance for Adult Children of Jewish-Gentile Intermarriages 202-265-7599

This Washington-based group has recently opened a chapter in New York to help descendants of mixed marriages cope with some of the problems they face in both the Jewish and Christian communities. Founded by two women whose parents intermarried, the group tries to help individuals integrate their two contrary sides, while also working with Jewish and Christian organizations to be more sensitive to the needs of these individuals.

Second Generation
350 Fifth Avenue, Suite 3508 594-8765

This group, which is affiliated with the International Network of Jewish Holocaust Survivors, holds monthly meetings, kinship groups, and publishes a newsletter.

Self Help Project 120 West 57th Street 582-9100

This department of JBFCS helps organizations and individuals start and maintain support groups in the Jewish community.

IMMIGRANT AID

At the turn of the century virtually all of New York's Jewish population were immigrants, struggling to find housing, jobs, and make their way in this new country. Jews have always had a strong communal responsibility, and it became the task of those who were already settled to help the newest arrivals—although with the help there was often a little scolding: "My brother-in-law said it wasn't nice . . . wasn't fitting to read a Jewish newspaper on the train," wrote one reader to the *Jewish Daily Forward* in 1939. Jews arriving in New York today are still political refugees, but the world has shrunk since 1910, so there is less culture shock. Still, there's a lot in New York that's different from Kiev or Teheran, and the Jewish community, continuing its obligation to help Jewish refugees, has many organizations to help these newcomers in the 1980s.

Federation Employment and Guidance Service
114 Fifth Avenue, 11th floor 10011 741-7110

FEGS has many programs, including vocational training for high school dropouts and the disabled, and it also offers vocational training to immigrant Jews from all countries (the majority of their clients are Russians and Israelis) The FEGS

Trades and Business School, 510 Sixth Avenue (741-7583), provides skills training in areas where there are employment opportunities, including home-appliance repair, heating, refrigeration, air conditioning, jewelry manufacturing, typewriter repair and general office work. The school has support services among which are ESL courses. FEGS's Taxi Driver Institute, 114 Fifth Avenue (741-7012), provides training in driving, taxi industry regulations, and—probably most important for immigrants—defensive driving and New York city geography. Project ARI (Action for Russian Immigrants) is located in Brooklyn, but FEGS's Central Placement Office in Manhattan provides information about it (741-6145).

HIAS (Hebrew Immigrant Aid Society)
200 Park Avenue South 10003 674-6800

The Hebrew Immigrant Aid Society is an international migration agency funded by UJA–Federation. The Society focuses on immigration procedures rather than resettlement, and assists Jewish (as well as non-Jewish) immigrants in dealing with the legal process here. Most of the people it works with are Soviet Jews who need help retrieving personal documents (many of which have been sent to Israel by the Russian government), securing letters of invitation to family members still in the U.S.S.R., and filing for American citizenship.

Jewish Board of Family and Children's Services
120 West 57th Street 10019 582-9100

JBFCS runs a variety of programs for immigrants in this country. Many of them are in communities outside Manhattan where recent immigrants have tended to settle, so those interested should call the main office of JBFCS for information.

New York Association for New Americans, Inc.
225 Park Avenue South 10003 674-7400

This organization, which is part of the UJA–Federation network, provides a variety of resettlement services for Jewish immigrants, including counseling, health services, vocational training, English language training and general acculturation. They also have adolescent and young adult groups and run holiday programs and cultural activities for all ages. Their major concentration has been with Soviet Jews, but they have also worked to help refugees from Hungary, Cuba and other countries.

FOR SOVIET JEWS

This is by far the largest group of recent Jewish immigrants to this country (Federation estimates about 35,000 in New York City). Many need housing and financial assistance since they usually are permitted to emigrate only if they are willing to leave everything behind. They also often need vocational training or professional retraining, since many of them lost jobs when they first applied for emigration (which may have been years ago) and many technological fields undergo rapid changes. Some programs are strictly for relief, others cater to particular groups such as the elderly, and others try to meet the social and cultural needs of Russian emigres in the New York community. Most have as their goal helping these new arrivals to become self-sufficient and self-supporting by retraining adults and integrating their children into the American education system. Since immigrants tend to settle as groups in various areas throughout the city, agencies and organizations often set up service centers within individual communities.

Chamah   78 Pearl Street 10004   943-9690

> Chamah, which is a cultural and educational organization for Russian immigrants, runs a daily radio program in Russian on WNYM (1330 AM) Sunday–Thursday 8–9 P.M. and Saturday 10–11 P.M. It also runs seminars for Russian-Jewish intellectuals and sponsors a Russian-language Jewish weekly magazine, published in Israel and sold in the U.S. Chamah also publishes a variety of Jewish books in Russian which are sold by mail order and advertised through its radio program. A catalogue is available.

Project COPE

Career Opportunities and Preparation for Employment
Agudath Israel   5 Beekman Street 10038   406-4400

> This is another Agudath Israel project, and it was founded to provide training and employment services to the religious community. For Russian Jews it provides vocational training, teaches ESL, and helps them to find jobs.

JASA-SHARE   Association of Older Jewish Immigrants from the Soviet Union
40 West 68th Street 10023   724-3200

> Earlier this year Mayor Koch gave Bella Bery, the former director of JASA-SHARE, the Ethnic New Yorkers' Award for

her work in building this tiny group (it numbered ten in 1979) of older Jewish immigrants into a network with 2000 members. In addition to classes and trips to prepare these older new Americans for life in New York, the group has founded a bilingual magazine that not only teaches about life in America but also preserves some of the cultural heritage of Soviet Jews. They meet in synagogues and centers throughout Manhattan, and the main JASA office provides the information.

Project RISE   Russian Immigrant Services and Education
5 Beekman Street 10038   791-1800

This project sponsored by Agudath Israel provides aid to Russian Jewish immigrants and encourages them to get interested in Jewish religious life, particularly Orthodox observance. (It publishes special Russian-language bulletins prior to each Jewish holiday, explaining the meaning and practices of each, and also distributes Russian-language Torah resource materials.) To this end, in addition to providing social services and assistance with medical and financial problems, it provides free circumcision services, finds Jewish schools and Torah-observant camps for children (it also helps in arranging for financial aid or scholarships), arranges one-to-one meetings with Orthodox American families and distributes religious articles.

Touro College
30 West 44th Street 10036   921-9847/575-1387

Touro College, which is located in the heart of the diamond district, offers a special college degree program for Russian immigrants. There are two-year and four-year programs in business administration as well as liberal arts. They accept transfer credits from Russian universities and offer scholarship assistance to those eligible. The day and evening courses are given in centers throughout the city, and include English language, American history, Jewish heritage and history, as well as business and professional courses.

YM–YWHA of Washington Heights and Inwood
54 Nagle Avenue 10040   569-6000

Many Russian immigrants, particularly the elderly, have settled in the Washington Heights section of Manhattan, and it is quite common to hear Russian spoken in any shop. Since most of the synagogues in the area are Orthodox, and most Russians at least initially have little interest in or knowledge of religion, they tend to gravitate to the Y as a welcome place to gather. The Y has an extensive Russian Program office, and offers a variety of services to this group. They receive information and assistance with immigration, Social Security,

Medicaid, and other necessary care, but the Y also tries to meet their social and cultural needs with classes, trips and entertainment. There are often as many as three ESL classes running at the same time (jointly run by the Y and Touro College), and there are Russian-language movies shown regularly, as well as Russian performances, singing and dancing. Trips are offered evenings and weekends—as well as during the day—for those who work, and of course, the Russian senior citizens are welcome to participate in any of the many programs at the Y's Senior Center.

VOCATIONAL GUIDANCE AND TRAINING

If you're going to work for the first time, or after a long time off, the options, opportunities or lack thereof can be pretty overwhelming. Similarly, if you're recovering from an illness, making a major career change, or just aren't happy doing what you're doing, there are some agencies and programs in the Jewish community that may be of help. The three major groups listed below have programs that are constantly changing, so we've tried to be general. For more information, and for an update on specific programs, call each agency. The National Association of Jewish Vocational Services, 386 Park Avenue South (685-8355), is the central coordinating body for vocational agencies in the Jewish community, and they will refer you to the appropriate agency.

American ORT Federation
817 Broadway 10003   677-4400

American ORT is the North American branch of Organization for Rehabilitation through Training, whose headquarters are actually in London. ORT operates vocational schools, tailoring relevant curricula for Jewish, general and technical education. In Manhattan, this happens at Bramson ORT Technical Institute, the first and only technical college under Jewish auspices in the United States. Bramson, 304 Park Avenue South (677-7420), provides courses in computer programming, sales and operations, electronic engineering technology, computer technology, ophthalmic technology, business management, secretarial studies, word processing and accounting.

B'nai B'rith Career and Counseling Services
823 United Nations Plaza 10017   490-0677

This division of B'nai B'rith International runs a career counseling and testing program that includes aptitude, interest and personality tests, and interviews, with an evaluation at the conclusion. Much of it is for college students, but the same services, where appropriate, are available for adults who are changing careers or want to begin second careers at retirement, and for women reentering the job market.

Project COPE Counseling Center

Career Opportunities and Preparation for Employment
Agudath Israel   5 Beekman Street 10038   406-4400

COPE was founded for the purpose of providing training and employment services to the religious community. It offers employers a fifty percent subsidy to train workers on the job. Through the COPE Institute, classes are offered in business skills, bookkeeping, and computer programming. English as a second language is offered to immigrants. Dislocated workers are helped and vocational guidance is provided. The largest number of people served at COPE are former homemakers, who are entering the job market after the loss or disability of a husband. Under the Fresh Start Program, women are not only given vocational counseling, but are helped through the transition period that occurs following a death, divorce or serious disability.

Federation Employment and Guidance Service

114 Fifth Avenue 10011   741-7110

FEGS, one of the largest private, nonprofit rehabilitation agencies in the country, offers a wide range of vocational services and treatment programs, not only for the disabled and elderly, which we have described elsewhere, but for those first entering the job market, reentering or changing careers. The names and descriptions of these programs change frequently (which means that some of the programs listed below may already be outdated) but FEGS' commitment to the overall goals does not. If you have a vocational question, or would like more information on FEGS programs outside Manhattan, call the main number and ask for help.

Career Development Services

510 Sixth Avenue 10011   741-7150

This is where you go at FEGS to figure out what you want to be when you grow up, even if you're already grown up. With trained counselors, in both an individual and group setting, you can explore options, find out what you're really good at as well as what you'd like to do, get help with resume writing, and learn about educational opportunities. There's a library with the latest materials in occupational and career planning. Also at this address is the Professional Development Institute, which provides training programs, workshops and seminars for corporations and individuals to further professional growth and career development.

Emergency Employment Mobile Job and Career Center
62 West 14th Street 10011 741-7154

This is FEGS' "Employment Office on Wheels," which travels through the greater metropolitan area to provide help in finding employment, give information about career opportunities, and offer workshops for people seeking career changes or entrance.

Skills Training Centers
Business School 114 Fifth Avenue 10011 741-6248
Trades School 510 Sixth Avenue 10011 741-5916

These Centers coordinate the various training institutes that are designed for people just entering the job market or who are in need of retraining. FEGS operates courses nine months in length, thirty hours per week, in various manufacturing and repair fields. There is also a special twenty-hour Taxi Driving Institute, conducted in conjunction with LaGuardia Community College.

Insurance Rehabilitation
114 Fifth Avenue 10011 741-7011

This program is designed to apply FEGS vocational and rehabilitative expertise to the needs of those whose employment has been affected by accident or illness. Victims are helped with claims recovery and rehabilitation.

Operation Success
62 West 14th Street 10011 741-7123

Responding to the forty-five percent dropout rate in the New York City public high school system, FEGS started a pilot program to bring some of its services into the schools. Sponsored by the New York State Education Department, the program was designed in cooperation with the Board of Education and the United Federation of Teachers. In Manhattan, Operation Success is run out of Seward Park High School, 350 Grand Street.

FEGS Corporate Services
114 Fifth Avenue 10011 741-6307

FEGS has begun to work with corporations by providing out-placement services to those who have been laid off, helping to upgrade employee skills, coordinating preretirement counseling, and management development.

Young Israel Employment Bureau
3 West 16th Street 10011   929-1525

About half the clients of Young Israel's Employment Bureau are Jewish, and there are specific criteria for eligibility, so applicants will be questioned about previous work history, income and welfare history. On-the-job training is provided in cooperation with companies who are interested in hiring.

DIVORCE

Those in the throes of divorce are often interested in getting some individual or family counseling; suitable programs under Jewish auspices are described in the section Those Under Stress, in this chapter. One special program for people trying to avoid lengthy and costly court battles is the Divorce Mediation Service of the Jewish Board of Family and Children's Services, 120 West 57th Street (582-9100). If you're in the process of a divorce and would like to avoid the court ordeal, the Divorce Mediation Service will help with separation agreements, property division, spousal maintenance, and child support and visitation. Also under the auspices of JBFCS is the Family Location and Legal Services, 235 Park Avenue South (460-0900). They can be helpful to those who cannot afford lawyers to handle divorce proceedings, and they also have a missing persons service.

According to Jewish law, in order for men and women to remarry after a civil divorce, each must obtain a *Get,* a Jewish divorce decree. Orthodox and Conservative rabbis, as well as many Reconstructionist rabbis, require such a document before officiating at a wedding where one or both parties has been previously married (the Reform movement considers the civil decree sufficient, though some Reform rabbis may not). If you saw the movie *Hester Street,* you may remember a horrifying scene of a *Get* being delivered in a dark room filled with men speaking Yiddish. While it may sometimes still be like that, when both husband and wife agree to it, the procedure is essentially paperwork and can often be done through messengers, without the couple being present or together. Even if you're not considering remarrying right away, obtaining a Jewish divorce at the time of your civil divorce may make sense. It's somewhat easier then, and can even be negotiated through your lawyers and written into separation agreements. It may even be a useful ritual, if you find the right rabbi and approach it as a life-cycle event that will help you move on to the next stage. In light of the rather cold and bureaucratic way in which many uncontested divorces are now handled, a sensitive delivery of a *Get* might provide a sense of closure for you and your ex-spouse. Some rabbis do their own *Gittin*. If you belong to a synagogue, check first with the rabbi. Either he or she will handle it for you or tell you where to go. As in other areas of ritual practice, the denominations do not always recognize each others' *Gittin*, causing serious problems for the innocent person in need. If you have no rabbi, you can call the denominational movements yourself. Each movement handles the procedure somewhat differently. For a *Get* under Orthodox auspices, there are a few choices:

Beth Din of America
275 Seventh Avenue 10001   807-9042

> This rabbinic court, under the auspices of the Rabbinical Council of America (consisting of Orthodox rabbis who tend to be modern in their outlook) will help you obtain a Jewish divorce. Be aware, however, that under Jewish law, only husbands can initiate Jewish divorce proceedings, and Orthodox women who have obtained civil divorces and whose husbands are unwilling to give them Jewish decrees are often in rather bad trouble. Although the Beth Din may try to help, unless the husband agrees to give the *Get*, the woman cannot marry within the Orthodox community.

KAYAMA   475 Fifth Avenue, Suite 1810   725-0578

> Formed to arrange Jewish divorces for men and women, KAYAMA brings together clergy, lawyers and family counselors to help those seeking divorce. They will accompany the husband or wife through the procedure and provide financial help where necessary.

G.E.T.   718-871-3407

> We're breaking our rule about not listing groups outside Manhattan, because G.E.T. (Getting Equitable Treatment) is one of the only groups trying to help men and women seeking a Jewish divorce where there is a problem—usually with a recalcitrant or missing husband. In accordance with Orthodox law, this group, made up of volunteers and a professional caseworker, uses persuasion where possible, and public demonstrations where necessary, to convince a husband to give his wife a Jewish divorce.

American Association of Rabbis
350 Fifth Avenue 10001 244-3350

> This professional organization of rabbis from a variety of backgrounds maintains what they call a *halakhic Bet Din,* a rabbinic court that complies with Jewish law, for the purpose of conferring Jewish divorces.

Rabbinic Alliance of America
156 Fifth Avenue 10010 242-6420

> This extremely Orthodox group has a rabbinic arbitration court as well as a *Bet Din* to handle Jewish divorces.

Other options include the Conservative and Reconstructionist movements, both of which will help you arrange a Jewish divorce:

The Rabbinical Assembly *Conservative*
3080 Broadway 10027 678-8858

> The *Bet Din* of the Rabbinical Assembly, the Conservative movement's rabbinic arm, confers Jewish divorces in what they say is a traditional manner, according to Jewish law. In the event that the husband refuses to issue a *Get,* the rabbinic court uses a Jewish legal procedure to annul the marriage, thereby enabling the woman to remarry, at least in a Conservative ceremony.

Reconstructionist Rabbinical Association
270 West 89th Street 10024 496-2960

> The Reconstructionist Rabbinical Association has instituted two new procedures for conferring Jewish divorces. When the husband refuses to grant the divorce (or can't be located), there is a female-initiated divorce issued. There is also an egalitarian divorce decree, for couples who want a Jewish divorce that better reflects their viewpoints about the equality of men and women.

DEATH

Many of us have no experience arranging a funeral and burial until we ourselves have to face the difficult task for a loved one. According to Jewish custom and law, these arrangements must be made quickly, so that burial can take place as soon as possible. The first thing to do is call your rabbi, or the rabbi of the person who has died. Normally she or he will aid you in choosing a funeral home and making the necessary arrangements. If you don't have a rabbi, you can choose one of the funeral homes listed below; most will provide a rabbi for the funeral. (Of course, if you use a rabbi from the funeral home, she or he will not have known the deceased, so if you would like something personal said, speak with the rabbi about having a member of the family offer a eulogy.) Most of the funeral homes listed below do funerals for non-Jews as well, and while most of their work is with Jews, they don't automatically assume that you wish a traditional Jewish funeral. Such a funeral includes several preceremony rituals, including preparation of the body and watching. If you're interested in a strictly traditional Jewish funeral, be sure to let the director or your rabbi know. One major burial organization in Manhattan, where arrangements are made in accordance with Jewish law and custom, is United Hebrew Community of New York: Adath Israel of New York, 201 East Broadway (674-3580). Although they also provide medical benefits and run a synagogue, this group's primary function is to help its members arrange for funerals and burial. They have plots throughout the New York–New Jersey area, and help members arrange funerals at funeral homes or at their facility downtown. One other resource, for people who are unable to afford the escalating costs of a funeral, is the Hebrew Free Burial Association, 1170 Broadway, Room 805 (686-2433). They provide free Orthodox burials throughout New York City.

FUNERAL CHAPELS

Gramercy Chapels
152 Second Avenue 10003   477-6334

Gutterman's Inc.
331 Amsterdam Avenue 10023   873-3500

Isador Nagel & Sons
152 Second Avenue 10003   674-3200

Parkside Memorial Chapels
49 East 7th Street 10003   533-5210

Park West Chapels, Inc.
178 West 76th Street 10023   362-3600

Riverside Memorial Chapel, Inc.
180 West 76th Street 10023   362-6600

West End Funeral Chapels
200 West 91st Street 10024   724-0600

Zion Memorial–Abraham Blau
153 East Broadway 10002 226-1617/674-2220

If you have any questions about funeral homes and practices, try calling the Jewish Funeral Directors of America, 122 East 42nd Street, Suite 1120 (370-0024). This is an umbrella organization of funeral directors, which maintains a New York committee.

CEMETERIES

Your funeral director can assist you in the selection of a cemetery if arrangements have not been previously made. If the person who died belonged to a fraternal or burial society, plots may be available through that group. A list of fraternal organizations appears in Chapter 8. Many Manhattan synagogues have plots in the metropolitan area. Those who will sell them to nonmembers are listed below.

Central Synagogue *Conservative*
123 East 55th Street 10022 838-5122 Brooklyn, N.Y.

Congregation Ansche Chesed *Conservative*
251 West 100th Street 10025 865-0600
Rochelle Park, N.J.

Congregation Beth Hillel of Washington Heights *Orthodox*
571 West 182nd Street 10033 568-3933 Paramus, N.J.

Congregation K'Hal Adath Jeshurun *Orthodox*
85 Bennett Avenue 10033 923-3582 Clifton, N.J.

Congregation Kehilath Jeshurun *Orthodox*
125 East 85th Street 10028 427-1000 Paramus, N.J.;
Queens, N.Y.

Congregation Nodah Bi Yehuda *Orthodox*
392 Ft. Washington Avenue 10033 795-1552 Fairfield, N.J.

Congregation Ramath Orah *Orthodox*
550 West 110th Street 10025 222-2470 Woodbridge, N.J.

Congregation Rodeph Sholom *Reform*
7 West 83rd Street 10024 362-8800 Queens, N.Y.

Congregation Shaare Hatikvah Ahavath
Torah v'Tikvoh Chadoshoh *Orthodox*
711 West 179th Street 10033 927-2720 Paramus, N.J.

Congregation Shaare Zedek *Conservative*
212 West 93rd Street 10025 874-7005 Fairview, N.J.

Congregation Ohav Sholaum *Orthodox*
4624 Broadway 10040   567-0900   Paramus, N.J.

East 55th Street Conservative Synagogue *Conservative*
308 East 55th Street 10022   752-1200   Queens, N.Y.

East End Temple *Reform*
398 Second Avenue 10010   254-8518   Fairview, N.J.

Fifth Avenue Synagogue *Orthodox*
5 East 62nd Street 10021   838-2122   Paramus, N.J.

Ft. Tryon Jewish Center *Conservative*
54 Ft. Washington Avenue 10033 795-1391 Woodbridge, N.J.

Garment Center Congregation *Orthodox*
205 West 40th Street 10018   391-6966

Inwood Hebrew Congregation *Conservative*
111 Vermilyea Avenue 10034   569-4010   Fairview, N.J.

Inwood Jewish Center *Orthodox*
12 Elwood Street 10040   569-4311   Paramus, N.J.

Park Avenue Synagogue *Conservative*
50 East 87th Street 10028   369-2600   Valhalla, N.Y.

Park East Synagogue *Orthodox*
163 East 67th Street 10021   737-6900   Queens, N.Y.

Society for the Advancement of Judaism *Reconstructionist*
15 West 86th Street 10024   724-7000   Queens, N.Y.

Stephen Wise Free Synagogue *Reform*
30 West 68th Street 10023 877-4050 Westchester Hills, N.Y.

Temple Emanu-El *Reform*
1 East 65th Street 10021   744-1400   Brooklyn, N.Y.

Temple Israel of the City of New York *Reform*
112 East 75th Street 10021   249-5000
 Hastings-on-Hudson, N.Y.

Washington Heights Congregation *Orthodox*
815 West 179th Street 10033   923-4407   Queens, N.Y.

Young Israel of Manhattan *Orthodox*
225–229 East Broadway 10002   732-0966

MONUMENTS

Marking the grave with a stone or metal monument normally
occurs sometime toward the end of the year of mourning, at a

ceremony called the unveiling. These rituals are largely customary, and there is very little of an actual service. Essentially, it's a time for the family to come together to note the passing of time since the death of a loved one. The monument is usually set in place before the family arrives and is sometimes covered with a piece of cheesecloth to be removed by the mourners during the unveiling itself. This cheesecloth is normally provided by the monument maker and may be given to the family both to put on the marker and take off. Sometimes those who place the monument will have already covered it, but don't assume this. The cemetery people almost never have cheesecloth for you, so be sure to ask about this when you're making arrangements for the monument. Below is a list of monument makers in Manhattan; there are many more located near cemeteries throughout the New York area.

Adler's Memorials
180 West 76th Street 10023   753-6330

Blevitzky Bros.
212 Forsythe Street 10002   477-4908

Forsyth Monuments
172 Suffolk Street 10002   473-2388

Lipstadt Memorial Co.
180 West 76th Street 10023   874-6843

National Memorials Inc.
84 Forsythe Street 10002   966-9683

Riverside Memorials
180 West 76th Street 10023   362-0900

Shastone Monuments
217 East Houston 10002   475-0360

Silver Monument Works Inc.
125 Stanton Street 10002   777-6691

Steinberg & Dubin
245 East Houston 10002   475-7697

Weinreb Bros. & Gross Memorials Inc.
172 Suffolk Street 10002   254-2360

Weitzner Bros. & Papper
25 Second Avenue 10003   254-8826

BEREAVEMENT COUNSELING

Because Jewish funerals take place so quickly following a death, sometimes it's only after all the rituals are complete that you find yourself in need of some emotional help. The New York Board of Rabbis, 10 East 73rd Street (879-8415), offers bereavement counseling by trained rabbis. The Jewish Board of Family and Children's Services sponsors Services to the Widowed, 120 West 57th Street (582-9100), which provides counseling and other kinds of help to those who have recently lost a loved one.

Chapter 12
LOOKING EAST: ISRAEL

The city with the largest Jewish population is naturally the city with the largest number of organizations whose primary concern is the state of Israel—its society, economy, political structure, its political, economic and social relationship with the United States, its agriculture, educational opportunities, social service and medical facilities, and its religious character.

This chapter describes the work of these groups, which have been listed under general categories like fund-raising, education, business and travel, *aliya*, societal issues and American-Israeli relations. Nowhere in this guide has the organization of organizations been more difficult, primarily because these groups tend to be multifaceted, with interlocking directorates, programs and purposes. As hard as we have tried be be comprehensive, there are undoubtedly more Manhattan groups whose primary function involves the state of Israel. Suffice it to say, if there is any aspect of Israeli life in which you are interested, there's a group for you in Manhattan!

ZIONIST ORGANIZATIONS

These organizations are primarily concerned with communicating Zionist aspirations and ideas to American Jews and others.

Umbrella groups in New York are the World Zionist Organization–American Section, the American Zionist Federation, and the World Confederation of United Zionists, all described below.

World Zionist Organization–American Section
515 Park Avenue 10022   752-0600

WZO is what its name implies—a world-wide Zionist umbrella organization that includes all Zionist groups. Housed at 515 Park Avenue, the central Zionist address in Manhattan, WZO disseminates information through its Education Department, runs trips to Israel and supports other Zionist organizations. One major program is the Theodor Herzl Institute, which sponsors Zionist Adult Education lectures and classes (see Chapter 6 for more information).

World Confederation of United Zionists
30 East 60th Street 10022   371-1583

This is an umbrella organization comprised of Hadassah, B'nai Zion and the American Jewish League for Israel. It is not affiliated with any political party in Israel, and works on behalf of Zionist educational programs throughout the Diaspora. The Confederation publishes *Zionist Information News*, which is printed in English, Spanish and French.

American Zionist Federation
515 Park Avenue 10022   371-7750

As its name implies, AZF is a Zionist organization, committed to the Jerusalem Program, which encourages *aliya*. Its educational and cultural programs seek to give Americans a greater appreciation of Israeli life. Organizations under the rubric of AZF include:

American Zionist Youth Council
515 Park Avenue 10022   751-6070

This council is comprised of the major Zionist youth groups, including Betar, B'nai Akiva, Young Kibbutz Movement, Ichud Habonim, Young Judaea, Masada, Hashomer Hatzair and others. It serves as a coordinating body and acts as a spokesperson for Zionist youth issues.

American Jewish League for Israel
30 East 60th Street 10022   371-1583

Each month the League sponsors a guest speaker at the America-Israel Friendship House, who generally speaks on events pertaining to Israel. They have also recently created a merit scholarship fund for high school students who would like to spend a year at an Israeli educational facility.

Americans for a Progressive Israel–Hashomer, Inc.
150 Fifth Avenue 10011   255-8760

Through local chapters and public events, API's goal is to provide an understanding of Jewish identity and progressive values. It is affiliated with the Kibbutz Arzti Federation in Israel. Here in New York, API also sponsors the Mordechai Anielewicz Circle, a group for young adults interested in progressive Zionist throught. API runs an ulpan for those interested in learning to speak Hebrew, and it sponsors trips to Israel.

Amit Women
817 Broadway 10003   477-4720

This is a religious women's organization that raises money for some twenty major Israeli educational facilities. It has local chapters throughout the area, and does cultural and educational programming concerning its work.

Association of Reform Zionists of America
838 Fifth Avenue 10021   249-0100

ARZA is particularly concerned with the building of Reform Judaism in Israel and the pursuit of religious pluralism. It is organized through Reform congregations, with local chapters planning individual programs.

B'nai Zion
136 East 39th Street 10016   725-1211

B'nai Zion, the oldest Zionist fraternal organization in the United States, with links to many larger Zionist groups, provides its members with health and other benefits as well as social and cultural programs. It supports several medical and educational facilities in Israel.

Emunah Women of America
370 Seventh Avenue, Suite 11N 10001   564-9045

This ultra-Orthodox women's Zionist organization has a network of chapters throughout the United States, with branches all over the world. It supports and maintains almost 200 Israeli institutions, mostly for children.

Hadassah, The Women's Zionist Organization of America, Inc.
50 West 58th Street 10019   355-7900

One of the largest women's Zionist organizations, with a membership of close to 400,000, Hadassah built and maintains Hadassah Hospital in Jerusalem, while also supporting several other health, educational and children's facilities in Israel. In the United States, it sponsors a youth program, Hashachar, which runs camps, trips and Zionist youth programs. There are 1700 Hadassah chapters in this country, whose activities include social, educational and cultural programs of Jewish and Zionist interest.

Herut-USA
9 East 38th Street 10016   696-0900

Formerly known as the United Zionist Revisionists of America, this organization provides information about the nationalist political party whose name it carries. Like Herut in Israel, it is committed to a strong military defense and opposes territorial compromise.

Labor Zionist Alliance, Inc.
275 Seventh Avenue 10001   989-0300

With chapters throughout the city, this group affiliated with the Labor movement in Israel is a fraternal, educational and cultural organization. It supports schools, camps and cultural activities throughout the United States, seeking to promote Labor goals of religious pluralism, equal rights, civil liberties and social justice. It also publishes a weekly Yiddish magazine.

Mercaz
155 Fifth Avenue 10010   533-7800

The Conservative movement's Zionist arm, Mercaz seeks to promote Conservative Judaism in Israel, and encourages Conservative American Jews to make *aliya* under its rubric.

Na'amat USA
200 Madison Avenue 10016   725-8010

Formerly Pioneer Women, this American group supports the work of its Israeli sister organization of the same name. It is part of the World Labor Zionist movement, and supports social service and educational facilities for women, children and others in Israel.

North American Aliya Movement
515 Park Avenue 10022   752-0600

NAAM coordinates *aliya* activities for individuals and groups. There are sixty NAAM chapters through the country that conduct meetings, workshops, lectures and conferences for future immigrants to Israel. The group sponsors several summer and short-term programs to Israel for people who are considering *aliya*.

Religious Zionists of America
25 West 26th Street 10010   689-1414

There was a time when the term religious Zionists was an oxymoron—the Orthodox were having nothing to do with the state of Israel. RZA was founded by those in the Orthodox community who did consider themselves Zionists. Affiliated with a political party in Israel, RZA raises money and promotes *aliya* under the rubric of Orthodoxy.

Zionist Organizaton of America
4 East 34th Street 10016 481-1500

This group was created to develop American Jewish support for Israel. Unlike some other Zionist organizations, however, it has no political affiliation.

Women's League for Israel, Inc.
515 Park Avenue 10022 838-1997

Affiliated with the American Zionist Federation, although not technically a constituent agency of the group, the Women's League for Israel has 5000 members in 39 regional and local women's groups, whose primary function is to support educational, vocational and social service programs in Israel.

Sephardi Federation of America
133 East 58th Street 10022 730-1210

An affiliate of the American Zionist Federation, though again not technically a constituent, this group disseminates and publishes information dealing with Sephardic tradition and culture.

American Zionist Youth Foundation
515 Park Avenue 10022 751-6070

AZYF is an independent branch of the Zionist movement primarily concerned with children and young adults. Through its Education Department, materials are developed for Zionist youth and camp programs. The Salute to Israel Parade, held annually in Manhattan, is coordinated through this agency, as are other special city-wide programs. The Israel Program Center runs a variety of trips to Israel for young people, which are described in Chapter One. The University Services Department coordinates college programs.

Jewish National Fund
42 East 69th Street 10021 879-9300

Mostly known for its tree planting program (which is actually located at 33 East 67th Street, 737-7441), JNF is a land-reclamation and development agency, which sponsors dinners, educational seminars, activities for young professionals, Tu b'Shevat drives, tours of Israel and summer camp programs. It is affiliated with the American Zionist Federation, whose own groups are in turn affiliated with JNF!

ORGANIZATIONS CONCERNED WITH ISRAELI SOCIETY

In a real way, every organization listed here (indeed listed in this book!) is concerned with Israeli society. The organizations under this section, however, are specifically concerned with working to improve aspects of Israeli society, and do not fall under the auspices of the American Zionist Federation. That doesn't mean they don't view themselves as Zionist groups. Some do fund-raising for specific institutions and programs in Israel, while others are chiefly educational groups. They belong to all sides of the complicated political structure in Israel, from right to left and in between.

American Committee for Israel Peace Center
345 East 46th Street 10017   972-5907

>   This is the American arm of the International Center for Peace in the Middle East, located in Tel Aviv, which functions as a think-tank on the issue of peace between Jews and Arabs.

Americans for a Safe Israel
147 East 76th Street 10021   988-2121

>   AFSI opposes making what they call "dangerous concessions" to the Arabs. Their message is communicated through a newsletter, public forums, publication of books and materials, and other activities through the national office and local chapters.

American Friends of Neot Kedumim
270 West 89th Street 10024

>   This group supports the work of the Biblical Landscape Preserve, which is located in Israel, between Jerusalem and Tel Aviv. Neot Kedumim seeks to better understand early rabbinic texts dealing with agricultural matters by actually trying to re-create their settings.

American Friends of Peace Now
27 West 20th Street 10011   645-6262

>   Shalom Achshav is a broad-based nonpartisan group working for peace in the Middle East. It calls for a moratorium on further settlement of land beyond the Green Line, as well as better communication between Jews and Arabs. Its American Friends lecture about its goals and raise funds for its work.

American–Israeli Civil Liberties Coalition, Inc.
15 East 26th Street 10010   696-9603

>   This is a nonpartisan group with an Israeli counterpart whose purpose is to work toward the development of civil liberties in Israel. The American group raises money for the program in Israel, which includes the development of educational materials on civil liberties.

American Professors for Peace in the Middle East
330 Seventh Avenue 10001 563-2580

This is a small organization of academicians, whose primary purpose is to promote better understanding on college campuses of Israel and its policies. Their work includes holding seminars and other programs on area campuses, as well as arranging exchange programs between Israeli and American faculty members.

Friends of New Outlook
295 Seventh Avenue 10001 691-9860

Established in 1957 under the guidance of Martin Buber, who wrote that "The time has come for the peoples of the Middle East to acquire a new outlook," this group tries to serve as a medium for the clarification of problems concerning peace and cooperation among all the peoples of the Middle East. The group publishes a monthly magazine and sponsors seminars and conferences. It established the Center for International Peace in the Middle East, and was nominated for the Nobel Peace Prize in 1985.

Gesher Foundation
421 Seventh Avenue 10001 564-0338

Gesher is an Israeli organization trying to build bridges between Israel's disparate groups, particularly between the religious and secular youth. Through dialogue, education and mass communication, those involved (it is a membership group) are committed to "putting Israel back together again."

Interns for Peace
270 West 89th Street 10024 580-0540

Bringing Arabs and Jews together in order to create healthy and productive communities is the primary goal of this group, which sponsors training seminars and sends volunteers to work in Arab-Jewish rural communities.

Neve Shalom
270 West 89th Street 10024 724-4864

This Arab-Jewish cooperative village outside Jerusalem also sponsors a school for peace. The Manhattan office conducts educational and fund-raising programs.

Givat Haviva Educational Foundation, Inc.
150 Fifth Avenue 10011 255-2992

Givat Haviva Institute in Israel brings Jews and Arabs, as well as Ashkenazim and Sephardim, together. Supported by Kibbutz Artzi here in the U.S., the group sponsors programs, brings Israelis to speak and sends Americans to Israel.

Zionist Academic Council

515 Park Avenue 10022 371-7750

Zionist professors concerned with academic support for Israel sponsor, through this council, conferences, studies and faculty exchanges.

GOVERNMENT, BUSINESS AND TRAVEL

Organizations and agencies listed here help Americans (and Israelis living here) to make business connections and financial investments in Israel. We've also listed government agencies that offer aid to Israelis here, as well as information on tourist travel to Israel.

Consulate General of the State of Israel

800 Second Avenue 10017 697-5500

This is the official representative of the Israeli government in New York. It disseminates information, holds meetings with American Jewish leaders and aids Israeli citizens living here.

Israel Government Tourist Office

350 Fifth Avenue 10118 560-0650

Located on the nineteenth floor of the Empire State Building, this is where you go if you're planning a trip to Israel and are looking for maps, information or advice. This is not a travel agency, but a government office ready to help make your trip enjoyable and interesting. The people here can help with arrangements for having a Bar or Bat Mitzvah ceremony in Israel. (See our section on Bar and Bat Mitzvah for more information.)

El Al Israel Airlines

850 Third Avenue 10022 751-7500

Israel's airline flies regular, nonstop flights to Israel, as well as flights with stopovers in Europe. Flights depart from the International Terminal at Kennedy Airport, and boast the tightest land and air security possible.

Israel Government Trade Center ˙

350 Fifth Avenue 10118 560-0660

At the same address as the Tourist Office, this is an arm of the Israeli Ministry of Trade, which helps generate the export of Israeli products to United States markets. Although they are primarily involved with American and Israeli business people, they will provide individuals with information about where to purchase Israeli products (such as Nimrod sandals, Gottex bathing suits, Beged Or leather goods, etc.).

Bequests and Legacies
350 Fifth Avenue 10118   560-0635

An arm of the Israeli Government Ministry of Justice, this office helps Americans who wish to leave money to Israel in their wills. They have a list of Israeli charities, and will help in will preparation.

Cosell Interair
210 East 36th Street 10016   213-0036

This is a courier service that has daily shipments to Israel, much like Federal Express, except that they go only to Israel.

American–Israel Chamber of Commerce and Industry
500 Fifth Avenue 10110   354-6510

This group provides trade assistance to those interested in working with Israeli companies or doing business in Israel.

AMPAL–American Israel Corp.
10 Rockefeller Plaza 10019

This is a private company that provides investment information on Israel for those interested in financial ventures.

Isralom–Israel Homes and Real Estate
800 Second Avenue 10017   532-4949

Here is where you might go if you're interested in purchasing real estate, homes or apartments in Israel.

Tefahot Israel Mortgage Bank
800 Second Avenue 10017   697-5020

In addition to exhibition material and brochures, this office handles subsidized mortgages for housing in Israel.

The following Israel Banks have Manhattan branches, where they offer the regular services of commercial banks and you can usually exchange Israel currency.

Bank Leumi
579 Fifth Avenue 10036   382-4407

Bank Hapoalim
10 Rockefeller Plaza 10020   397-9650

Israel Discount Bank
511 Fifth Avenue 10036   551-8500

UMB
630 Fifth Avenue 10019   541-8070

FUND-RAISING FOR ISRAEL
AND ITS INSTITUTIONS

Although many organizations in this chapter raise money for programming, educational materials and staff, the groups in this section are actually fund-raising organizations, whose chief purpose is to support either specific institutions or programs in Israel, or to raise money for general aid to the country. Many of them also do educational programming or sponsor trips to Israel. We've listed first those organizations that need notation. After that, organizations whose names indicate what institution they represent are listed only with name, address and telephone number.

American Committee for the Advancement of Torah Education in Israel, Inc.
1 West 85th Street 10024 496-1618

This American-based organization raises money for two religious institutions for college-age youth in Israel.

American Friends of the Alliance Israelite Universelle
135 William Street 10038 425-5170

This group helps to support over thirty-five educational facilities in Israel and other developing countries.

American Friends of Israel
10 Rockefeller Plaza 10020 582-8431

AFIL is a small private charity that supports schools for gifted children in Israel.

Fund for Higher Education
1500 Broadway 10036 354-4660

This private foundation raises money for Israeli and American universities, to foster better relations and communication.

Histadrut House
33 East 67th Street 10021 628-1000

Histadrut is the general Federation of Labor in Israel, and here in New York the American group raises money for Histadrut's social welfare, educational and health programs in Israel.

Israel Cancer Research Fund
1290 Sixth Avenue 10104 969-9800

This group sponsors cancer research in Israel, and brings together scientists from America and Israel who are involved in cancer research.

Israel Tennis Centers Association, Inc.
133 East 58th Street 10022 308-7266

When tennis started its rise in the United States, some people thought it would be a great sport for Israel too. This group raises money to build courts and develop tennis programs throughout Israel, especially in new settlements and development towns.

Jerusalem Foundation
500 Fifth Avenue 10036 840-1101

Under the auspices of its Jerusalem group and Mayor Teddy Kolleck, this foundation raises money for the city of Jerusalem.

Kolel Shomre Hachomas
5 Beekman Street 10038 732-0300

This Orthodox group raises money for various religious institutions in Israel.

National Committee for Labor Israel
33 East 67th Street 10021 628-1000

This group of trade unions, labor Zionists, and other interested organizations supports the work of Histadrut, the Israel labor union. Through education and fund-raising, the group supports health and educational facilities in Israel. The Israel Histadrut Foundation, at the same address, helps people write wills and otherwise make financial arrangements for the benefit of Histadrut programs.

National Council of Jewish Women
15 East 26th Street 10010 532-1740

The Council has a program called Ship-A-Box, which collects and sends toys and educational materials to disadvantaged children in Israel. They also have a Research Institute for Innovation in Education at Hebrew University.

National United Jewish Appeal
99 Park Avenue 10016 818-9100

Created by the American community in response to *Kristallnacht,* this was the first really centralized fund-raising body to gather resources to help Jews in crisis. Its fund-raising efforts have contributed to the rescue and resettlement of Jews throughout the world, particularly in Israel, Europe and South America.

New Israel Fund
111 West 40th Street 10018   302-0066

Calling itself an "innovative partnership of Israeli and American Jews dedicated to supporting the growing movement for positive social change" in Israel, the New Israel Fund raises money and conducts educational forums in support of a broad spectrum of projects and institutions in Israel that do not receive traditional funding. Groups like a rape crisis center, a battered women's shelter, an Israel–U.S. Civil Liberties Law Program, and the Association for Support and Defense of Bedouin Rights in Israel have received New Israel Fund grants in the past.

PEF Israel Endowment Funds, Inc.
342 Madison Avenue 10173   599-1260

This long-standing group has quietly sent over $56 million to Israel, with no fund-raising organization. It is a public charity, and welcomes contributions, which can be earmarked for specific Israel organizations. Money is given to a wide range of institutions and special projects.

P'eylim–American Yeshiva Student Union
3 West 16th Street 10011   989-2500

Yeshiva students and graduates formed this group to help Israeli immigrant youth from Arab countries. They sponsor summer camps, send rabbis and teachers to development towns, and run religious programs for new immigrants.

Poale Agudath Israel of America
156 Fifth Avenue 10010   924-9474

PAI builds and maintains various religious communities and institutions in Israel.

State of Israel Bonds
730 Broadway 10003   677-9650

Not a fund-raising or charitable organization per se, State of Israel Bonds aids in the development of the state of Israel through the sale of its bonds, which may be purchased directly from them or from Israeli banks.

United Charity Institutions of Jerusalem
1141 Broadway 10001   683-3221

This group raises money for the support of a variety of educational and social service institutions in Jerusalem.

United Israel Appeal
515 Park Avenue 10022   699-0800

United Israel Appeal is not a fund-raising organization, but rather the bridge between United Jewish Appeal–Federation and the state of Israel. As the primary beneficiary of UJA money, as well as United States financial aid, UIA provides Israel's Jewish Agency with funds to help educational, immigration, agricultural and social service organizations.

Women's Social Service for Israel, Inc.
240 West 98th Street 10025 666-7880

This women's group raises money for its hospitals and homes in Israel.

United Tiberias Institutions
5 Beekman Street 10038 349-8755

This group raises money to support educational and social service programs in the city of Tiberias, Israel.

ALYN–American Society for Handicapped Children in Israel
19 West 44th Street 10036 869-8085

American Associates, Ben Gurion University
342 Madison Avenue 10173 687-7721

American Association for the Welfare of Soldiers in Israel
15 East 26th Street 10010 684-0669

American Committee for the National Sick Fund of Israel, Inc.
60 East 42nd Street 10165 599-3670

American Committee for the Weitzmann Institute of Science
515 Park Avenue 10022 752-1300

American Committee for Shaare Zedek Hospital
49 West 45th Street 10036 354-8801

American Committee for Shenkar College of Textile Technology and Fashion
855 Sixth Avenue 947-1597

American Friends of Beth Hatefutsoth
515 Park Avenue 10022 752-0246

American Friends of Beit Halochem
136 East 39th Street 10016 725-1211

American Friends of Everyman's University–Israel
330 West 58th Street 10019 713-1515

American Friends of Haifa Medical Center
136 East 39th Street 10016 725-1211

American Friends of Haifa University
20o Fifth Avenue 10010   696-4022

American Friends of Hebrew University
11 East 69th Street 10021   472-9800

American Friends of the Israel Museum
10 East 40th Street 10016   683-5190

American Friends of the Israel Philharmonic
250 West 57th Street 10019   245-6760

American Friends of the Jerusalem Mental Health Center
10 East 40th Street 10016   725-8175

American Friends of the Kibbutzim in Israel, Inc.
150 Fifth Avenue 10011   255-8760

American Friends of Laniado Hospital
18 West 45th Street 10036   944-2690

American Friends of Life Care Jerusalem
5 Beekman Street 10038   608-1699

American Friends of Lifeline for the Old
1450 Broadway 10018   221-6050

American Friends of the Mirrer Yeshiva in Jerusalem
1133 Broadway 10010   243-3987

American Friends of Neveh Zion
3 West 16th Street 10011   929-1845

American Friends of Ohr Somayach
39 Broadway 10006   344-2000

American Friends of the Rambam Medical Center
475 Fifth Avenue 10036   689-6846

American Friends of Ramat Hanegev
118 East 25th Street 10010   460-8708

American Friends of Tel Aviv University
360 Lexington Avenue 10017   687-5651

American Friends of Yeshivat Kerem B'Yavneh
6 East 45th Street 10017   687-0805

American Friends of Yeshivot Bnei Akiva in Israel
50 West 34th Street 10001   947-6787

American Friends of Yeshivat Sha'alvim
156 Fifth Avenue 10011   924-9475

American–Israeli Lighthouse
30 East 60th Street 10022   838-5322

American Red Magen David for Israel
888 Seventh Avenue 10106   757-1627

American Society for Technion–Israel Institute of Technology
271 Madison Avenue 10016   889-2050

Ariel American Friends of Midrasha and United Israel Institutions
10 East 40th Street 10016   725-0308

Bar Ilan University
853 Seventh Avenue 10019   315-1990

Hebrew University–Technion Joint Maintenance Appeal
11 East 69th Street 10021   988-8418

Jerusalem Institutions for the Blind–Keren-Or, Inc.
1133 Broadway 10010   255-1180

AMERICA-ISRAEL RELATIONS

America-Israel Cultural Foundation, Inc.
485 Madison Avenue 10022   751-2700

> Each year this group holds a major cultural event in Manhattan, bringing talented young Israeli musicians here to perform, in an effort to build cultural bridges between the two countries.

America-Israel Friendship League
134 East 39th Street 10016   213-8630

> Initiated by B'nai Zion, this nonsectarian organization distributes books and other materials to university libraries, provides funds for seminars and programs about Israel, and generally works to improve communication and understanding between the United States and Israel.

American Israel Public Affairs Committee
370 Lexington Avenue 10178   557-2408

> Based in Washington, D.C., AIPAC is a registered lobby of the Israel government, and lobbies for legislation affecting Israel, Soviet Jewry, and other Jewish-Israeli interests.

ALIYA

If you're thinking about making *aliya*—living in Israel permanently—there are some places that provide help. At 515 Park

Avenue (752-0600), a central Zionist address in Manhattan, a few offices can help you with *aliya*. Israel Aliya Center recruits Jewish families and individuals for *aliya*, and will help you in all aspects of the decision and move. The North American Aliya Movement (NAAM) sponsors sixty chapters in thirty-seven cities to promote *aliya* and provide support for future immigrants. NAAM runs several specialized and general trips designed to help the prospective immigrant get a true sense of life in Israel. Both the Reform and Conservative movements help people make *aliya*, specifically to kibbutzim under their auspices. For more information call ARZA (249-0100) or MERCAZ (533-7800).

Kibbutz Aliya Desk
27 West 20th Street 10011   255-1338

This is a central office for all Israeli kibbutzim, and the place you should go if you're considering making *aliya* to a kibbutz. The desk is staffed by representatives of religious as well as nonreligious kibbutzim, and also kibbutzim identified with social and labor government factions. There is a wide range of programs available. At the same address you'll find the Young Kibbutz Movement, which has local groups of young people, eighteen to thirty-five, who are interested in exploring options of kibbutz life in Israel.

Eretz Yisrael Movement
15 East 26th Street 10010   684-7370

Dedicated to the principle of *aliya*, this group provides information and counseling for people who are interested in settling in Israel, though it doesn't actually handle the nuts and bolts issues. It is affiliated with the World Zionist Organization, and sponsors various summer trips to Israel, including one designed for families wishing to get a "taste of Israel."

If your child has made *aliya*, and you would like to connect with other parents for support, there is one resource in Manhattan: Parents of North American Israelis, 515 Park Avenue 10022 (935-5805). Formerly called the Association of Parents of American Israelis, this group holds meetings to help deal with the concerns of parents whose children live in Israel. The group has a free loan fund for emergencies such as trips home in the event of a death in the family, and emergency medical care. With forty-one chapters across the United States and Canada, PNAI has five chapters in the metropolitan area.

Chapter 13
THE LARGER PICTURE

Because of the large number of Jews in the New York area, virtually every major Jewish organization in the United States—and even throughout the world—has an office here. There are communal and community relations groups, which look out for Jewish interests, especially when they are threatened or can be enhanced, and fund-raising oganizations that raise money for a variety of causes (groups that raise money specifically for Israel are described in the preceding chapter). We've described religious organizations, which promote denominational ideologies or seek to strengthen Judaism in the United States and overseas. A section also lists political organizations, which take an active role in lobbying, demonstrating and marshalling Jewish energy for issues of concern to the Jewish community. Many of the Jewish professional organizations have Manhattan addresses; these "unions" seek to create community among their members and to provide them with occupational opportunities and security. We've described educational and cultural groups, which promote Jewish educational and cultural life through programming and the publication of materials. Finally, we've enumerated those groups devoted to keeping the memory of the Holocaust alive, through programs, printed and visual material, and education. Some of these groups also provide aid to survivors.

Although many groups in this chapter have programs for New Yorkers (and we've described them throughout the book), their major focus is the national or international Jewish community. Clearly, though, the New York Jewish community is enriched by their presence.

COMMUNITY RELATIONS AND JEWISH WELFARE ORGANIZATIONS

American Jewish Committee
165 East 56th Street 10022   751-4000

The Committee, founded in 1906 to help Jewish victims of pogroms, has continued to see its role as safeguarding the freedom of Jews throughout the world, but its emphasis on civil rights for all cuts across denominational boundaries. It is one of the largest Jewish organizations in the United States. The New York chapter sponsors public forums on national Jewish issues, an oral history project on Jews in politics in New York City, workshops on homelessness, and other programs for its 5000 area members and others. A new group, the "Successors," is designed to meet the needs of people between the ages of twenty and forty who are interested in community involvement. The AJC publishes *Commentary* and *Present Tense*.

American Jewish Congress
15 East 84th Street 10028   879-4500

Originally founded to protect Jewish rights in countries around the world, particularly those of Jews in Europe between the World Wars, the Congress has worked to protect Jews from discrimination in housing, education and employment, and works for affirmative action for *all* minority groups. It is active on the Jewish cultural scene through the Martin Steinberg Center. Its local office provides a variety of programs and legal assistance. *Judaism* is published here.

The American Jewish Joint Distribution Committee, Inc. 60 East 42nd Street 10017   687-6200

For more than seventy-five years, the "Joint" has been the primary way that American Jews have helped others overseas. When famine struck in Ethiopia, it was to the Joint that people sent checks for food. When the earthquake in Mexico City threatened to destroy the community, it was to the Joint that Jews contributed. Amongst its varied activities, the Joint supports ORT, the Alliance Israelite Universelle and Ozar Hatorah.

Anti-Defamation League of B'nai B'rith
823 United Nations Plaza 10017 490-2525

ADL fights discrimination and threats to democracy, particularly where they concern the Jewish community. It disseminates information, works with other communal organizations and their leaders, conducts seminars and programs about Judaism, participates in interfaith activities, and sees itself as a watch dog for the Jewish people. Its headquarters are here, with twenty-seven regional offices throughout the United States.

Associated YM–YWHA of Greater New York
130 East 59th Street 10022 751-8880

This is the coordinating arm for the many Jewish community centers in the New York area that provide social, cultural, educational, and health and physical education programs for their members.

Association of Jewish Family and Children's Agencies
40 Worth Street 10013 608-6660

Over 100 children's and family agencies in the Jewish community belong to this umbrella group, which is a national organization that strengthens the work of its member agencies by providing consultative services and sponsoring conferences.

B'nai B'rith
823 United Nations Plaza 10017 490-2525

The world's largest and oldest Jewish service organization sponsors not only the ADL, but Youth Activities (see "Children"), Community Volunteer Services programs, services for senior adults, Israel programs, Jewish adult education programs, career and counseling services, and many more programs of interest to the Jewish community. Activities are coordinated through its local chapters, District No. 1 and the Empire Region.

Conference of Presidents of Major American Jewish Organizations
515 Park Avenue 10022 752-1616

Almost every Jewish organization is represented at the Conference of Presidents. The group tries, where possible, to speak for the Jewish people on matters of concern in the Jewish and general community.

Council of Jewish Federations
730 Broadway 10003 475-5000

Comprised of 200 Federations throughout the country, CJF provides leadership training, campaign planning, community building, personnel services and a host of other services to its members.

Jewish Community Relations Council of New York
111 West 40th Street 10018 221-1535

This umbrella group represents forty-five member organizations that work on relations between various Jewish communities, and the Jewish community's relations with the rest of the world. To this end it functions as a liaison with New York City, State, and federal offices; it participates in or sponsors the Task Force on Missionaries and Cults, Jewish Coalition for Higher Education, Commission on Jewish Security and Police Liaison, as well as committees on Israel, international politics, and Holocaust concerns. In Manhattan, local community relations councils—each with its own neighborhood programs, projects and concerns—are located at:

United Jewish Council of Lower East Side
235 East Broadway 10002 235-6037

Greenwich Village–Soho & Lower West Side Community Council
Educational Alliance 51 East 10th Street 10003 420-1150

Mid-Manhattan Jewish Community Council
344 East 14th Street 10003 674-7200

Upper East Side Jewish Community Council
92nd Street Y 1395 Lexington Avenue 10028 427-6000

West Side Jewish Community Council
210 West 91st Street 10024 496-0401

Jewish Community Council of Washington Heights and Inwood
121 Bennett Avenue Room 11A 568-5450

JWB 15 East 26th Street 10010 532-4949

This umbrella group acts as a consultant to Jewish community centers throughout the nation, working with them in planning, staff development, and boosting their effectiveness as centers of Jewish life. Their departments include the Jewish Music Council, Jewish Book Council, Jewish Media Service, and Lecture Bureau.

National Jewish Community Relations Advisory
Council 443 Park Avenue South 10016 684-6950

This is a coordinating body of Jewish organizations throughout the United States, whose purpose is promoting cooperation between all these groups. It works with its member organizations to get them to try to formulate policy jointly and to exchange information.

National Conference of Christians and Jews
71 Fifth Avenue 10003 206-0006

NCCJ provides educational materials to religious groups of all denominations in order to promote communication and cooperation among America's religious faiths.

The Radius Institute
19 West 44th Street, Room 311 10036 719-9383

A unique organization in American Jewish life, Radius works like a management consultant firm to small, or new and developing, Jewish organizations. It sponsors workshops for communal leaders on topics such as networking and fund-raising.

UJA–Federation of Jewish Philanthropies
130 East 59th Street 10022 980-1000

Once upon a time, there was the UJA of Greater New York, which raised money mostly for Israel, and the Federation of Jewish Philanthropies, which raised money for constituent social service, education and cultural organizations in the metropolitan area. Bit by bit, however, in city after city, UJA and Federation offices were merging. And now New York has merged as well, with the new organization called UJA–Federation of Jewish Philanthropies. Within this new structure, the Domestic Division will allocate money to organizations and agencies in the metropolitan area, while the Overseas Division will coordinate allocations to those groups dealing with needs in Europe, South America, Africa and Israel, or wherever else a need arises overseas. Among its many departments, the Jewish Information and Referral Service (753-2288) provides New Yorkers with all kinds of information and aid concerning both Jewish and secular agencies, organizations and programs.

World Jewish Congress   1 Park Avenue 10016   679-0600
Established by the American Jewish Congress in 1936, the WJC aims to serve as an international watchdog for Jewish interests.

RELIGIOUS ORGANIZATIONS

Agudath Israel of America
5 Beekman Street 10038   791-1800

Through its many educational and social service programs, this Orthodox group, led by the heads of major Orthodox Yeshivot, is dedicated to strict adherence to Jewish law. Through its office of Government Affairs, it advocates legislation protecting Orthodox Jews in areas such as *kashrut,* Shabbat observance, education, and immigration.

CLAL–The National Jewish Center for Learning and Leadership   401 Seventh Avenue 10001   714-9500
This organization, which has undergone several metamorphoses over the years, spans the denominational movements and seeks to educate leaders to help perpetuate

the Jewish people within the framework of a modern, open society. With an emphasis on denominational communication and cooperation, CLAL and its leader Irving Greenberg run rabbinic and lay workshops throughout the country.

Federation of Reconstructionist Congregations and Havurot   270 West 89th Street 10024   496-2960

Reconstructionism, the newest denominational movement in American Jewish life, views Judaism as an evolving religious civilization, comprised of art, culture, music, dance, literature, law, philosophy and religion. Committed to living in two civilizations—American and Jewish—Reconstructionists seek to create Jewish communities dedicated to the highest ideals of both cultures. The Federation (FRCH), as the organizational center of fifty-five Reconstructionist congregations in the United States, provides advice, education and support for these synagogues, and participates in the broader Jewish community as well. It publishes *The Reconstructionist.*

National Council of Young Israel
3 West 16th Street 10011   929-1525

Over 300,000 members of Young Israel synagogues throughout the country are members of this National Council, which services Young Israel congregations and provides help in the metropolitan area to seniors, young adults and children. Its social services include an employment bureau and two health facilities. The group publishes *The Young Israel Viewpoint.*

National Havurah Committee
270 West 89th Street 10024   496-0055

The NHC serves as an advisory and support center for all *havurot* (fellowships) throughout the country. It sponsors annual institutes of study, worship and cultural programs, and publishes *New Traditions,* a quarterly journal.

New York Federation of Reform Synagogues
838 Fifth Avenue 10021   249-0100

This is the New York regional office of the Union of American Hebrew Congregations, the synagogue arm of the Reform movement. Dedicated to advancing the programs and ideology of liberal Judaism, the New York regional office services approximately 104 Reform congregations. It provides outreach to intermarried couples as well as some specific services to needy Jews in the New York area.

Synagogue Council of America
327 Lexington Avenue 10016 686-8670

An umbrella organization with a leak (representing three of the four denominational groups in American Jewish life—

Reconstructionists have not yet been included), Synagogue Council conducts research, sponsors programs and tries, when possible, to speak with a unified voice on issues of concern to the Jewish community.

Union of American Hebrew Congregations
838 Fifth Avenue 10021   249-0100

UAHC provides a wide range of religious, cultural, administrative and educational aid to its 750 Reform-affiliated congregations throughout North America. Among its publications are *Keeping Posted* and *Reform Judaism*.

Union of Orthodox Jewish Congregations of America
45 West 36th Street 10018   563-4000

This national organization for thousands of Orthodox congregations seeks to perpetuate traditional Judaism through service to synagogues and youth. It maintains a kosher certification service. The New York Region office services more than 200 affiliated synagogues as well as nonaffiliated synagogues that call for its services, which are religious, educational and social. It is active in public affairs and coordinates activities among the communities in the New York area.

Union of Sephardic Congregations
8 West 70th Street 10023   873-0300

This group is comprised of Sephardic synagogues throughout the United States. It prints Sephardic prayerbooks in Hebrew and English.

United Israel World Union
1123 Broadway, #723 10010   688-7557

Founded in 1943 as a universal movement committed to Mosaic principles, this group has chapters throughout the country and the world. Its motto is "One God, One Law, for all humanity."

United Synagogue of America
155 Fifth Avenue 10010   533-7800

This is the synagogue arm of the Conservative movement in the United States, and it coordinates and lends support to more than 800 member congregations. It helps with their educational and administrative programs and also provides staffing. Affiliated with the Jewish Theological Seminary of America and the Rabbinical Assembly, it communicates the goals of Conservative Judaism, which include a commitment to both tradition and change. The Metropolitan Region coordinates local activities.

Women's Tefilla Network   928-2001

This is an umbrella organization for Orthodox women's davening groups all over the country. In the Metropolitan area, such groups exist in Manhattan, the Bronx, Queens and Brooklyn, as well as in the suburbs. The Network provides resources and information for these groups, whose worship style and schedules vary.

World Union for Progressive Judaism
838 Fifth Avenue 10021   249-0100

This is an international group of Reform, liberal and progressive Jews that promotes the ideology of liberal Judaism through programs, publications and advocacy.

World Council of Synagogues
155 Fifth Avenue 10010   533-7800

An international group of Conservative Jews, the World Council promotes the development of Conservative synagogues throughout the world, and represents the Conservative movement at the World Zionist Organization.

POLITICAL ORGANIZATIONS

Several Jewish organizations with political concerns have Manhattan offices and programs. Groups concerned with general issues of social justice as well as with specific political struggles engage in educational programming, news conferences, letter-writing, demonstrations and other activities supporting their causes.

American Committee for the Rescue and Resettlement of Iraqi Jews   1200 Fifth Avenue 10029   427-1246

The 1000 members of this group work for the rescue of Jews imprisoned in or wishing to leave Iraq.

American Council for Judaism
295 Fifth Avenue 10001   947-8878

This group maintains that Israel is a homeland only for its own citizens, and fights against notions of Jewish nationalism.

American Jewish Alternatives to Zionism
133 East 73rd Street 10021   628-2727

This is another anti-Zionist group, which calls for a "de-Zionized Israel," and takes active public stands against what it calls "Zionist aggression."

The Center for Russian Jewry–Student Struggle for Soviet Jewry   210 West 91st Street   10024   928-7451

SSSJ stages rallies, disseminates information and holds public forums to emphasize the plight of Soviet Jews.

Coalition to Free Soviet Jews
8 West 40th Street   10018   354-1316

Formerly the Greater New York Conference on Soviet Jewry, this coalition of eighty-five organizations in the metropolitan area organizes Solidarity Sunday, the day-long parade for Soviet Jews. Through its many programs in schools and communal facilities, as well as its publications, press conferences and negotiations, the Coalition advocates the religious, cultural and civil rights of Soviet Jews, particularly their right to emigrate.

Commission on Social Action of Reform Judaism
838 Fifth Avenue   10021   249-0100

Long committed and in the forefront on issues of social justice in the Jewish community, the Reform movement's national commission supplies information to its local committees, which plan community programs on a wide spectrum of social justice issues.

Jewish Defense Organization
134 West 32nd Street   10001   239-0447

Like the California-based JDL, the Jewish Defense Organization has karate and other self-defense classes, as well as patrols in crime-ridden Jewish neighborhoods in the city.

Jewish Labor Committee
25 East 21st Street   10010   477-0707

With a membership of 500,000, this coalition of trade unions and other groups fights totalitarianism, anti-Semitism and racial discrimination.

Legal Coalition for Syrian Jewry
111 West 40th Street   10018   221-1535

This is an association of lawyers, public officials, law professors and others concerned with the plight of Syrian Jews. The group disseminates information to synagogues in the New York area.

National Conference on Soviet Jewry
10 East 40th Street   10016   227-5885

This group coordinates nationwide efforts on behalf of Soviet Jews. With local affiliates throughout the country, and over forty member agencies, the conference conducts seminars, distributes materials and works with governmental officials to rescue Soviet Jews.

New Jewish Agenda 14a Church Street 10007 595-0214

This is a group of progressive Jews concerned about nuclear disarmament, economic justice, Israeli-Palestinian relations, feminism and other issues it sees as important to the Jewish community. There are local chapters throughout the country, with approximately 4000 members.

North American Conference on Ethiopian Jewry
200 Amsterdam Avenue 10023 595-1759

This group supplies speakers and slide presentations for Jewish groups interested in Ethiopian Jews.

PROFESSIONAL ORGANIZATIONS

Those who work in a professional capacity in the Jewish community have been quick to form organizations that support and guide them in their various tasks as communal, rabbinic, cantorial and educational professionals. In addition to providing comradeship and advice, many of these groups have placement services for their members, health benefits, journals and other programs and services.

American Association of Rabbis
350 Fifth Avenue 10010 244-3350

This is a union for ordained rabbis who are not affiliated with any of the denominational movements. It provides placement for its members.

American Conference of Cantors
838 Fifth Avenue 10021 737-5020

The professional organization for Reform cantors, this group maintains a placement service and publishes books and music pertaining to Jewish worship.

American Jewish Correctional Chaplains Association
10 East 73rd Street 10021 879-8415

Under the auspices of the New York Board of Rabbis, this is a professional group for Jewish chaplains who serve area prisons.

American Jewish Public Relations Society
234 Fifth Avenue 10001 697-5895

Public relations workers at Jewish communal organizations come together here to advance professional goals and standards. Employment assistance is provided.

Association of Jewish Center Workers
15 East 26th Street 10010 532-4949

Made up of workers at community centers, YM–YWHAs, youth organizations, synagogues and other facilities, this association offers professional growth opportunities, benefits and publications.

Cantor's Assembly 150 Fifth Avenue 10111 691-8020

Cantors in Conservative congregations throughout the United States and the world belong to this group, which publishes a journal and maintains a placement service.

Central Conference of American Rabbis
21 East 40th Street 10016 684-4990

The CCAR is the rabbinic arm of the Reform movement, with 1500 members. It publishes a journal and other materials, provides professional benefits to its members, works for the advancement of Reform Judaism, and maintains a placement service.

Conference on Jewish Social Studies
2112 Broadway 10023 724-5336

This is an academic group of social scientists, communal workers, historians and educators who are interested in Jewish social studies. The group publishes a journal, *Jewish Social Studies.*

Council for Jewish Education
114 Fifth Avenue 10011 675-5656

This is a group of teachers of Hebrew in universities, heads of educational agencies, and other Jewish educators, who come together to promote Jewish education, raise professional standards, support Jewish educators and strengthen Jewish life. It maintains a placement service.

Council of Jewish Organizations in Civil Service, Inc. 45 East 33rd Street 10016 689-2015

There are over 120,000 Jewish civil servants in city, state, and federal levels of government. This group, which is made up of thirty-nine organizations, combats discrimination, protects the rights of civil service employees and provides benefits to its members.

Council of Young Israel Rabbis
3 West 16th Street 10011 929-1525

Rabbis serving Young Israel congregations throughout the United States and the world belong to this group, which promotes traditional Judaism and encourages study. It maintains a charitable program and placement service.

Hebrew Actors Union
31 East 7th Street 10003 674-1923

This is a small union of Jewish actors, many of whom are involved with Yiddish theatre. The group has two hundred members, to whom it provides professional, cultural, and educational assistance.

Jewish Educators Assembly
15 East 26th Street 10010 532-4949, ext. 206

This educators' group affiliated with United Synagogue helps make policy for Conservative Jewish schools, provides professional standards for teachers, and provides a placement service.

Jewish Ministers Cantors Association of America
3 West 16th Street 10011 675-6601

This was the first cantorial organization in the United States, founded to perpetuate the profession in its traditional form. It provides its members with classes, library resources, financial aid and placement help.

Jewish Music Educators Association
426 West 58th Street 10019 245-8200

This group seeks to promote Jewish music in Jewish education and to maintain professional standards for Jewish music teachers.

Jewish Teachers Association
45 East 33rd Street 10016 684-0556

The JTA is a group of 28,000 Jewish educators in public and private schools around the United States. It combats discrimination and provides personal and professional services to its members.

National Association for the Advancement of Orthodox Judaism
132 Nassau Street 10038 513-0100

This group of rabbis and scholars promotes traditional Judaism and provides placement to foreign-born rabbis and others.

National Conference of Yeshiva Principals
160 Broadway 227-1000

There are over 1000 members of this organization, which brings together principals of Hebrew day schools, sponsors seminars and compiles statistics on Jewish education.

National Council for Jewish Education
426 West 58th Street 10019 245-8200

Housed at the Board of Jewish Education, this is a professional association of principals and teachers in Jewish schools.

New York Board of Rabbis
10 East 73rd Street 10021   879-8415

One of the few places that Reform, Reconstructionist, Conservative and Orthodox rabbis come together for mutual support, educational programs, professional assistance, and service to the larger community is at the New York Board of Rabbis. Despite its title, this group is actually national in scope, but most of its members live in the metropolitan area. The Board's various services to the community have been listed throughout this book; in addition, it is a professional organization that supports rabbis through a wide array of programs.

Rabbinical Assembly   3080 Broadway 10027   678-8060

The union of Conservative rabbis, the RA has about 1200 members and is dedicated to promoting Conservative Judaism and fostering comradeship among its members. It publishes a journal and prayerbooks, has a rabbinical court, and maintains a placement service. The Manhattan region coordinates local programs.

Rabbinical Alliance of America
156 Fifth Avenue 10010   242-6420

This ultra-Orthodox rabbinical organization has about 400 members and maintains a rabbinical court for divorce and arbitration. It publishes journals and provides support for Orthodox rabbis.

Rabbinical Council of America
275 Seventh Avenue 10001   807-7888

Another professional group for ordained Orthodox rabbis, the RCA participates in intradenominational programs and sponsors various seminars in the metropolitan area. It publishes journals, helps to place rabbis in congregations, and works for the advancement of Orthodox Judaism.

Shomrim Society   1 Police Plaza 10038   964-5547

Founded in 1922 to lobby for members' rights, this group of Jewish policemen and women has about 2300 members, including active and retired officers. The group is involved in social service activities and provides some benefits for its members.

Union of Orthodox Rabbis
235 East Broadway 10002   964-6337

Five hundred Orthodox rabbis belong to this union, which seeks to protect the interests of religious Jewry.

World Conference of Jewish Communal Service
15 East 26th Street 10010   683-8056

Founded by Jewish communal workers throughout the world, this umbrella organization serves as a meeting place for those who work in and for the Jewish community. They hold a conference in Jerusalem every four years and provide members with educational and professional resources.

EDUCATIONAL ORGANIZATIONS

American Academy for Jewish Research
3080 Broadway 10027   878-8864

The Academy fosters Jewish learning and research by holding periodic meetings of scholars, issuing publications and promoting cooperation among Jewish scholars in the United States and other countries.

American Society of Sephardic Studies
500 West 185th Street 10033   960-5235

This is an organization of Jewish scholars in Sephardic studies that has academic presentations and maintains a speakers' bureau.

Association of Advanced Rabbinical and Talmudic Schools   175 Fifth Avenue, Room 711 10010   477-0950

This is the accrediting agency for rabbinical and Talmudic schools all over the United States.

Association of Jewish Libraries, New York Metropolitan Area   c/o National Foundation for Jewish Culture
122 East 42nd Street 10168   490-2280

This association of professionals working in Jewish libraries or with Judaica collections in other settings offers workshops and support for its members.

Board of Jewish Education of Greater New York
426 West 58th Street 10019   245-8200

This large central agency for Jewish education has a broad range of activities aimed at improving the quality of education in Jewish day schools and religious schools throughout the area. They operate workshops and continuing education programs for teachers, advise on and provide curriculum, and provide service to day schools in administration, management, food services, curriculum and programming. In addition BJE also operates a media center to help schools evaluate and obtain audiovisual materials.

The Center for Computers in Jewish Education
304 Park Avenue South 10010   677-7420

Sponsored by Bramson ORT, the vocational school, this unique center is a resource for educators interested in Jewish software for use in day schools and supplementary schools. Though the center does not sell anything, those interested in reviewing a particular piece of software can do so here. Seminars are also held for educators.

Coalition for Alternatives in Jewish Education
468 Park Avenue South, Room 904 10016   696-0740

This organization operates a curriculum bank and provides a marketplace for career opportunities. It sponsors an annual conference each summer with intensive workshops for lay and professional Jewish educators.

Jewish Chautauqua Society
838 Fifth Avenue 10021 570-0707

This affiliate of the Union of American Hebrew Congregations endows courses in Judaism at universities in the New York area. It is especially interested in campuses and organizations where there is no Jewish presence.

Jewish Education Service of North America
730 Broadway 10003   260-0006

JESNA is the coordinating agency for Jewish education that works with both local and national agencies in assessing needs and evaluating existing educational institutions. It provides consultation in the areas of curriculum, staff development and methodology, works to upgrade Jewish education professionals, and does research on all aspects of Jewish education.

The Melton Research Center for Jewish Education
3080 Broadway 10027   678-8031

Housed at the Jewish Theological Seminary, Melton seeks to "improve the quality of Jewish education through the development of programs, materials, and texts that deal with contemporary society and its effect on ethical and religious life."

National Council for Torah Education
25 West 26th Street 10010   689-1414

This educational organization is sponsored by the Religious Zionists of America, and promotes intensive Jewish education in both day and supplementary schools.

National Society for Hebrew Day Schools
229 Park Avenue South 10010   674-6700

Torah U'mesorah, as this group is known, is a national association serving religious day schools. It also helps new schools get started, and sponsors educational programs.

United Parent–Teachers Association of Jewish Schools 326 West 58th Street 10019 245-8200

Part of the Board of Jewish Education, this group functions as an umbrella organization for all parent-teacher groups in day schools and supplementary schools in the Greater New York area. It runs seminars, provides information, and gives advice to these groups.

CULTURAL ORGANIZATIONS

American Society for Jewish Music
155 Fifth Avenue 10010 533-2601

This organization seeks to encourage composition, performance and research in both secular and liturgical music. To this end it sponsors performances of new and rarely-heard works, publishes a scholarly journal, and works to establish links between Jewish universities and music institutions throughout the world.

Association of Jewish Book Publishers
838 Fifth Avenue 10021 525-3844

This organization represents thirty-five Jewish book publishers in the United States, many of whom are located in New York.

Congress for Jewish Culture
25 East 21 Street 10010 505-8040

An umbrella group of writers, educators, and cultural organizations concerned with Yiddish culture, the Congress for Jewish Culture promotes all kinds of activities, including art exhibits, literary events, concerts, and publication of Yiddish books.

Jewish Genealogical Society
P.O. Box 63898 10128

For those inspired by *Roots, The Immigrants,* and all the other multigenerational sagas, this group may provide some resources for tracing your family history. There are meetings and the group publishes a newsletter giving tips on how to find information about ancestors in devastated European communities. For information about the group's activities, call Steve Siegel at 427-6000, ext. 215.

Jewish Historical Society
8 West 70th Street 10023 873-0700

Founded to promote research in American-Jewish history, this group has no research library, but sponsors education programs, lectures and walking tours, and publishes a newsletter.

Jewish Music Alliance 1133 Broadway 10010 924-8311

This group devotes itself to distributing Jewish music and reading material, and is affiliated with a number of Jewish and Yiddish choral groups.

JWB Jewish Book Council
15 East 26th Street 10010 532-4949

The Jewish Book Council, whose board is made up of authors, educators, publishers and representatives of Jewish organizations, sponsors Jewish Book Month, the National Jewish Book Awards, *Jewish Book World* (a quarterly publication), book fairs, and other programs that promote awareness of Jewish books.

JWB Jewish Media Service
15 East 26th Street 10010 532-4949

This is JWB's clearinghouse for audiovisual resources, and in addition to doing consultation and referrals to synagogues, Jewish community centers and other educational institutions, it operates a film and video distribution service.

JWB Jewish Music Council
15 East 26th Street 10010 532-4939

This department of JWB serves as a coordinating body for Jewish music activities and encourages composition and research in Jewish music.

League for Yiddish
200 West 72nd Street, Suite 40 10023 787-6675

This organization seeks to perpetuate and enhance Yiddish as a living language and sees itself as the spiritual home for people who love Yiddish. It publishes a literary quarterly and sponsors programs of Yiddish writers and speakers.

Martin Steinberg Center, American Jewish Congress
15 East 84th Street 10028 879-4500

This community for Jewish artists seeks to promote Jewish art; it supports the artists with workshops, study groups and forums in which to display their work. It also publishes the *Jewish Arts Newsletter* providing information about coming events and the work of artists or groups in the United States. The National Jewish Artisans Guild is also part of the Martin Steinberg Center.

National Foundation for Jewish Culture
122 East 42nd Street, Suite 1512 10168 490-2280

As the national agency for Council of Jewish Federations, this organization provides consultation and support to other Jewish cultural and educational institutions, and serves as a clearinghouse for information about Jewish culture. It supports projects that develop and preserve Jewish cultural life in the U.S., including national conferences and festivals in theater, music, Yiddish translation and research.

National Hebrew Culture Council
14 East 4th Street 10012   674-8412

This group provides educational materials, and runs contests and teacher seminars in public schools to foster the teaching of the Hebrew language.

HOLOCAUST ORGANIZATIONS

American Federation of Jews from Central Europe
570 Seventh Avenue 10018   921-3871

As the coordinating agency for American Jews who fled central Europe during the Holocaust, this organization does research on the history, immigration and settlement of this group, holds conferences, and sponsors social service programs with other agencies. It also works on restitution.

American Friends of the Anne Frank Center
135 East 55th Street 10022   759-2080

The Anne Frank Center, 245 East 60th Street, which has exhibits, audiovisual materials, speakers, and resource material about the life of Anne Frank and the Holocaust, is supported by this group. It also has ties to the Anne Frank Foundation in Holland.

The Blue Card, Inc.   2121 Broadway 10023   873-7400
Victims of Nazi persecution are given financial help by this organization when there is no other source available.

Conference on Jewish Material Claims Against
Germany   15 East 26th Street 10010   696-4944

The Conference works to get settlements from Germany for Holocaust survivors.

Emanu-El Midtown YM–YWHA Holocaust Project
344 East 14th Street 10003   674-7200

This project, conducted in cooperation with the Center for Holocaust Studies in Brooklyn, trains participants to be interviewers of Holocaust survivors in an attempt to use oral history to document this period. Participants work directly with survivors and also attend lectures, films and discussions to help with understanding the Holocaust.

Foundation for Future Generations
393 West End Avenue 10024 724-4556

Of the six million victims of the Holocaust, one million were children. This new group, committed to remembrance of these children, provides scholarships, fellowships and grants to students in Israel and the United States majoring in Jewish Studies. Each award bears the name of a child killed by the Nazis.

Group Project for Holocaust Survivors and Their Children 345 East 80th Street, #31 J 10021 737-8524

Holocaust survivors, many of whom have felt neglected by society or have had long-term difficulties as a result of their experiences during this tragic period, need emotional support. The Group Project offers psychotherapeutic services on individual, family and group bases, and holds bi-monthly intergenerational meetings for survivors and their children. It also provides seminars for interested professionals in the New York area and has supervised research and publications about the psychological impact of the Holocaust on survivors, their children, and the general Jewish population.

Holocaust Survivors Memorial Foundation
350 Fifth Avenue, Suite 3508 10018 594-8765

This is an educational organization founded by Holocaust survivors and their children to teach about the history of the Holocaust.

International Center for Holocaust Studies
Anti-Defamation League of B'nai B'rith
823 United Nations Plaza 10017 490-2525

This organization sponsors conferences and workshops on the Holocaust as well as a literary competition on Holocaust subjects. It also publishes *Dimensions: A Journal of Holocaust Studies.*

International Network of Children of Jewish Holocaust Survivors, Inc. 1 Park Avenue, Suite 1900 10016

This group coordinates the activities of the many groups for children of Holocaust survivors.

Jewish Philanthropic Fund of 1933
570 Seventh Avenue 10018 921-3871

The Philanthropic Fund was founded by Jewish immigrants who fled from central Europe during the Nazi era, and provides funds for the support and maintenance (including social services) of needy and elderly Jews from this community. It is affiliated with the American Federation of Jews from Central Europe, and supports other organizations that similarly provide services to older Nazi victims or that supply information about European Jewry before World War II.

New York City Holocaust Memorial Commission
111 West 40th Street 10018   221-1573

The Holocaust Memorial Center in Manhattan will include a museum, archives and conference center. The commission was set up to organize this project. It also does educational outreach and serves as a liaison with local Holocaust organizations.

Research Foundation for Jewish Immigration
570 Seventh Avenue 10018   921-3871

Affiliated with the American Federation of Jews from Central Europe, this institution researches and publishes studies of German-Jewish immigrants of the Nazi period and their resettlement in this country. It maintains an archive of biographical material on approximately 25,000 German-speaking Jewish refugees from central Europe. This archive is available to qualified scholars and researchers.

Second Generation
350 Fifth Avenue, Suite 3508 10018   594-8765

This group, affiliated with the International Network of Children of Jewish Holocaust Survivors, sponsors monthly meetings and kinship groups for children of survivors, and publishes a newsletter.

Self Help Community Services
300 Park Avenue South 10010   533-7100

717 West 177th Street 10033   781-6677

This large organization, affiliated with UJA–Federation provides a wide range of social services for elderly survivors of the Holocaust. Their programs include counseling, telephone support, full-time and short-term home care, help with household management and financial support. In addition, survivors are participating in Yale University's Video Archives for Holocaust Testimonies project.

Thanks to Scandinavia   745 Fifth Avenue   486-8600
In appreciation of Scandinavia's efforts to rescue Jews during World War II, this organization gives scholarships and fellowships to American universities and medical centers to students from Denmark, Finland, Norway and Sweden.

United Restitution Organization
570 Seventh Avenue, 16th Fl. 10018   921-3860

This organization handles claims against West Germany.

Simon Wiesenthal Center
342 Madison Avenue 10017   370-0320

This is one of the offices of the Wiesenthal Center (whose main location is in Los Angeles), named after the famous hunter of Nazi war criminals. This is probably the largest organization dedicated to the study of the Holocaust and the preservation of awareness as our main tool in preventing a recurrence. The Center does public outreach and media projects; it also works with governments and diplomats on the prosecution of Nazi war criminals, and in combating contemporary anti-Semitism and genocide.

World Federation of Bergen Belsen Associations
P.O. Box 232, Lenox Hill Station 10021   752-0600

This fraternal organization for survivors of the Bergen Belsen concentration camp has branches all over the United States, Canada and Israel. They are affiliated with the World Federation of Jewish Fighters, Partisans and Camp Inmates, and have participated in the American Gathering of Jewish Holocaust Survivors.

World Federation of Hungarian Jews
136 East 39th Street 10016   683-5377

This fraternal organization of Hungarian Jews, many of them Holocaust survivors or refugees from the Nazi era, does charitable work, provides educational programming and represents Hungarian interests in matters of restitution against the German government.

Index

NANCY DAVIS is a writer and editor. She published a series of travel guides at Business Travelers, Inc., where she was vice-president and editorial director. A graduate of Bryn Mawr College, Davis has worked in several publishing houses. She lives in Montclair, N.J., with her husband, Edward, and their three children, Michael, Alex and Elizabeth.

JOY LEVITT is a rabbi. She's a graduate of the Reconstructionist Rabbinical College. She edited *A Guide to Jewish Philadelphia*. Rabbi Levitt is a vice-president of the Reconstructionist Rabbinical Association, and serves the Reconstructionist Congregation of the North Shore in Roslyn, N.Y., with her husband, Rabbi Lee Friedlander. They have a daughter, Sara.